than it is to say, 'God is love.' Of course, God is more than those characteristics, but certainly not less. It also explains why the university and hospital movements arose predominantly in the Christian West. In *Logic and the Way of Jesus*, Dickinson helps us see the good of training our minds and how to do so. Moreover, he helps us see why, as Christians, loving God with our heads in addition to [our] hands and hearts is essential to Christian discipleship in pursuing the good life. This is a good resource for individuals, small groups, and classrooms."

—**Corey Miller**, president and CEO, Ratio Christi

"Travis Dickinson is a Christian scholar with a pastor's heart of equipping believers for ministry and maturity. *Logic in the Way of Jesus* brings all of this together in a readable way. The real importance of the book lies in the way Dickinson depicts, explains, and illustrates crucial concepts as aspects of Christian discipleship: worldview, rationality, inductive and deductive logic, truth, and much, much more. This book is crucial reading for pastors, students, and everyday Christians. I highly recommend it."

—**JP Moreland**, distinguished professor of philosophy, Talbot School of Theology, Biola University

"Some tell us we should think well, and that is important. Others teach us how to think well, and that is also important. This is a book that gives the why and how: a white swan event. Whether teaching basic logic in a Christian context or hoping to learn how to be a better reasoner, this is an outstanding resource."

—**John Mark Reynolds**, president and professor of philosophy, The Saint Constantine School

"Those of us who teach logic and critical thinking in Christian universities, colleges, and seminaries have long dreamt of a book like this. Travis Dickinson's *Logic and the Way of Jesus* is the new gold standard in the field. There is no close second. Not only does it teach the fundamentals of logic in remarkably clear and practical terms; it demonstrates how a basic grasp of critical thinking skills is essential to loving God with our minds, forming a consistent Christian worldview, and following Jesus—our Lord and the preeminent Logician. This book is required reading for all who would 'contend for the faith' in our spiritually confused, post-Christian generation!"

—**Richard Brian Davis**, professor of philosophy, Tyndale University

"*Logic and the Way of Jesus is* an incisive, thoughtful, and carefully designed look at what it means to think Christianly about all aspects of life. In this outstanding book, Travis Dickinson brilliantly and insightfully connects intellectual curiosity, an understanding of logic, critical thinking, the place of faith and reason, and the importance of developing a Christian worldview. In doing so, he winsomely and persuasively invites Christ followers to think and live in a renewed and holistic way in order to change lives, strengthen churches, enhance Christian entities, advance the gospel, and bring glory to the one, true, and living God. Heartily recommended!"

—**David S. Dockery**, president, International Alliance for Christian Education, and distinguished professor of theology, Southwestern Baptist Theological Seminary

"Brilliant! This is the book I've been waiting for: a clarion call to reject anti-intellectualism and love God with all our minds. Dickinson's *Logic and the Way of Jesus* is one part inspiring and one part practical: a perfect blend, showing the brilliance of Jesus, the Master Logician, and the call of his followers to think critically and Christianly in a world gone mad."

—**Paul M. Gould**, associate professor of philosophy of religion, Palm Beach Atlantic University

"*Logic and the Way of Jesus* is an accessible guide that helps equip followers of the Way to cultivate a more responsible, intellectually virtuous character, one that is modeled by Christ himself and rooted and nourished in the life-giving reality of the triune God. Dickinson reminds us that the intellectual pursuit of God is to be understood primarily in the context of the first and greatest commandment: to love the Lord our God with every aspect of our being. This is no ordinary introduction to logic textbook! Dickinson is a seasoned, pastoral guide to the logical and moral dimensions of a well-ordered, Christ-shaped mind."

—**Ross D. Inman**, associate professor of philosophy, Southeastern Baptist Theological Seminary

"The call to Christlikeness is a call to love God with a well-ordered and virtuous mind. *Logic and the Way of Jesus* brilliantly equips readers to answer this call. Appealing throughout to the example of Jesus, Travis Dickinson shows us—with patience born of true expertise—the way to recover the intellect as central to Christian discipleship. Dickinson's engaging readability and skillful explanations guarantee that *Logic and the Way of Jesus* will serve equally well in classical schools or college classrooms, small groups, and personal studies."

—**R. Keith Loftin**, headmaster, Kingdom Preparatory Academy

"There has been a need for this book for a long time. *Logic and the Way of Jesus* explains why critical thinking is important for Christians and offers a practical road map for how to think like Jesus. This is now my top recommendation for a book of its kind."

—**Sean McDowell**, associate professor of Christian apologetics, Talbot School of Theology, Biola University

"The incarnation of the Son of God saliently revealed the ground of logic and love, of rationality and hospitality. It is no less true to say, 'God is logic'

LOGIC AND THE WAY OF JESUS

LOGIC AND THE WAY OF JESUS

Thinking Critically and Christianly

TRAVIS DICKINSON

Foreword by PAUL COPAN

ACADEMIC®
BRENTWOOD, TENNESSEE

Logic and the Way of Jesus

Published by B&H Academic
Brentwood, Tennessee

ISBN: 978-1-5359-8327-3

Dewey Decimal Classification: 160
Subject Heading: LOGIC / JESUS CHRIST /
THOUGHT AND THINKING

Cover design by Darren Welch.
Cover illustration: *Jesus Preaching in the Synagogue* by Gustave Doré, sourced from ivan-96/istockphoto; geometric pattern by briddy_/istockphoto

Printed in the United States of America

4 5 6 7 8 9 10 VP 29 28 27 26 25

CONTENTS

ACKNOWLEDGMENTS

Special thanks are due to Brett Coppenger and Keith Loftin for reading through the manuscript and making invaluable suggestions. Thanks to Cristina VanWerkhoven for help with creating the practice problems. Thanks to B&H Academics' Audrey Greeson and Renee Chavez for extending virtually every deadline and, along with their editorial team, for helping make this a reality. Special thanks to my former students at Scarborough College who took my Critical Thinking and Worldview class, where many of these ideas were worked out and refined. And to my new students at Dallas Baptist University, I look forward to continuing this conversation. Thanks to the late Dallas Willard, whom I never got to meet, and JP Moreland, who, in many different ways, inspired the idea for the book.

And the most special thanks are due to my wife, Shari, who patiently endured many off-the-clock writing hours and carried the parenting load with excellence. Thanks also to our kids, Kaelia, Delaney, Emery, and Kade, for providing many opportunities to do more important things all along the way. I love you all very much.

It is my sincere hope that this book is an encouragement to the church, is used in high school and college classes, and is read by any who love Jesus and desire to think more carefully and Christianly.

FOREWORD

The apostle Paul writes in the book of Colossians that Jesus Christ is "the head of the body, the church" (1:18). He continues his description of the preeminent Christ—the one in whom "are hidden all the treasures of wisdom and knowledge" (2:3). In that same chapter, Paul reminds his readers not to become caught up in false, human-generated worship; while it may appear full of piety and "holy" self-denial, he says, such religiosity is in fact a departure from Christ. The person who does so has "lost connection with the head, from whom the whole body, supported and held together by its ligaments and sinews, grows as God causes it to grow" (2:19 NIV).

Travis Dickinson has written an important book reminding us of how many professing believers in the church have, in various ways, "lost connection with the head"—with Jesus Christ. They have failed to see Jesus as the most brilliant thinker ever—a master logician and the wisdom of God in human form. They have been slipshod in their thinking, and they have not shown interest in loving God with all their minds. Because many in the church have not seen the value of thinking Christianly—of having a thoughtful, well-informed faith—they have not viewed Jesus rightly, and they therefore do not represent him well. And most church leaders don't seem interested in remedying this problem.

Whether in our worship or in our theology or our view of the world, failing to be thoughtful, soundly reasoning Christians will be detrimental to our spiritual lives and our witness in the world. We will have a blurrier vision of God and how to worship him "in truth" (John 4:23–24); we will probably not view the Christian faith as a serious knowledge tradition (Luke 1:1–4); we will be unable to give reasons for the hope within us in our witness (1 Peter 3:15); and we will fail the next generation of believers because we have not properly equipped them to proclaim and defend the gospel in the marketplace of ideas.

Dickinson's book takes important steps forward to remedy this problem. Dickinson makes a solid case for grounding rationality in God himself and that we as his image bearers can better represent and reflect and honor God by being more thoughtful Christians. He shows how Jesus is the ultimate logician, the wisdom of God incarnate, and that we can learn from his example. This book also furnishes us with tools to help us become more clear-minded, careful reasoners who are not tossed about by false doctrines or pseudophilosophies or fallacious logic.

Because the mind is like a muscle, the more we exercise it, the better thinkers we'll become. While it takes effort to read thoughtfully and then to apply the tools in this book to sharpen our thinking, the rewards will be great in every way—assuming we are humble learners who aren't puffed up in the process. So take up this book, and read it with care—and, by God's grace, become a wiser, more thoughtful worshipper of God and disciple of Christ and more effective Spirit-empowered witness in the world.

Paul Copan
Pledger Family Chair of Philosophy and Ethics
Palm Beach Atlantic University
West Palm Beach, Florida

The Intellectual Pursuit of God

Our world, today, is post-Christian. What this means is that Christianity deeply influenced our culture here in the globalized West,[1] but the culture has moved on. The culture has embraced a broadly secular worldview. This has been a sweeping change. There are, of course, still remnants of a Christian culture including many churches and Christians. But the cultural influencers in the globalized West do not today express a Christian worldview.

[1] The "globalized West" refers to the culture that started in Christian Europe in the Middle Ages and then spread to many parts of the world, with the United States being one of the more influential. Today this culture and way of thinking has truly become global, affecting people in all parts of the world, with the advent of mass communications and mass media. There are certainly places that are still largely unaffected by Western culture, but there are many countries in the East (such as Japan) where it is firmly established.

Losing Our Minds

An early pioneer of Christian rock music once asked, "Why should the devil have all the good music?"[2] The line of this 1970s song laments the fact that Christians produced none of the popular music at the time. The "good" rock music was to be found only in secular bands. Well, we might also ask why the devil should have the whole culture. Why are Christian beliefs and values so diminished in the world around us?

Again, it hasn't always been this way. There was once a time when Christians indeed had good music. The church also had good art, philosophy, literature, science, and so on, and occasionally Christians produced culture-shifting masterpieces.

We could note many examples. Take sixth-century Roman statesman and philosopher Boethius as an example. Along with being a member of the Roman senate, Boethius was a devout Christian and wrote a variety of influential philosophical works. But he also wrote works in music theory, geometry, and arithmetic. His manual for music theory and composition lasted as a central text for centuries of scholars. In the fourteenth century, we have the Italian poet Dante Alighieri. His epic poem, *The Divine Comedy*, which is an allegorical vision of the Christian life, is regarded as one of the world's greatest works of literature. In the scientific revolution of the sixteenth and seventeenth centuries, many of the primary figures were devout Christians, including Francis Bacon, Robert Boyle, Johannes Kepler, and Isaac Newton. Finally, there is the eighteenth-century songwriter Isaac Watts, who wrote such classic hymns as "Joy to the World" and "When I Survey the Wondrous Cross." Watts also wrote a textbook on logic, the full title of which is *Logick: or, the Right Use of Reason in the Enquiry after Truth, with a Variety of Rules to Guard Against Error, in the Affairs of Religion and Human Life, as well as in the Sciences*. This book had not only an impressive title but was the standard

---

[2] Larry Norman, "Why Should the Devil Have All the Good Music," track 9 on *Only Visiting This Planet*, Verve, 1972, vinyl LP.

logic textbook at universities all over the Western world for nearly 200 years. This is only a sampling of the long and varied tradition of Christians who saw their Christian faith as not only consistent with influencing and producing culture but also motivating this cultural work.

Consider also that Christians founded most of the world's greatest universities, with overt Christian teaching as a primary part of the curriculum. This includes Oxford, Cambridge, Harvard, Yale, Princeton, and Columbia universities, as well as many others throughout Europe and the United States. Christian thought dominated the idea centers of the culture. For better or worse, it was sometimes difficult to be successful in areas of scholarship and the arts without being a Christian.

To be clear, the church's deep influence on the culture sometimes led to abuses of power. When Galileo Galilei (1564–1642) became convinced the earth orbited the sun, he was served a sentence of life imprisonment because this idea was taken to be in conflict with the idea of a fixed and immovable earth in the Bible.[3] Even though there were abuses of power, the point is that Christianity was a major player in the creation of the culture of what is today the globalized Western world.

Sadly, today, Christianity has lost much of its cultural influence. Not only is the Christian worldview no longer dominant in the universities, the arts, science, philosophy, literature, and so forth, it doesn't always even get a hearing. When Christians are too public and enthusiastic about their Christian faith, especially in scholarship or art, they are met with suspicion and sometimes scorn. This is the modern world in which we live. Where are the Christian artists, musicians, writers, and thinkers who are producing culture-shifting masterpieces that express a Christian worldview? There are some who are doing good and faithful work, to be sure, and we need

---

[3] As one translation of Ps 93:1 says, "Thou hast fixed the earth immovable and firm" (NEB). Galileo was also at odds with the scientific community, so his troubles were not purely theological.

lots more of these. But things have shifted and, in this shift, the Christian impact on culture has greatly diminished.

How Did We Get Here?

Why has our impact on culture become so paltry?

It's certainly not because we lack the numbers to have an impact. In the United States, as of 2015, evangelical Christians alone made up around 25 percent of the population.[4] Combining all other broadly Christian views (Roman Catholic, mainline Protestant, etc.), the percentage jumps up to around 70 percent of the US population. That means one out of four people in this country is an evangelical, and close to three out of four are broadly Christian. That is a large majority of the population, yet Christian values and beliefs are radically underrepresented in culturally important areas.

In his insightful book *Love Your God with All Your Mind*, J. P. Moreland explains how the culture has shifted to a post-Christian one. He, along with others,[5] identifies a major shift in the church that occurred in a variety of revivals and awakenings in the seventeenth and eighteenth centuries in America. The shift was to an emphasis on a more emotional and experience-based conversion rather than one with a reflective and intellectual emphasis. One came to Christ on the basis of momentary feelings of conviction rather than on the basis of a deep consideration of the truth of Christianity. Though tremendous good came from these spiritual awakenings, this marked a distinct change in how people came to be Christians and has had a deep impact on the church today.

---

[4] *America's Changing Religious Landscape: Christians Decline as Share of U.S. Population; Other Faiths and the Unaffiliated Are Growing*, Pew Research Center, May 12, 2015, available at https://www.pewforum.org/2015/05/12/americas-changing-religious-landscape/.

[5] See most notably Mark A. Noll, *The Scandal of the Evangelical Mind* (Grand Rapids: Eerdmans, 1994).

Let's be clear: coming to faith in Christ in repentance is going to be an emotional experience. This is to be expected. Emotions, however, are fickle things, and they are not—by themselves—a good way to determine truth and maintain belief and commitment. Emotional moments may cause us to change our minds and make commitments, but they do not necessarily entail a lasting commitment. In big emotional moments we may not even know to what we are committing. As we are swept up in the emotions of a movement, we have to stop and ask whether it is a good idea. It is noteworthy that two of what are now worldwide religious movements, Mormonism and Jehovah's Witnesses, came out of a certain area that was, in effect, ground zero of the Second Great Awakening, called the "burned over district" in upstate New York. Many recent converts to Christianity, in turn, converted to these alternative Christian views. It seems they didn't have the theological depth to understand the differences between these views and traditional Christianity.

The point is that when it is all about emotion and fervor, then we fail to have a guide to truth. Emotions simply are not good indicators of truth. And if you can be emotionally drawn into joining Christianity, you can be drawn into another community with similar emotional appeal perhaps without even realizing you've made a change. Even all those converts who remained in Christian communities didn't necessarily remain because they had good reasons to believe Christianity was true. For many, the commitment had nothing to do with having good reasons for belief, let alone a foundation of deep knowledge of the Bible and Christian doctrine. It was, at bottom, an emotional and sentimental commitment they didn't want to give up.

Therefore, the church, though having grown in number, became dominated by a less intellectually grounded faith. This became especially problematic because the church was unable to meet the significant intellectual challenges it inevitably came to face from a world that looked to throw off previous eras' shackles of religious dogma. There were, for example, a variety of scholarly attacks on the historicity of the Bible (focused especially on miracles and supernatural events). Though these were scholarly and there were difficult challenges along the way, the critiques were often extremely speculative. For example, one eighteenth-century German scholar, Karl Friedrich Bahrdt, denied Jesus's resurrection and instead proposed an elaborate conspiracy. Bahrdt claimed that Jesus only pretended to die, having been given medication from Luke, who was a physician, to withstand the pain of the crucifixion. Shortly thereafter, Joseph of Arimathea resuscitated Jesus to pull off the ruse that he rose from the dead.[6] Now, this is a theory that's hard to take seriously, but Christians weren't in the game to offer a response to claims such as this and a defense of the claims of Scripture.[7]

The world attacked, and most Christians weren't ready for it. In this situation, the church, it seems, had three options. First, it could have attempted to intellectually face down the challenges. Second, it could have simply conceded that Christianity is false on the basis of these challenges. Neither of the first two options were tenable for the church. As we've said, a new popular majority wasn't prepared to face down the challenges, and of course the church was not interested in conceding that Christianity was false. There was only one option left if the church was to survive. The third option is to detach faith from reason. Here one would be saying the challenges don't matter because faith has nothing to do with intellectual reasons. With this view of faith, intellectual pursuits are not only unnecessary for Christians, but they may even be harmful. After all, this is where all the challenges are.

The church may have survived but this had devastating effects. The problem is that if faith is detached from reason, then, by definition, people do not have a reason to consider what Christians have to say. There is no

---

[6] See Douglas Shantz, "Karl Friedrich Bahrdt (1740–92): Pietism, Enlightenment, and the Autonomous Self in Early Modern Germany," *Canadian Society of Church History* (2012): 53–68.

[7] For a defense of the reliability of the Bible, see Craig L. Blomberg, *The Historical Reliability of the New Testament: Countering the Challenges to Evangelical Christian Beliefs* (Nashville: B&H, 2016); and Paul M. Gould, Travis Dickinson, and R. Keith Loftin, *Stand Firm: Apologetics and the Brilliance of the Gospel* (Nashville: B&H, 2018), chap. 5.

point to (rationally) engage something that's disconnected from reason. And so, with this popular majority way of thinking of faith, the church becomes more and more marginalized. As Moreland puts it, "this shift itself expresses a growing anti-intellectualism in the church, resulting in the marginalization of Christianity in society—its lack of saltiness, if you will—and the emergence of the most secular culture the world has ever seen."[8] The diagnosis here is Christians have ceased to emphasize and value a Christian intellect. We have, in a way, lost our minds. Mark Noll, in his influential book *The Scandal of the Evangelical Mind*, famously says, "The scandal of the evangelical mind is that there is not much of an evangelical mind."[9] That is, we have failed to think critically about life, and consequently we fail to think Christianly about our world. A wide majority of Christians do not even know what constitutes the basic doctrines of Christianity, and this is a big problem with big consequences. If a typical Christian cannot spell out what it is to be a Christian, then he or she will only be a Christian accidentally, if at all. For most, they are Christian in slogan and in certain practices (such as occasionally attending a Sunday morning service) but fail to fully live out the Christian life. How will we impact our culture with Christian beliefs and values if Christians themselves do not even know what those are?

What does this post-Christian society look like? It, too, has become devoid of intellectual depth. Moreland describes it:

> Our society has replaced heroes with celebrities, the quest for a well-informed character with the search for flat abs, substance and depth with image and personality. In the political process, the makeup man is more important than the speech writer, and we approach the voting booth, not on the basis of a well-developed philosophy of what the state should be, but with a heart full of images, emotions, and slogans all packed into thirty-second sound bites. The

---

[8] J. P. Moreland, *Love Your God with All Your Mind: The Role of Reason in the Life of the Soul*, rev. ed. (Colorado Springs: NavPress, 2012), 15.

[9] Noll, *The Scandal of the Evangelical Mind*, 3.

> mind-numbing, irrational tripe that fills TV talk shows is digested by millions of bored, lonely Americans hungry for that sort of stuff.[10]

Rather than setting the pace for the culture and being the antidote for this loneliness and anxiety, the church has come to reflect the secular worldview. We have, for example, the phenomena of celebrity pastors who often seem to prioritize Christian image over being biblical (and faithful!). People often join a church on the basis of the production and enjoyment value of its weekly services rather than a considered review of its doctrine and mission. The values of a church often look no different from secular enterprises. Many churches aim to give people a great experience and then grow, grow, grow. This is no different from the basic model of Disney or Starbucks. But churches can't do it as well as Disney or Starbucks. Consequently, biblical Christianity creates little more than a slight disturbance among the broader culture.

This shift from an intellectual faith to a faith of experience and emotions is a serious problem in the church, and it has had catastrophic consequences for our impact on our culture. To stem this tide, we must, as Christians, recover two things. We must learn to think critically and to think Christianly about all of life.

Thinking Critically

The reason, historically, people didn't become Christians merely on the basis of emotional appeals is that churches were once intellectual centers. The pastor, often the most educated person in town, was an intellectual as much as he was a spiritual adviser. It was often the pastor who educated school-age children in a variety of subjects. That was part of his job in addition to providing deep theological education. People didn't separate faith and reason precisely because Christianity provided the most reasonable worldview for understanding and getting around in the world.

---

[10] Moreland, *Love Your God with All Your Mind*, 14.

John Wesley was an eighteenth-century evangelist and theologian who, along with his brother Charles, founded Methodism. He once gave an address to clergy on what qualities and abilities every minister should possess. We should make note of his emphasis on the intellectual qualities. For Wesley, ministers must have a thorough "knowledge of all the Scriptures," which, for him, meant being able to read Greek and Hebrew.[11] But Wesley also urges ministers to have some knowledge of "the sciences." By this, Wesley does not necessarily mean only what is learned in a typical science class today. The term *sciences* had a much broader application. In fact, the two examples he gives of the sciences are logic and philosophy.

He says of logic, "For what is [logic], if rightly understood, but the art of good sense? of apprehending things clearly, judging truly and reasoning conclusively? . . . What is there, then, in the whole compass of science, to be desired in comparison of it?"[12] Wesley sees no conflict in being a Christian and becoming adept at using the principles of logic. In fact, he thinks there is no intellectual pursuit in the sciences more important for a minister. Think about it. Shouldn't a minister be able to judge truly and reason conclusively? Isn't this relevant to having good theology and being able to rightly divide the Word of God (2 Tim 2:15)? It's a great tragedy that so many Christians think the principles of logic and critical thinking are irrelevant to and even opposed to being a faithful minister.

Wesley goes on to say:

> Should not a Minister be acquainted too with at least the general grounds of natural philosophy? Is not this a great help to the accurate understanding several passages of Scripture? Assisted by this, he may himself comprehend, and on proper occasions explain to others, how the invisible things of God are seen from the creation of the world; how "the heavens declare the glory of God, and the

---

[11] John Wesley, "An Address to Clergy," in *The Christian Reader*, ed. Mary Gerhart and Fabian Udoh (Chicago: University of Chicago, 2007), 108.

[12] Wesley, 109.

> firmament showeth his handiwork"; till they cry out, "O Lord, how manifold are thy works! In wisdom hast thou made them all."[13]

Notice how the study of what he calls "natural philosophy" (or what is sometimes called "natural theology" today) is connected to understanding Scripture and evangelism. It helps make the case to others about the reality of God through what can be seen in creation. Shouldn't the minister be able to show someone how God can be seen in creation (Ps 19:1; Rom 1:19–20)?

If this wasn't enough, Wesley goes on to say that ministers should have some knowledge of geometry. What reason could Wesley have for recommending a general knowledge of geometry for Christian ministry? He says that this is valuable because a knowledge of geometry gives one a "clearness of apprehension, and an habit of thinking closely and connectedly."[14] In short, a knowledge of geometry cultivates the habit of thinking well. If one can think carefully and connectedly with geometric theorems, then one will likely be able to think carefully and connectedly when it comes to Scripture and theology. A lot of students struggle to see why studying higher-level mathematics is relevant to their life. But if studying mathematics helps us to think well, then this seems of great value to the minister.

Notice the general thrust of what Wesley is urging: he implores ministers to be intellectuals for greater ministerial effectiveness. Christianity provides answers to life's most difficult challenges. But to understand and articulate these things, as a minister, one needs well-developed intellectual abilities. There are two ways in which intellectual ability is required. First, he says we will have a greater depth in our own Christian worldview. Wesley leaves no doubt that this begins with knowledge of the Bible. But, if one were to only memorize copious amounts of Bible verses, Wesley thinks one will not be equipped to minister effectively. We must first of all understand what these verses say (which is not always easy), but a minister should also be able

---

[13] Wesley, 109.

[14] Wesley, 109.

to see how they connect and fit into a broader theological picture. To do this well, we must understand the principles of Bible study and interpretation (sometimes called hermeneutics) and areas like biblical and systematic theology. These are all well-worked-out fields of inquiry. As any first-year seminary student will tell you, learning biblical languages, the principles of Bible interpretation, and theology can be intellectually overwhelming. What underlies all of this is a significant exercise of critical thinking. Thus, to be well equipped as a minister in our knowledge of the Bible and theology, we have to be well equipped intellectually. But this shouldn't stop with only Bible and theology. Wesley envisions being equipped broadly.

The second reason there will be greater ministerial effectiveness is because we can provide rational grounds for the Christian faith. Wesley seems to allude to Rom 1:19–20, which says that God's invisible attributes can be "clearly seen" in the world around us. He also has in mind King David's claim, "The heavens declare the glory of God. . . . Day after day they pour out speech" (Ps 19:1–2). The idea is we can look at the world and see obvious ways it points to the reality of God. This is perhaps best exemplified by Paul's ministry in Athens (Acts 17:16–34). Paul presented a case for the gospel grounded in "some of [their] own poets" (v. 28) and the Greek philosophical thought familiar to the Athenians. Paul's familiarity with Greek philosophy and poetry made him effective in Athens. All of this requires significant and well-honed intellectual skills. Without developing the critical thinking skills necessary for believing and living out Christianity, our cultural engagement runs the risk of ringing hollow. We are not all going to go into formal ministry. But because we are all called to impact the culture for Christ, being intellectual and thinking critically about our faith is not optional.

Thinking Christianly

We must not simply think critically. If we are to have a positive impact on our culture, we must also think *Christianly.*

Consider how you would answer the question, What is Christianity? Many would respond with a rehearsal of some Christian doctrines and beliefs (e.g., the doctrine of the Trinity or a statement of the gospel, etc.). This is, of course, a crucial part of what Christianity is. But Christianity is not merely a certain set of beliefs. What kind of a thing is Christianity? Well, you might say, it is a religion. This is also true, but defining the term *religion* is notoriously difficult. Religions all have certain beliefs and religious practices or rituals, but so do people who play golf, say, every Sunday morning. If you believe Christian doctrines and gather on Sunday mornings, is that all there is to Christianity? Surely there is more to it than just that.

What we have to understand is that Christianity is a whole way of life. It is a worldview in the fullest sense of that term. There is a Christian way of seeing the world and understanding your place in it, and this gives meaning to every aspect of the world for the Christian. Let's try a thought experiment. Suppose you decided to pretend to be an atheist for a week. You will act for one week as if God does not exist. How much would your week have to change? If your week would virtually remain the same, then it's likely you haven't understood Christ's call on our life: "If anyone wants to follow after me, let him deny himself, take up his cross, and follow me" (Matt 16:24). Jesus explains discipleship by analogy to a death sentence! Dietrich Bonhoeffer agreed: "When Christ calls a man, he bids him come and die."[15] This is certainly extreme, and that's the point. Following Christ is a whole life commitment.

Let's say you want to decide what you will do as a career. If you simply look for a profession that pays the best and is the most enjoyable, then you are not thinking Christianly about your future career. Money and the enjoyment of life are not unimportant things, but they certainly aren't what life is all about, on the Christian view. Our career choice should be determined by what Christ has called us to do. We should then do our job in service to

---

[15] Dietrich Bonhoeffer, *The Cost of Discipleship* (New York: Macmillan, 1963), 99.

Christ's kingdom, no matter where and no matter what that is. In short, we should do our careers Christianly.

Your career is a big decision. But having a Christian worldview should also impact what you do with your day today. You make an enormous number of decisions in a twenty-four-hour period, and these often add up in big and consequential ways. Indeed, they begin to constitute the general direction of your life. It's the innumerable small decisions where one's character really shows. The point is that Jesus should be a part of those small, everyday decisions too. When we do this, Jesus is part of the general flow of our lives. If we were to pretend to be an atheist for a week, this would require radical change.

The problem is that we often compartmentalize our lives. We have our spiritual pursuits on the one hand, and our career pursuits (or education or hobbies or relationships, etc.) on the other. But Jesus, if he is Lord, must be Lord over all. The Christian worldview applies to how we live out our days in the big and momentous things as well as the mundane. Much more than being part of a Sunday morning club, we are to think and live Christianly as it relates to all parts of life.

Curiosity

Engaging the culture for Christ is not the only reason for intellectual pursuits. The Bible presents a picture of humans as created to be intellectual. Being intellectually curious is part of God's design.

The great philosopher Aristotle recognized a fundamental drive in every human being. He famously begins one of his most important books by saying, "All men by nature desire to know."[16] His thought is that all people naturally *seek after* knowledge with an intrinsic desire to understand the world around us. Christian philosopher John Mark Reynolds says, "In one of the most

---

[16] Aristotle, *Metaphysics*, in *Aristotle Selected Works*, 3rd ed., trans. and ed. Hippocrates Apostle (Grinnell, IA: Peripatetic, 1991), 980a21.

powerful opening sentences ever written, Aristotle presumes that human beings as human beings are mentally restless. Human curiosity knows no limits, and humans can be defined as a species that wants to know *more*."[17] This desire can no doubt be stifled by boredom or laziness, or it can be cultivated and fed. The point is the God-given desire is there in all of us to some degree.

This isn't, of course, to say we all desire academic learning. Formal academic pursuits are only one way we pursue knowledge. Some folks may have no formal academic training but can throw out sports statistics until your head spins. Others regularly research and know everything there is to know about fashion styles. Still others are brilliant when it comes to the trades even if they never went to college or even finished high school. These individuals are not often seen as intellectuals in the traditional sense, but they certainly are engaged in exercising their minds and have in-depth knowledge in relevant areas.

We can see this natural desire most obviously when people are young. Children are typically extremely curious about life. Anyone who works with kids will tell you that they never have to teach children to be curious. Kids just naturally wonder how the world works and consequently ask amazing questions. We all start out this way, but, as we get older, we have a tendency to get bored with the world, and we stop asking questions about a world filled with mystery and intrigue. But our natural state is one of wonder and curiosity.

This natural curiosity is part of the original purpose for which humankind was created. In Gen 1:28, God gives to Adam and Eve what's known as the "creation mandate." God says, "Be fruitful, multiply, fill the earth, and subdue it." The Hebrew word for "subdue" has a specifically gentle and nonviolent connotation. In other words, we are not to burn nature to the ground, but we are to shape it and control it for good purposes. Using trees for lumber or iron ore to make steel is not evil and, in fact, fulfills

---

[17] John Mark Reynolds, *When Athens Met Jerusalem: An Introduction to Classical and Christian Thought* (Downers Grove, IL: InterVarsity Press, 2009), 194; emphasis in original.

this mandate as we do it responsibly as stewards of these resources. But, here's the thing: to use these resources requires knowledge. And to use these resources responsibly often requires knowledge and extreme innovation. As a result, fulfilling this mandate requires us to investigate and unlock the mysteries of the world around us.

We should notice this mandate in Gen 1:28 comes immediately after the creation of humans. There's a striking difference in the creation of humans that makes us unique from all the rest of the created order. The preceding verse says:

> So God created man
> in his own image;
> he created him in the image of God;
> he created them male and female. (Gen 1:27)

God created humanity in his image. This is an extremely rich theological claim, and unfortunately we don't have the space to thoroughly explore it here. But the picture we see in Genesis 1 is God creates the world, and this world is good. He creates humans to be God-like in that we are to reflect his creative image to care for and subdue the world. Animals, who are not made in the image of God, have the cognitive abilities to merely survive the world. It is only humans, in God's design, who are made to seek understanding and knowledge. So part of the reason we are put on this planet, according to the creation mandate, is to discover, understand, and create (craft and build) things with the world as we find it. We were never meant to be passive onlookers and mere receivers regarding the world. God's intention for humans is to actively discover and be creative.

The point is that developing the intellectual skills needed to know the world is part of a biblical picture of our design. Some discoveries along the way have happened by accident. But to understand the discovery and to be able to use it (i.e., to subdue it) takes careful thinking and significant intellectual skill. Thus, to appropriately live out this mandate, we must value our intellectual lives. This is quite literally the design of God.

Loving and Knowing God with All of Our Minds

We were designed to be intellectually curious, but not all objects of knowledge are equally satisfying. The ultimate object of knowledge is God himself. Our ultimate purpose is to know God, and without this knowledge we are left wanting. Blaise Pascal once said:

> What else does this craving, and this helplessness, proclaim but that there was once in man a true happiness, of which all that now remains is the empty print and trace? This he tries in vain to fill with everything around him, seeking in things that are not there the help he cannot find in those that are, though none can help, since this infinite abyss can be filled only with an infinite and immutable object; in other words by God himself.[18]

We will naturally seek to know many things, but it is not until we have true knowledge of God that we find wholeness and peace. This is far more than simply having intellectual knowledge of God, but it is certainly not less than an intellectual knowledge.

Jesus commands us to pursue God intellectually. In fact, this is part of the greatest and most important of the commands in all of Scripture.

There's a point in Jesus's ministry during which elite religious leaders and scholars of his day repeatedly challenged him (Matthew 22). We will have a lot more to say about these challenges later in the book. However, for now we should notice that Jesus was pressed with some serious intellectual challenges. Jesus, with stunning intellectual grace and ability, refuted them to the point that the top intellectuals of the day were left speechless.

After a number of failed attempts to challenge Jesus, an expert in the Hebrew law asked, "Teacher, which command in the law is the greatest?" (Matt 22:36). Now, this passage might be a bit too removed from its original

---

[18] Blaise Pascal, *Pensées* (New York: Penguin, 1995), 45.

context for us to appreciate how difficult this question really is. If one knows anything about the Old Testament, one likely knows that the Jews had *a lot* of laws, and in Jesus's day, the Jews had added a whole new layer of extra laws just to ensure no one breaks the actual laws. So Jesus was tasked with having to pick the greatest law out of all the Jewish laws.

Jesus was up to the intellectual task, however, and responded seemingly without hesitation: "Love the Lord your God with all your heart, with all your soul, and with all your mind. This is the greatest and most important command" (Matt 22:37–38). Even though he was asked only for the greatest, Jesus did the religious expert one better. He gave as the second greatest commandment, "Love your neighbor as yourself" and then said, "All the Law and the Prophets depend on these two commands" (vv. 39–40). What's extraordinary here is that Jesus gave not only the two greatest commandments but justified their greatness by pointing to them as the basis of all the laws and all of God's word to humankind given to the prophets. The expert in Hebrew law had no response. Jesus's logic was unassailable.

So we, as Christ followers, should take careful note. Jesus just told us, of all the things to do, this is most important. We are commanded to love God with all of who we are: our hearts, our souls, and *our minds*. I think we have some handle on what it means to love God with all of our hearts and our souls. This, among other things, means we should love God emotionally and with the deep parts of who we are. But Jesus also commanded us to love God with all of our minds.

Now, what does it even mean to love God with all of our minds? I'd like to suggest that the command here is to pursue God intellectually. This means we should intellectually seek after God in love and in our relationship with him in order to know him in a deep and full way.

To help us understand this idea, let's imagine a young couple who have fallen head over heels for each other. In those first few months of young love, the couple can't bear to be apart for more than a few moments. They walk everywhere together, sit together, study together, eat together, and simply stare at each other as much as humanly possible. There is an intense (almost sickening, for the rest of us) curiosity. They tell each other *everything*. They ask each other *everything*.

Couples in the early stages of love seek eagerly to know everything there is to know about each other. Part of this pursuit is knowing and expressing their thoughts, ideas, and deepest beliefs—that is, a big part of this pursuit is intellectual. Unfortunately, as time goes by, the interest and curiosity can wane, and older couples can sometimes lose their curiosity for each other. If a married couple has lost all their curiosity toward each other, the marriage is in serious trouble. A healthy marriage is one in which the curiosity has moved on to a greater depth. But in these early stages, when we fall deeply in love, we certainly love emotionally, but we also love with a deep intellectual curiosity. We love with our minds.

In a similar way, we ought to love God with all of our minds. This means we are called to pursue God intellectually as we love him and seek to know him. What does this look like? It starts with being curious about God, his Word, and his world. When we are curious and pursue someone intellectually, we ask questions. Some of these will be deep and difficult questions: Why, if God exists, is there so much evil and suffering in the world? Why isn't God more obvious? Why is there so much killing and violence in the Old Testament?

There is a certain attitude and posture with which we should ask the deep and difficult questions about God. We shouldn't, for example, ask questions simply to gain head knowledge. Again, two people deeply in love aren't just learning facts about each other; they want to know the *whole person* whom they love. Those in love also do not ask questions to be a nuisance or to attempt to trip each other up. We should approach God genuinely seeking to know him in a deeper way; we should ask these questions precisely because we want to know and love God more fully.

There is, to be sure, a skeptical and cynical way to approach God. What I have in mind here is someone who is asking questions but not really looking for answers. Kids often ask, "Why?" Sometimes they are not curious and not really looking for an answer. Suppose I tell my daughter that it is bedtime. She asks, "Why do I have to go to bed?" I explain that it is a school night. But then she asks, "Why do I have to go to bed early on school nights?" I answer that she needs her rest for school, and she questions this as well. And this goes on for a series of "why" questions for every answer I give. When something like this happens, she's not really asking to get an answer. She just doesn't want to go to bed (and, as it turns out, has successfully forestalled going to bed for at least a few minutes). Similarly, it is sometimes the case that when people ask questions of God they are not actually seeking truth. They don't really want an answer in that they are already opposed to any possible answer you are going to give. This is decidedly not what it means to love God with your mind.

Instead, we should ask questions and seek knowledge of God to know him deeply and intimately. This is part of being in love with God: pursuing with intellectual curiosity an intimate knowledge of God.

Faith and Reason

Now, it is sometimes thought that we are called to a life of faith and that this is something different from an intellectual life. A long history of debate exists about the roles of reason and faith. Many Christians are suspicious of any account that highlights the role of reason, thinking that this is dangerous for faith. But much of this suspicion amounts to a misunderstanding of the concepts of faith and reason.

What, first of all, is faith? Faith is quite an important concept for us as Christians, and yet it is not often defined carefully.[19] I suggest we understand faith as "ventured trust." The thought is that we have faith when we risk

---

[19] Like many terms, there are a few uses of the term *faith* in the Bible. It sometimes uses the term *faith* to mean the collection of our Christian beliefs. For example, Jude urges his readers "to contend for *the faith* that was delivered to the saints once for all" (1:3, italics added). Jude is calling for his readers to fight against false doctrine that had crept into the church and fight for true doctrine, i.e., the faith. Notice how different this is from the use in 2 Cor 5:7 where Paul says, "For we walk by faith, not by sight." The point of this passage is we shouldn't walk and do

ourselves in dependence on someone or something. We can stand at a distance and believe that, say, an airplane is safe and reliable. This may be some form of trust, but it isn't faith. It's faith when we board the airplane. It's a ventured trust in that we *venture* ourselves on a person or thing. Faith is not just trusting from a distance but entrusting ourselves. We can have faith in big or small ways. We can place our faith in a friend for a ride home. We would be depending on this person, but there's not much at stake if the person does not come through for us. By contrast, there's a whole lot that can go wrong when we take off in an airplane. We really entrust our whole lives to the plane (and the pilot, the mechanics, the designers, etc.) when we get on board.

Another great example is the faith between two people when they join themselves in marriage. The Bible often compares our relationship with God to a marriage relationship between a husband and wife. Notice that each spouse ventures themselves and their well-being on the other. The happiness and general well-being of the spouses is deeply wrapped up in how well they can mutually depend upon and trust the other.

This brings us to the role of reason. How does one know whether it's a good idea to get on an airplane? If the airplane is rusted out, leaking fluids, and parts are falling off, then we shouldn't place our faith in that craft. How does a spouse gain trust? One will need varied experiences of fidelity. If a potential spouse always blows it, then one should not place one's faith in that person.

Now, it's clear one could get on an airplane in an irrational way. One can also get married to someone who clearly is not trustworthy. We've all had moments when we've trusted without any good reason. Take, for example, the slick door-to-door salesperson who is selling a useless product. The salesperson comes to your door and tells you why your life is not complete without purchasing this product, and, before you know it, you own it. We so often regret these sorts of high-pressure sales decisions. We later wonder what we were thinking and why we didn't just say no. The point is we *can*

---

life beholden to our present circumstances—i.e., just what we see—but we should walk *trusting* Christ.

place our faith in people or things without sufficiently good reason; however, we shouldn't. Faith without reason is a really bad idea!

How does one know who or what should be trusted? We are going to have to use our reason. What other options do we have? How else, other than using reason, can we know who and what to trust? Now we need to be clear. I'm using the term *reason* in quite a broad sense. I'm not using it in a technical, academic sense. We don't use science experiments or formalize arguments to figure out whether your love interest is the person you should marry. But we definitely use (or should use) reason. If you are wondering whether to place your faith in a person in marriage, then the fact that this person has cared for you even at your low points suggests that he or she is worth depending on. You have a very good reason.

Though we can always improve our reasoning, we all use reason to decide where to place our trust. I suggest that all of us came to faith on the basis of *some* reasons. Perhaps someone preached on the tortures of hell, and it sounded so horrible you made a decision to give your life to Christ. Though a fear of hell is probably not the best reason to believe, it is a reason. For many of us, we heard a testimony of how Jesus changed a person's life when that person came to faith, and this was a primary reason for coming to faith. Hearing a testimony like this, it seems, is a pretty good reason for coming to or at least being interested in faith. Most of us, as we grow in Christ, hear many such testimonies, have our own experiences, meet with God through the words of Scripture, consider apologetic arguments, and otherwise get confronted with the reality of God and the truth of the gospel in coming to faith. These have compelled us to venture our trust in Christ.

Objection 1: Doesn't This Put Reason over Faith?

While it may seem obvious that we have some reasons for coming to faith, it is sometimes objected that developing an intellectual faith dangerously makes reason an authority over faith and the dictates of Scripture. Consider, for example, Abraham offering up Isaac as a sacrifice (Gen 22:1–19). The thought is often that Abraham had all the reason in the world not to go through with the sacrifice but nevertheless chose to place faith in God. He put faith over reason. Or did he? Is it correct to say that Abraham put faith *over* reason? It seems to me that Abraham made a *very* rational choice.

How was Abraham's choice rational? We should keep in mind that, in the story, God spoke verbally to Abraham (give that one a second) and told him to sacrifice his son. By this time, Abraham had come to believe (for good reasons) that God is the one and only almighty God. It wasn't so long before this event that Abraham's wife, Sarah, had had Isaac. God had made promises about what he would do through Abraham and his offspring.[20] The problem was that Abraham and Sarah were childless and, at this point, elderly. The birth of Isaac was a *miracle*—imagine how impactful this was on Abraham's understanding of God. It undoubtedly expanded his understanding that God is steadfastly faithful and able to fulfill his covenant promise, even if doing so takes a miracle.

With all of this as backdrop, when the almighty and steadfastly faithful God of the universe shakes the sound waves and tells you to do something, it is eminently rational to act accordingly. Abraham surely didn't understand how this all fits in with the overall plan. Isaac was, after all, the promised child through whom God would fulfill his covenant with Abraham (Gen 12:1–3; 26:2–5). Hebrews even tells us that "Abraham *reasoned* that if Isaac died, God was able to bring him back to life again" (11:19 NLT, italics added). It's true that Abraham had competing reasons that suggested sacrificing his only son was not a good idea. But when we step back and consider Abraham's overall intellectual situation, these competing reasons pale in comparison to the reasons he had for going through with what God asked him to do. If Abraham wasn't utterly convinced that God was speaking to him, it seems unlikely (again, for intellectual reasons) he would go up to sacrifice his son. So it's not that faith won out over reason. It's that Abraham had his reason properly ordered and thus acted in faith. Abraham believed God.

---

[20] See Gen 17:19.

Another example we may consider is Peter's experience on the Sea of Galilee (Matt 14:25–32). For a moment Peter walked on the water. This was an amazing act of faith. But then he started looking around and saw some compelling reasons that suggested walking on the water in a violent storm was not such a good idea. Matthew says, "But when he saw the strength of the wind, he was afraid, and beginning to sink he cried out, 'Lord, save me!' Immediately Jesus reached out his hand, caught hold of him, and said to him, 'You of little faith, why did you doubt?'" (vv. 30–31). Peter quickly ceded his trust away from Christ and began to sink. He failed to trust Christ. Did Peter put reason over faith? No! It is not as if Peter lacked reasons for trusting Christ. In fact, Peter had all the reason in the world for faith given all he had seen and come to believe about Jesus at this point in Jesus's ministry. Jesus clearly had the power to enable Peter to walk on water, and he should not have given in to these competing reasons. Unlike Abraham, Peter failed to trust despite the good reasons he possessed. But it was his doubt that was the irrational choice.

Here's the reality: as Christians, we always have more reasons to trust God when he has called us to something. It may be difficult, at times, to discern what God has called us to, but venturing our trust in God will always be the rational choice.

The struggle Christians have with reason and intellectual pursuits is most often a matter of misunderstanding its role. Reason plays an important but limited role. It tells us where to place our faith, and that's it. We still have to exercise faith, and we can, like Peter, all too easily ignore what reason is telling us is true. We should be like Abraham and believe God. We shouldn't be like Peter and irrationally doubt. As we pursue God intellectually, our faith in him should only grow deeper and more mature.

Objection 2: I've More Important Things to Do

Some people believe that intellectual pursuits are a waste of time compared to doing something "useful" with our lives. Pragmatism, the view that usefulness is the primary value, is deeply embedded in our culture. We should be out there actually getting something done or building something or helping people. Some even think that it is selfish to sit around bettering ourselves intellectually.

This pragmatist outlook has a spiritual version as well. Here the thought is we should all be out on the streets sharing the gospel and not wasting our time in a classroom learning how to think. All we need is the Holy Spirit, perhaps some practical ministry training, and we should be good to go. The rest is distraction.

There are many problems with this line of thinking. The most obvious problem is that it violates the commands of Scripture. We've already looked at what Jesus calls the greatest commandment—to love God with all of our hearts, souls, and minds (Matt 22:37). Pursuing God intellectually is not optional.

In another passage, the apostle Peter tells us to be "ready at any time to give a defense to anyone who asks you for a reason for the hope that is in you" (1 Pet 3:15). Notice he didn't say we should get out there and just start doing work. The primary force of the passage is to *be ready*. Of course, one shouldn't read this to mean we never need to get out there and do the ministerial work. The context of 1 Peter 3 is how to live in a hostile world. It is implied in the passage you are going to need this readiness because challenge is coming your way.

The term *defense* is a legal term similar to what a contemporary lawyer would do in defending a client. Imagine you are on trial, having been charged with a crime for which you are innocent. How would you feel if your lawyer came in without any kind of deep knowledge of your case but assures you that he has done this many times and has some great practical strategies for convincing juries? I'm not sure any of us would be comfortable with this. In a trial, someone's life and well-being hangs in the balance. Similarly, when it comes to evangelism, someone's eternal soul hangs in the balance. Thus, spending time being prepared intellectually to make a defense for the truth of the gospel is not wasted time.

Objection 3: But I'm Not Cut Out for the Intellectual Life

I often hear people say they lack intelligence and the smarts required to pursue academic subjects. "I'm just not an intellectual," it is sometimes said. Well, it may be that you don't have the intellectual resources to become a world-class scholar. Join the club! Most of us will not reach that rarefied air, but my experience with teaching students for more than twenty years is that most can do far more than they think.

Here's a typical situation. A student comes into a class and begins to hear unfamiliar terminology. Other students in the class seem to know these words, but, to this student, it sounds like everyone is speaking a different language. The student feels completely overwhelmed. Our culture of immediate gratification doesn't help us here, as the student begins to look for the nearest exit.

Here's the reality. It may be that a student doesn't get metaphysics or organic chemistry or econometrics immediately. Again, join the club. These are difficult subjects. Everyone who walks into a brand-new subject feels this way at some point—even the world-class scholars did early on in their careers. If a student will just stick it out and simply work hard at understanding the terminology and concepts, these things will begin to feel familiar. It is going to take hard work, but this will set a student up to do well.

The call, in this chapter, is not necessarily to be an academic scholar. Academic pursuits are important, and it is my hope this book will inspire some to pursue the highest levels of academia. That calling, however, is not for everyone. Having an intellectual faith is pursuing a deep knowledge of God. Again, academic study of the Bible and theology in formal settings truly can be helpful, but they certainly are not necessary. One can ask the deep and difficult questions about the faith and pursue answers no matter whether one is a professional academic or lacking any formal education. Most of us will find ourselves somewhere in between these two. What's important is we take our background at whatever level we are and strive to know and love God as deeply as we can.

How to Have an Intellectual Faith

So, how does one develop an intellectual faith?

Unfortunately, there's no magic bullet here. Though this is going to sound obvious, it's worth saying: to develop an intellectual faith requires one to develop oneself intellectually. We will turn to doing exactly this in the coming chapters. We will spend a considerable amount of time looking at how to reason well and think critically. We need to be careful that we have good arguments for our beliefs and are able to evaluate the objections and counterarguments that pose problems for our beliefs.

However, only developing ourselves intellectually will not necessarily give us an intellectual faith. We must also develop ourselves to think Christianly about the world. How do we do this? The first thing I suggest is taking our faith and pursuit of knowing God seriously. We should make it a first priority to dig into understanding who God is. Just like the couple in youthful love, we have to prioritize our relationship with God. This should involve gaining a knowledge of the Bible and general theology. God has revealed himself specifically in Scripture. We can't know him intimately without knowing him through our devotional study of the Bible. As noted earlier, this knowledge of God and Christian belief is crucial because we can't be intentional Christians if we don't even know what Christianity is. We will only be Christians accidentally if Christians at all.

Taking faith seriously should also involve asking the deep and difficult questions about the faith. As we begin to have a greater familiarity with Christian beliefs, I suggest we develop the habit of asking, "Why think this Christian belief is true?" This can be difficult, but again, tremendous resources are out there that address the deepest and most difficult questions about the faith. We should remember these are lifelong pursuits. We will never figure it all out. The point is to keep pursuing these things as a way to know God deeply and develop our Christian worldviews.

My second suggestion for developing an intellectual faith is to develop and follow *your* interests. You are a unique creation of God with specific interests. What one person is captivated by is possibly of little interest to another. And that's okay. Some things interest me that you would likely find rather mind-numbing. Other areas enjoyed by many don't pique my interest, even though they may be valuable areas of study. As you pursue God with all of your mind, ultimately you will discover certain things that really interest you. You should follow these interests.

There is freedom here. It wouldn't be good if we all were experts in one area, say, philosophy or science. One benefit of following your interests is that you are better able to sustain your efforts. As mentioned, intellectual work is difficult and laborious. This is exponentially harder when you have lost all interest in the topic. But when you are working in an area of great interest, you are better able to sustain your efforts as you go.

Now, it's a big world, and there are many distinct disciplines and areas of study. You really won't know if something is an interest until you get your feet wet with it. You should get exposure to a wide variety of topics and see what piques your interest. I have known many people who found themselves completely surprised to fall in love with a topic. It can even happen that they have had a bad experience in a certain class or topic previously, but then, at some point, they give it another shot and become deeply interested. It also happens in the other direction. You may realize you are not all that interested in something you thought you would be. You really never know until you try. As a result, looking at a variety of topics (perhaps taking classes in these areas, if you are a student), reading widely, and speaking with people from a variety of areas of thought will greatly help you discover your interests.

My third suggestion is to be patient and take your time because the intellectual life is a lifestyle, not a destination. You will not get everything figured out overnight, and it will often feel like you have a long way to go.

Once again, join the club. We all have a long way to go because there is not some destination where we will, at some point, finally arrive. We can make progress on this journey, but we never arrive. So if you are a student, don't be in a big rush to get done with your studies. In a rush to get to the next thing in life, we often sacrifice the current thing. This was my story, actually. I saw college as a way to get a diploma and get on to "real life." If I'm honest, I wasn't after the knowledge—I was after the slip of paper that said I was a college graduate—and I missed out on learning and cultivating a more intellectual faith. Thankfully, in graduate school, I realized this error, and I slowed down to learn. If you are currently in college, I suggest you take full advantage of all the intellectual challenges around you right where you are.

In developing an intellectual faith, we should value the deep, difficult, and sometimes boring study of the fundamental areas of our Christian faith and realize this takes considerable time. If you do this in a formal setting, then choose the school, do the major, and take the elective courses that will be most beneficial for your development as an intellectual. Take your time and focus on developing your intellect and knowledge.

A final suggestion is to find a community of like-minded folks with whom you can develop intellectually. It is important to find people who are like-minded in desiring to develop themselves intellectually. You need people who are on a similar journey so that you can discuss and work out the ideas you are wrestling with. Though you can do quite a bit on your own, it is far more effective to develop yourself intellectually with a group of like-minded people.

Conclusion

I have argued in this chapter that we have lost our impact on the culture because we have neglected the development of an intellectual faith. I have claimed that faith and reason are perfectly compatible since reason is a tool that tells us where to place our faith. Thus, we, as Christians seeking to know God in a deep and full way and to engage the culture for Christ, should develop ourselves intellectually. In the coming chapters, we will provide a further ground for seeing this pursuit as thoroughly Christian. We will look at how Jesus, as a brilliant thinker, regularly astonished crowds with his intellectual abilities. In this, he modeled for us how we should live. We will then look at the concept of worldview. We will see how the Christian worldview makes good sense of logic that, in turn, constitutes an argument for Christian theism.

Are you ready for this? Do you want to have a positive impact for Christ on the culture around you? Then you must become a Christian who thinks both critically and Christianly. In short, you must have an intellectual Christian faith.

Jesus the Logician

Dallas Willard once said, "Few today will have seen the words 'Jesus' and 'logician' put together to form a phrase or sentence, unless it would be to *deny* any connection between them at all. . . . There is in our culture an uneasy relation between Jesus and intelligence."[1] As Christians, we think of many things when we think of Jesus, but his intelligence and logical skill are often not among those things. It's true that most Christians will affirm Jesus's omniscience, in his deity, but we do not seem to think of him as a generally brilliant thinker and subtle logician.

Elsewhere Willard says:

> Here is a profoundly significant fact: In our culture, among Christian and non-Christians alike, Jesus Christ is automatically

[1] Dallas Willard, "Jesus the Logician," *Christian Scholar's Review* 28, no. 4 (1999): 605, italics in original.

> disassociated from brilliance or intellectual capacity. Not one in a thousand will spontaneously think of him in conjunction with words such as "well-informed," "brilliant," or "smart." Far too often he is regarded as hardly conscious. He is looked on as a mere icon, a wraithlike semblance of a man, fit for the role of sacrificial lamb or alienated social critic, perhaps, but little more.[2]

Given that we fail to see Jesus as an intellectual, we of course don't model our intellectual lives after him.

Why don't we see Jesus as an intellectual? It might be that we think of Jesus as divinely omniscient. Perhaps we think his omniscience is simply out of reach for us to attain. We can't match Jesus's omniscience, so what's the point of modeling our lives after his intelligence? But Jesus was also omnibenevolent—that is, he was perfectly, morally good—and we usually don't have a problem attempting to model our lives after Jesus morally. Matching Jesus's perfection in his moral character is no more attainable than matching his intellect. It seems we should strive to be like Jesus in both areas. That is, if we are his disciples, we should, however imperfectly, strive to be like him in all ways.

When I was in high school, the WWJD campaign became a worldwide phenomenon. Youth pastors everywhere urged their students, before they acted, to ask, "What would Jesus do?" and people across the world wore colorful WWJD bracelets as reminders. The emphasis with this campaign was to conform our *actions* to be like Jesus. And that's certainly a worthy aim. Jesus is the perfect human, and he lived a life in which he fully flourished as a human being. Thus, we should act like him in every way. But notice what's missing from the WWJD question. We are not urged to ask what Jesus would *think* or how Jesus would *reason*. This is a problem because our thoughts and ideas are clearly more fundamental than our actions. It is all

---

[2] Dallas Willard, *The Divine Conspiracy: Rediscovering Our Hidden Life in God* (New York: HarperCollins, 1998), 134.

too easy to do the right action but do it for the wrong reason. For example, we could, when someone insults us, turn the other cheek, as Jesus commends. But if we did this in a passive-aggressive way or in a manipulative way, then we've seriously missed the point. We may have done what Jesus would do but with flawed thinking. Thus, we need to take a careful look at how Jesus thought and reasoned.

Jesus Is Logically Astonishing

By all accounts, people clamored to be near Jesus. This is, in part, because he did extraordinary things. For example, he performed miracles, and who wouldn't want to be near someone who multiplies food and heals people of their sicknesses? These things gathered a crowd, to be sure. These instances, however, occurred relatively infrequently throughout Jesus's ministry. More often, the crowds gathered to hear him teach. In addition to the miracles and healing, Jesus regularly put on display his intellect and wisdom, and people gathered and were often as astonished by this sort of display as they were by his miracles.

The Bible records several places where the people were "astonished" by Jesus's teaching. Matthew 7:28–29 says, "When Jesus had finished saying these things, the crowds were astonished at his teaching, because he was teaching them like one who had authority, and not like their scribes." In fact, this was, in part, why the religious leaders desired to kill Jesus. Mark 11:18 says, "They were afraid of him, because the whole crowd was astonished by his teaching."

At one point in Jesus's ministry, he returned to his hometown of Nazareth. As he began to teach in the synagogue, the people were again astonished by his teaching. But they were confused because they knew Jesus and his family. There were likely people present who had watched Jesus grow up and knew his background. Jesus's family were commoners, not educated and not brilliant thinkers. Consequently, the people responded, "Where did this man get this wisdom and these miraculous powers? Isn't this the carpenter's son? Isn't his mother called Mary, and his brothers James, Joseph, Simon, and Judas? And his sisters, aren't they all with us? So where does he get all these things?" (Matt 13:54–56).

At another point, having heard his teaching, the Jews asked in amazement, "How is this man so learned, since he hasn't been trained?" (John 7:15). We don't know exactly what Jesus's educational experience was as he grew up, but we can speculate a bit based on what we know a typical Jewish person would have experienced. Jesus was the son of a carpenter and likely apprenticed with his father, Joseph, to learn carpentry skills. Jesus also would have had some form of semiformal education in the local synagogue to learn about the Hebrew Scriptures. But he clearly became a full-fledged rabbi in the eyes of the people. How did a carpenter's apprentice become a rabbi without extensive training? The people were astonished because he had all the skills of an extremely talented rabbi without ever having been discipled under and trained by a rabbi.

We get some insight into the intellectual development of Jesus in a short passage in Luke 2 when Jesus was only twelve years old. In fact, this is the first time the Gospels record people being astonished by Jesus's intellect was when he was twelve years old. Two verses mention the wisdom of Jesus as he grew. In v. 40, Luke says, "The boy grew up and became strong, filled with wisdom, and God's grace was on him." Then in v. 52, Luke concludes the chapter saying, "And Jesus increased in wisdom and stature, and in favor with God and with people." Jesus not only grew physically, but he grew in his wisdom and intellectual skill. The point is that Jesus, as the twelve-year-old incarnate God, had need to develop his intellectual potential and talents.

What does it look like for an adolescent to be filled with wisdom? Sandwiched between these two statements of Jesus's wisdom is a story that helps answer this question. Having been in Jerusalem for the Jewish Passover festival, Jesus's family departed Jerusalem to head back to Nazareth. Much to his parents' surprise (and, likely, the horror that comes from having a missing child), Jesus wasn't with them. It took them three days to find "him in the temple sitting among the teachers, listening to them and asking them questions" (Luke 2:46).

Let's notice a few things about this passage. First, Jesus was sitting *among* the temple teachers. These were the elite Jewish scholars and likely some of the exact individuals Jesus would later confront. He was not sitting at their feet but sitting among these elite scholars as a twelve-year-old.

Second, though he sat among them, Jesus had the posture of a learner. He listened and asked questions. Jesus developed and grew in his intellectual skill and knowledge as he grew physically.[3] Here in the temple, Jesus was the learner. A person who would become intellectually skilled must do a lot of listening, especially to those who are experts. Let's just say twelve-year-olds are not well known for being good listeners, but Jesus was among these teachers listening. And he not only listened passively; he also asked questions. He sought understanding. In short, Jesus was seeking to be a critical thinker.

The teachers, as Luke goes on to tell us, were "astounded at his understanding and his answers" (Luke 2:47). Even his parents were "astonished" by the scene of their twelve-year-old sitting among the temple teachers when, in their minds, he was supposed to be on the way back to Nazareth (v. 48). These are the first of many times in the life of Jesus, as recorded in the Gospels, that people were astonished by Jesus.

This passage is important because it is a window into Jesus's formative years. Jesus was an eager and inquisitive learner who displayed significant intellectual skill in his understanding. In a way, if we want to know how to grow to be like Jesus, this passage tells us how Jesus himself grew. We can't skip the process of being formed in our intellectual abilities. Jesus may not have had a rabbi under whom he apprenticed in an official capacity, but we do. We have Jesus himself as the perfect exemplar of fully formed intellectual skill, and we should strive to be like him in this.

---

[3] This is, of course, not to deny the omniscience of Jesus. He was both fully God and fully man, so this is to say only that, in his humanity, he grew physically and also developed intellectually.

The Logical Skills of Jesus

It is important to note that though Jesus displayed great logical ability and we can learn a lot about logic and critical thinking from him, he didn't teach logic itself or develop some sort of theory or system of logic. Willard says:

> Now when we speak of "Jesus the logician" we do not, of course, mean that he developed theories of logic, as did, for example, Aristotle and Frege. No doubt he could have, if he is who Christians have taken him to be. He could have provided a *Begriffsschrift*, or a *Principia Mathematica*, or alternative axiomatizations of Modal Logic, or various completeness or incompleteness proofs for various "languages." (He is, presumably, responsible for the order that is represented through such efforts as these.)[4]

Jesus no doubt could have done these things, but that was not his mission on earth. Rather he *used* logic with astounding subtlety to bring people (especially those with a humble heart) to understanding. He clearly had a command and mastery of logical principles and used this in service of the gospel. The hope is, in a similar way, you, too, will become familiar with the principles of logic and critical thinking.

Let's look more closely at the logical skills of Jesus.

Rebutting Intellectual Challenges

We can see Jesus's logical skills on display in three areas. The first is in his brilliance in rebutting challenges. Jesus's response to the many intellectual challenges he faced is perhaps the most obvious way we see his logical skills and intellectual abilities on display.

Religious leaders frequently challenged Jesus, as they often saw him as a threat to them. They could not legitimately challenge Jesus morally because

[4] Willard, "Jesus the Logician," 605–6.

he lived in a way that was beyond reproach. So they had to challenge him intellectually. Remember that these challengers were the top religious scholars of the day. Many had devoted their lives to the study of Scripture and especially the Jewish law. They were truly the intellectual and religious elites in that culture. The challenges to Jesus often came on the matters of the law, an area that should be their sweet spot. No doubt they thought they had the upper hand against this carpenter's son. An intellectual contest on religious topics between someone with Jesus's background and the scholars of the day would typically not be a fair fight. But not so with Jesus.

A primary example of Jesus's logical skills in rebutting intellectual challenges comes in Matthew 22. We already discussed the Great Commandment (vv. 37–39), where Jesus summarized the entire law with the command to love God with all of one's heart, soul, and mind and to love one's neighbor as oneself. What's interesting is the overall context. Jesus tells us we ought to love God with all of our minds in the context of responding to a variety of sustained intellectual attacks against him. These intellectual elites attempted to theologically trap and intellectually confound Jesus. This did not go well for them.

The religious group known as the Pharisees began. They pressed Jesus about whether it is lawful to pay taxes to Caesar (vv. 15–22). This is a serious intellectual trap because if he said yes, then he recognized Caesar as an authority when the Jews were not supposed to have any authority except for God. In this case, he could be accused religiously. But if he said no, he broke Roman law and could be accused legally. In response, Jesus requested a coin and asked who is pictured on the coin. The Pharisees conceded it was Caesar. I always imagine Jesus flipping the coin back to them saying, "Give, then, to Caesar the things that are Caesar's, and to God the things that are God's" (v. 21b). This is a mic-drop moment. Matthew tells us the Pharisees were amazed and simply walked out (v. 22). Their challenge was soundly met.

The Sadducees were next. They approached Jesus with an elaborate thought experiment intended to refute the idea of a general resurrection (i.e., the idea that all people will rise from the dead in the end times). Unlike many Jews of the day, the Sadducees did not believe in a general resurrection (Acts 23:8). For Jesus to reject the general resurrection would have put him at odds with many of his followers who believed in a general resurrection.

In raising this challenge, the Sadducees pressed a well-known principle of the Mosaic law: "if a man dies, having no children, his brother is to marry his wife and raise up offspring for his brother" (Matt 22:24). They then gave the thought experiment: "Now there were seven brothers among us. The first got married and died. Having no offspring, he left his wife to his brother. The same thing happened to the second also, and the third, and so on to all seven. Last of all, the woman died" (vv. 25–27). We are to imagine a wife who has married, in turn, seven brothers after the brother before has died. The question is then asked of Jesus whose wife she will be in the resurrection.

What exactly was the challenge here? It looks like Jesus must say the woman is married to all seven brothers at once or deny the resurrection. In first-century Jewish culture, it would have been unthinkable for a woman to be married at once to seven husbands. There are, of course, instances of plural marriage in Scripture, but it is never a woman with multiple husbands. Moreover, plural marriage in Scripture is rare and usually the exception and was not widely practiced by this time of history. In any case, the Sadducees clearly thought she couldn't be married to all at once. And it would be arbitrary to think she would be married to any one of the brothers in particular. The implication is that the notion of resurrection should be rejected because it leads to absurdity.

The implied form of argument here is called a *reductio ad absurdum* (literally, reducing to the absurd). In a reductio (for short), we assume the truth of a claim for the sake of the argument and then show that the assumption entails a logical absurdity (in a formal sense, this would be a logical contradiction). How it works in common everyday settings is by showing that if a claim is true there would be some crazy or unthinkable (i.e., absurd in a less-technical sense) consequence. Thus, given that it entails an absurdity, the assumption should be rejected.

We can put the argument in a formalized way. That is, we make clear exactly what the premises and the conclusion are. If we do this with the Sadducees' reductio argument, it would look something like this:

1. Assume, for the sake of the argument, one day there will be a resurrection of the dead.
2. If there is a resurrection from the dead, then it is possible for a woman (who has been married to a series of seven brothers) to be married to seven brothers at once.
3. Being married to seven brothers at once is absurd.
4. Therefore, there is no resurrection of the dead.

The logic of the argument requires Jesus, since he is going to affirm the resurrection, to say why affirming the resurrection does not entail this absurdity. But Jesus clearly saw his way through this intellectual challenge.

He gave two responses. First, he said the Sadducees didn't properly understand "the Scriptures or the power of God" (v. 29). This, of course, got their attention. Jesus was, in effect, saying they had bad theology. And with a proper and biblical understanding of resurrection, the problem doesn't even arise. The Sadducees seemed to be thinking of heaven as a further continuation of this earthly life. But, as Jesus pointed out, resurrection life will be different than the life we know now. If people "neither marry nor are given in marriage" (v. 30), the conundrum does not arise. Jesus, in effect, denied the second premise above. It is not the case that if there is a resurrection from the dead, then a woman could be married to seven brothers at once. This would be to misunderstand resurrection life.

Second, he quoted Exod 3:6 and made quite a subtle point. Jesus said, "Now concerning the resurrection of the dead, haven't you read what was spoken to you by God: I am the God of Abraham and the God of Isaac and the God of Jacob? He is not the God of the dead, but of the living" (Matt

22:31–32). Now Jesus's argument here is not immediately obvious. Of this passage J. P. Moreland says:

> As a young Christian, I was puzzled by Jesus' response because I myself could have cited better verses than this one—for example, Daniel 12:2, which explicitly affirms the resurrection. Or so I thought. Jesus' genius is revealed when we recognize that He had studied Sadduccan theology and knew that they did not accept the full authority of the prophets, including Daniel. He also knew that the very passage He used was one of the very defining verses for the entire Sadducean party! His argument hinged on the tense of the Hebrew verb. Jesus does not say, "I was the God of the Abraham, etc.," but, "I am (continue to be) the God of Abraham, etc." a claim that could be true only if Abraham and others continued to exist.[5]

The point Jesus made, by using what they considered to be authoritative Scripture, was that their own preferred passages assumed people live beyond death. This was again another logical mic drop. It is not only that the argument they made against the resurrection was refuted, but Jesus also showed them the resurrection was implied by what they considered to be authoritative Scripture. Once again these religious scholars had no response. With this very brief but penetrating argument, the crowds were, again, "astonished at his teaching" (v. 33).

Despite Jesus's handling of this Sadducean objection, the Pharisees reconvened. They came up with one last challenge, this time from an "expert in the law," to test Jesus: "Teacher, which command in the law is the greatest?" And here comes the Great Commandment we explored in chapter 1. Jesus said we are to love God with all of who we are—with all our hearts, souls, and minds and love people as ourselves (vv. 36–39).

---

[5] Moreland, *Love Your God with All Your Mind*, 53 (see chap. 1, n. 8).

Turnabout is, as they say, fair play. So Jesus followed his handling of these challenges with a question for them (vv. 41–46). He asked them whose son is the Messiah. "David's," they responded. Jesus asked, "How is it then that David, inspired by the Spirit, calls him 'Lord'?" and quotes a messianic passage, Ps 110:1, wherein David explicitly referred to the Messiah as "Lord." Jesus asked them, "If David calls him 'Lord,' how, then, can he be his son?" The term "Lord" here is one the Jews would have used only of God. The point of Jesus's question was to show they hadn't rightly understood the Messiah. He is in the lineage of David, but, as Psalm 110 implies, the Messiah is no mere man or ordinary political king. Even David, the greatest king in Israel's history, called him Lord. These elite scholars had the Messiah right in front of them, and yet they were too dull in their understanding to see it. They wanted a political leader like David, and yet Jesus was so much more than that. Matthew 22 ends by saying, "no one dared to question him anymore" (v. 46).

It is noteworthy that the command to love God with all of our minds is embedded in a broader passage where Jesus refuted the top scholars of his day. Jesus fully exemplified intellectual virtue and skill. It seems we, too, should be astonished.

Jesus's Use of Story

The second area in which we see the brilliance of Jesus is in his use of story. Now, being a good storyteller does not necessarily make one brilliant. But Jesus was not merely a good storyteller. Jesus often, seemingly on the spot, had the ability to package profound truths in stories that perfectly applied to his hearers and brought insight and conviction. People love stories. They impact us deeply because we often let our guards down in getting sucked into a good story. This is not easy to pull off, especially on the spot. But Jesus did this brilliantly.

One common way in which Jesus used story to make important points was in the use of parables. A parable is a short story that has a specific moral or spiritual lesson. The story lines of the parables were usually fictional in most of the details. They often had unexpected elements in the story that Jesus used to make incisive points. For example, in the parable of the good Samaritan (Luke 10:30–35), it is the Samaritan who is the hero of the story and not the religious leaders (the priest or the Levite). This is most unexpected because Jews often had racial animosity toward the Samaritans.

The parable of the prodigal son (Luke 15:11–32) is a great example of a profound and brilliant lesson that Jesus gave. The story, in short, is about a father with two sons. One son is rebellious but humbled, and the other is obedient but moralistic. The younger son demands his inheritance early, and the father fulfills his request. There were likely a few gasps from the crowd at this moment. Both of these facts would have come as a shock because a son was not meant to receive his inheritance until the father had passed away. In effect, the son said, "I would like it to be as if you are dead." It is, in a way, even more shocking that the father gave in since he certainly didn't have to. In fact, in real life at the time, the son would have gotten a beating and perhaps been turned out for insurrection. And yet the father in this story concedes.

Given the patriarchal culture of Jesus's day, his listeners would already be hooked into this story. What son would do this? And, moreover, what father would allow this? With the power of a good story and the skill of a good storyteller, one can't help but want to hear what comes next.

After squandering the father's fortune with what the King James Version calls "riotous living," this rebellious and broken son returns home ready to beg a slave's position in his father's household. But his father sees him from a distance on his way home and *runs* to him. It is a beautiful picture of unconditional love and forgiveness. It seems this father has been keeping an eye on the road and then breaks conventional etiquette and sprints to his boy. Etiquette dictated that a father would never condescend to run to a son, especially a rebellious one. Yet this father runs and embraces the rebel as a son and throws him a party to celebrate his return.

Though this is the part of the story everyone knows, it doesn't end here. The first half is both shocking and simultaneously heartwarming, but it is the second half where Jesus made the central point of the parable. In the story, the older son has missed all of these events because he is faithfully working for the family. There's a stark contrast between the father's response and the older son's response. The older son does not view the younger son with love and forgiveness, but with anger. Where's the older son's party? After all, he's earned the father's favor by faithfully working for all of these years. Against typical etiquette, the father, again, goes out and meets his oldest son. But the father is met with self-righteousness and complaints.

It's a powerful story, but we have to understand who Jesus was talking to so that we don't miss his brilliance here. He was talking to a mixed crowd. He had "sinners" and the religious elite, the Pharisees and scribes, listening to the story. What gets really interesting are the ways in which each may have found themselves in the story. Clearly the so-called sinners (as if the religious leaders weren't also sinners) would have found themselves relating to the younger rebellious son. They may not have demanded an early inheritance and squandered away a fortune. They, however, perhaps would have related to taking advantage of loved ones and the brokenness, embarrassment, and humiliation of a sinful lifestyle, especially in such a moralistic society. And they would have longed for the grace, unconditional love, and forgiveness of a father like this one who would run to them with embrace and restoration. They would have been powerfully pointed to *the* Father whom Jesus had been preaching.

The religious leaders, by contrast, would not have related to the younger son. They clearly were meant to relate to the older son. The older son is obedient, but he has no love or forgiveness in his heart. He ironically feels as if the father has violated *his* rights by welcoming the younger son with a big party. It becomes clear that both sons have only sought after the father's wealth and have not loved the father for who he truly is. The younger son was bold enough to demand his father's wealth early. The older son remained obedient but only, as it turns out, in order likewise to gain his father's stuff. Tim Keller has said:

> Neither son loved the father for himself. They both were using the father for their own self-centered ends rather than loving, enjoying, and serving him for his own sake. This means that you can rebel against God and be alienated from him either by breaking his rules or by keeping all of them diligently. It's a shocking message: Careful obedience to God's law may serve as a strategy for rebelling against God.[6]

The difference between the two sons is that the younger son was lost but finds repentance and humility, while the older son seems equally lost but his lostness remains. Jesus's point was that the religious leaders were as lost as the so-called sinners, but the sinners, in their brokenness, knew they needed a savior while the religious leaders thought they had earned their rights.

What's amazing is that we can find ourselves in this story. Many of us can see ways in which we have shockingly rebelled against God. As we find that our sin only brings hurt and brokenness, we can take solace in knowing the Father is watching for our return and is ready to restore us. But others of us can find ourselves in our moralistic religious efforts where we, too, act as if God owes us for our service. We are good Christians, we may think, because of all of our spiritual efforts. Both behaviors are spiritually destructive, and we need to turn (or perhaps return) to the Father in repentance.

This is brilliant! It is a carefully crafted story with seemingly endless insights and applications. We find the same depth in Jesus's other parables such as the good Samaritan (Luke 10:30–37), the lost sheep (Matt 18:12–14; Luke 15:3–7), the talents (Matt 25:14–30), and others. It is only a serious intellect that can pull off the richness of such profound stories. We should

---

[6] Timothy Keller, *The Prodigal God: Recovering the Heart of the Christian Faith* (New York: Penguin, 2008), 42–43.

be impressed by Jesus's intellect, and we should strive to be like Jesus in his intellectual ability to use story for the kingdom of God.

The Depth of Jesus's Gospel Message

The final way Jesus's logical skills were put on display was in the depth of Jesus's message. He was not the Messiah people expected. The Jews expected a conquering king who would free them from the grips of Roman control and reward the faithful religious establishment. But Jesus came to free people from a different sort of bondage. He said, "If you continue in my word, you really are my disciples. You will know the truth, and the truth will set you free" (John 8:31–32). Jesus clarified this is a freedom from the slavery of sin and all of us need it, even (perhaps especially) the religious establishment.

Jesus's message is one that calls for repentance in light of God's grace and love. It is a fundamentally humbling message because it says we can't work our way to salvation. We must surrender. It is that the "the last will be first, and the first last" (Matt 20:16). This is a fundamentally subversive message, and it ultimately got Jesus killed because it flipped the script on the religious establishment. It's a difficult message for us to hear in our pride; however, it's brilliant. It ultimately speaks to the depth of our human condition. Our sin runs deep. And Jesus's message is that no amount of religious service will ever address the depths of our sin. We need a new heart. In C. S. Lewis's *Mere Christianity*, in the essay titled "Is Christianity Hard or Easy?," he says: "If I am a field that contains nothing but grass-seed, I cannot produce wheat. Cutting the grass may keep it short: but I shall still produce grass and no wheat. If I want to produce wheat, the change must go deeper than the surface. I must be plowed up and re-sown."[7] Many other religions do nothing more than give us a list of good deeds to perform. But

---

[7] C. S. Lewis, *The Complete C. S. Lewis Signature Classics* (New York: HarperOne, 2002), 158.

all of us have a far more fundamental problem than needing to do different and more good deeds.

In the early years of Christianity's history, people who joined the Christian movement were called followers of "the Way" (Acts 9:2; 19:9, 23; 22:4; 24:14, 22). Jesus claimed to be the Way at one point in his ministry. In John 14, Jesus told his disciples he was going away but his disciples couldn't come. Jesus said, "If I go away and prepare a place for you, I will come again and take you to myself, so that where I am you may be also. You know the way to where I am going" (vv. 3–4). Not understanding his meaning, Thomas asked, "Lord, we don't know where you're going. How can we know *the way*?" (v. 5, emphasis added). And Jesus's brilliant but also radical statement was, "I am *the way*, the truth, and the life. No one comes to the Father except through me" (v. 6, emphasis added). D. A. Carson says, "[Jesus] so mediates God's truth and God's life that he is the very way to God . . . the one who alone can say, *No one comes to the Father except through me*."[8] So the followers of the Way were, of course, followers of Jesus's teaching—but more importantly they were followers of Jesus himself as the way, the truth, and the life.

Just what is Jesus the way to? In other words, what is the destination to which Jesus is the way? Jesus is the way to peace, love, and reconciliation with the Father. Needless to say, this is an allusion to the gospel itself. The gospel, in short, is that God creates the world to bring glory to him with humans as the crescendo of creation. Humans, however, go against this purpose in bringing glory to themselves. That is, humans sin and are thereby fallen. But in God's great love, he sent Jesus to die on the cross for our sins and defeated death in his resurrection. We must repent of the ways in which we seek glory for ourselves (our sin) and accept what Jesus did on our behalf by placing our faith and allegiance in him. When we do this, we begin an eternal life marked by worship unto God.

---

[8] D. A. Carson, *The Pillar New Testament Commentary: The Gospel according to John* (Grand Rapids: Eerdmans, 1991), 491, italics in original.

This is a brilliant message. In fact, I believe there is no more profound message in all the world and in all of history.

It is also a message that can handle the deepest challenges. For example, the Christian gospel provides hope as we face times of suffering. How does it do this? First, the Christian gospel makes clear that the created world is not intended to satisfy our every pleasure. It is about the glory of God and all created things recognizing the supremacy of God in worship. And so the fact that our lives aren't pleasure filled at all moments and are sometimes truly difficult is not necessarily inconsistent with God's good plan for the universe.

Second, the Christian gospel involves our fall and general sinfulness. Our world is broken, evidenced by our own sinfulness. We live in a state of moral rebellion, apart from Christ, and choose to sin and reject God as King over us. The gospel doesn't soft-pedal this reality. In some ways, we should expect suffering in this world precisely because our fallenness predicts it.

Third, and most important, in our redemption from the state of rebellion, God enters into our imperfect world and secures our hope in Christ. In quite an insightful piece, Peter Kreeft says:

> He came. He entered space and time and suffering. He came, like a lover. Love seeks above all intimacy, presence, togetherness. Not happiness. "Better unhappy with her than happy without her"—that is the word of a lover. He came. That is the salient fact, the towering truth, that alone keeps us from putting a bullet through our heads. He came. Job is satisfied even though the God who came gave him absolutely no answers at all to his thousand tortured questions. He did the most important thing and he gave the most important gift: himself.[9]

Kreeft goes on:

---

[9] Peter Kreeft, *Making Sense Out of Suffering* (Cincinnati: Servant Books, 1986), 133.

> Jesus did three things to solve the problem of suffering. First, he came. He suffered with us. He wept. Second, in becoming man he transformed the meaning of our suffering: it is now part of his work of redemption. Our death pangs become birth pangs for heaven . . . Third, he died and rose. Dying, he paid the price for sin and opened heaven to us; rising, he transformed death from a hole into a door, from an end into a beginning.[10]

When we reflect on this, we see how truly unique Jesus's ministry was. Because of what Jesus did, we have an inextinguishable hope. In taking on the sins of the world on the cross, Jesus went through more suffering than we could ever dream. And he did it for us. This is a brilliant and beautiful message. This is not to make light of the experience of suffering. It is to say that we can face these difficult times with the hope of Christ's work on the cross and his defeat of death in the resurrection.

Why Don't We See Jesus as a Brilliant Thinker?

With this as backdrop, it's a wonder that we even need to make a case for seeing Jesus as a brilliant thinker. One reason he is not seen as a brilliant thinker is that Jesus's teaching was always in particular teaching contexts. It was very much on the go, as it were. We don't get a well-worked-out treatise like we do with other thinkers. He always addressed a certain crowd or perhaps confronted certain challenges by religious leaders of the day. Much of this occurred on street corners and hillsides. For example, Jesus taught people in a revolutionary way that the last will be first and the first last. But he didn't expand on this, and he didn't provide a philosophical theory to underlie this idea. Jesus put this revolutionary idea out there, and

[10] Kreeft, 138.

perfectly lived it out, and along with his other thought turned the world upside down.

The mistake here is thinking that because Jesus didn't give us a full development of his ideas, then those ideas were not held with intellectual sophistication. The richness of his thought and his ability to use logic didn't come by accident. This was certainly intentional, and as we saw earlier, he pursued these skills even as a twelve-year-old sitting among the temple teachers. But writing a treatise was not part of Jesus's mission. He was here to save sinners and give us a vision of human flourishing.

Perhaps a more salient reason we don't appreciate the intellect of Jesus is that we fail to make Jesus Lord of our intellectual lives. We seem to think a Christlike intellect is optional for us. We either don't notice Jesus's powerful intellect, or we think this just comes along with being divinely omniscient. But one way or another, we often don't take seriously the call to follow Jesus in having an intellectual faith.

As Christians, we look to Jesus (and the rest of Scripture) for the right things to believe. We look to Jesus for perhaps *what* to think theologically, but we do not look to Jesus as our model for *how* to think and *how* to embody the Christian life. But the call of Jesus is to follow him in discipleship. It is not simply to mimic his moral actions or to mimic his beliefs. It is to be Christians—literally little Christs. It is to be his disciples and live our lives not only with similar actions and beliefs but with a similar heart and a similar mind behind the actions and beliefs.

Jesus should be, for us, the primary thought leader for all areas of life—including our disciplines, careers, and hobbies. If he is not, then Jesus is not Lord of our whole lives. That is, if we, as Christians, do not conform our thinking to his in every area of our lives and every one of our pursuits, then Jesus is simply not Lord over our entire lives. We have only given him part of who we are. We may have even unwisely split our lives between sacred pursuits (going to church, devotional time, etc.) and the rest (going to school, work, etc.), which are, in effect, secular.

But this seriously misunderstands the fact that Jesus is to be Lord over all. Paul described Jesus, in Col 1:16, in the following way:

> For everything was created by him,
> in heaven and on earth,
> the visible and the invisible,
> whether thrones or dominions
> or rulers or authorities—
> all things have been created through him and for him.

He goes on to say of Jesus, "In him are hidden all the treasures of wisdom and knowledge" (Col. 2:3). If we take these verses seriously, then we will see Jesus as Master over all intellectual domains. It's his world, created by him and for him, and all the treasures of wisdom and knowledge are hidden in him. Thus, there's nothing we can do in life for which Jesus doesn't have something to say. We should therefore conform our thinking and our lives to him in every area.

These verses also make perfect sense of the ways in which Jesus displayed his brilliance in the gospels. Willard has said:

> Paying careful attention to how Jesus made use of logical thinking can strengthen our confidence in Jesus as master of the centers of intellect and creativity, and can encourage us to accept him as master in all of the areas of intellectual life in which we may participate. In those areas we can, then, be his disciples, not disciples of the current movements and glittering personalities who happen to dominate our field in human terms.[11]

I don't have the ability (or the space) to say what it looks like for Jesus to be Lord over every one of our pursuits (I will have more to say about this in chap. 13). This, of course, doesn't merely mean that a Christian businessperson must wear Christian T-shirts, not swear (at least, out loud),

---

[11] Willard, "Jesus the Logician," 613–14.

and play Christian music in his or her place of business. These things are all well and good, but the claim is that there is more to being a Christian businessperson (or scientist, plumber, politician, philosopher, teacher, etc.) than this. Too often the Christian businessperson is indistinguishable from a secular businessperson. The call is to do business Christianly, making Jesus Lord over it all. This will involve drawing business practices from uniquely Christian principles and asking, "How would Jesus think and live if he were in my job?" This makes a big difference. Jesus is a brilliant thinker indeed. His level of intellectual skill is unmatched. I close this chapter with a final quote from Dallas Willard:

> [Jesus] is not just nice, he is brilliant. He is the smartest man who ever lived. He is now supervising the entire course of world history (Rev. 1:5) while simultaneously preparing the rest of the universe for our future role in it (John 14:2). He always has the best information on everything and certainly also on the things that matter most in human life. Let us now hear his teachings on who has the good life, on who is among the truly blessed.[12]

---

[12] Willard, *The Divine Conspiracy*, 95.

Critical Thinking and Worldview

People who live in New Jersey, where I grew up, tend to have quite a distinctive accent. This may be a bit hard to believe, but I grew up thinking people from the state didn't have an accent at all. Everyone just talked normal, as far as I was concerned. Then I went to college out of state and was around many people from different parts of the country. When I eventually returned to New Jersey, I suddenly noticed how distinct residents' accents really were. It was at that moment that I realized I, too, had an accent. Coming to this realization took being around people who had different accents from me. When you get around others, you quickly realize everyone, including yourself, has an accent.

A worldview is much like an accent in this respect. We all grow up with worldviews, but many of us do not realize what our worldview is or that we even have one until we interact with people who think very differently about the world than we do. If you grew up in a Christian household, you maybe thought, like I did, that everyone goes to church, believes in God, and prays regularly, and that Christianity is true. It can come as quite a shock to realize that some people actually think there is no God at all or think a different religious view is true.

One of the most important steps in becoming a critical thinker is thinking critically about our worldviews. Or, as it is sometimes said, we need to learn to think *worldviewishly* about the ideas we consider. We can be thoughtful about a lot of life without ever thinking on the level of worldview. It takes going below the surface of our ideas. To think worldviewishly is also hard work, and it can even be a bit scary to honestly and genuinely evaluate our most fundamental ideas, commitments, and values. But to be a critical thinker, understanding and evaluating our worldview is really not optional. One of Socrates's most famous sayings is that "the unexamined life is not worth living." Socrates's method (as pictured in Plato's dialogues) with his dialogue partners was always to push them to examine the underlying thoughts and ideas of what they were saying. Jesus often did the same. Part of what it is to flourish as a human being is to reflect on and examine whether our familiar ways of thinking are correct. This is crucial to having an examined life. We must think reflectively about and evaluate our own worldviews, as well as the worldviews of others.

What Is a Worldview?

As the name suggests, a worldview is how we view or see the world. It's important to understand that it is *how* we see the world and not necessarily *what* we see. Let's say a Christian and an atheist are doing some stargazing on a really clear night in an area without much light pollution. In one sense both the Christian and the atheist will see the same thing. Let's say they see an exquisite display of stars and the moon across the horizon. And we may suppose that both will likely be in awe at this scene. But *how* they each see this scene will no doubt be quite different indeed. The Christian may see the starry sky as a sign of God's incredible power and majesty and may long to worship and to know better this artistic creator God. The atheist could see it as an amazing display of physical reality and be moved to understand the starry heavens through science but would see it as something of a happy accident. The difference here is a difference of worldview.

A worldview is often something we assume in experiencing the world, rather than being at the forefront of our minds. Still, as I will argue below, we can reflect on our worldviews and reject them, in part or in whole, and embrace a new worldview when we are convinced of its truth. But, when we are not reflecting on it, it is something we largely assume as we move throughout the world. It largely resides at a subconscious level, affecting the way we act—and especially react—to the world as we find it. As such, a worldview acts as a kind of interpretive lens through which we see and understand the world. Just as rose-colored glasses affect how we see, our worldview colors our experiences.

One of the most influential thinkers on the topic of worldview, James Sire, defines a worldview as:

> a commitment, a fundamental orientation of the heart, that can be expressed as a story or in a set of presuppositions (assumptions which may be true, partially true or entirely false) that we hold (consciously or subconsciously, consistently or inconsistently) about the basic constitution of reality, and that provides the foundations on which we live and move and have our being.[1]

Let's look at this definition in greater detail.

A worldview is a *fundamental orientation of the heart.* Sire uses the biblical term *heart* in his definition of worldview. At times this term is quite misunderstood. The Bible does, sometimes, refer to the heart in the literal, blood-pumping organ sense. But far more often, it talks about the heart in a

[1] James Sire, *The Universe Next Door: A Basic Worldview Catalog* (Downers Grove, IL: InterVarsity Press, 2009), 20.

nonphysical sense. For example, Prov 4:23 tells us the heart is "the source of life" and that we should guard it above all else. Solomon is not here telling us to guard the organ in our chests but means it in a nonliteral sense. The sense used here, and in many places throughout the Bible, is the deep place of the self. It is the interior of a person, including one's intellect, character, and spiritual self, as well as one's emotions.

David Naugle says that the biblical concept of "heart" is "the central, defining element of the human person . . . the spiritual nucleus of the person about which life orbits."[2] This orientation of the heart is not then only intellectual, even though our beliefs and reasons are part of the picture since those are quite fundamental to the human person. The point, however, is that we are merely intellectual. Wilkens and Sanford put it this way: "To isolate the intellectual component as the exclusive concern of worldview formation, as many worldview books do, is reductionistic. It condenses a real multidimensional person to a single aspect of his or her actual existence. To be sure, our intellect is important, but if taken in isolation it fails to put complete and real people in the picture."[3] So when Sire defines a worldview as a fundamental commitment and orientation of the heart, he is saying that it is a deep commitment of our interior self in all of its constituent aspects.

Sometimes our worldview can be seen most clearly in the ways in which we react to things. For example, let's say you grew up in a house surrounded by woods. Your best memories from growing up are all related to being with your family outside in these woods. Let's say being in nature like this becomes really important to you personally as you grow older. Spending time hiking and camping in the woods is more than a mere hobby. It is how you recharge and come to grips with life.

---

[2] David Naugle, *Worldview: The History of a Concept*, 5th ed. (Grand Rapids: Eerdmans, 2002), 268–69.

[3] Steve Wilkens and Mark Sanford, *Hidden Worldviews: Eight Cultural Stories That Shape Our Lives* (Downers Grove, IL: InterVarsity Press, 2009), 16.

But let's say you find yourself on an urban development committee that is debating whether to develop a beautiful portion of wooded public land into a large and lucrative new subdivision. As you think about how to vote on this committee, there is undoubtedly a certain orientation of your heart regarding this situation. You would likely be committed to keeping the woods rather than doing the development. But not everyone will agree. Suppose one committee member grew up in the city and doesn't value nature like you do. Let's also suppose this person is primarily concerned with the financial bottom line in these sorts of situations. This person has quite a different orientation of the heart toward this matter.

Imagine the ensuing debate between you and this other member, who may continue to emphasize how much money will be involved, thinking that you are just not understanding how lucrative this will be for the city. You may keep emphasizing the value to the city of keeping the woods and preserving nature, thinking this is obvious. This is a clash of worldviews, and it can be frustrating when one is not realizing the differences at that level. When we don't engage on the level of worldview, we'll find ourselves talking past one another. Progress is often only possible if we take the time to think worldviewishly about how each person is approaching the issues.

Secondly, *a worldview can be expressed as a story or in a set of presuppositions*. When we want to think about or discuss our worldviews, we have to use descriptions and make claims. So while a worldview itself is a fundamental orientation of the heart, we will talk about worldviews either using a story or a set of claims.[4]

---

[4] Sire says that a worldview can be expressed as a set of "presuppositions." While this is no doubt true, I would suggest these need not be things that are only strictly presupposed. We can express our worldviews as a set of claims that we actively believe. For example, part of my worldview is believing that God exists and created the universe. I may merely presuppose this, at times, when I, say, look up at a night sky. However, I can also reflect on this idea, consider the evidence for God's existence, and believe it as an explicit claim.

The Bible expresses a full Christian worldview, but it doesn't exactly give it to us in outline form. In fact, it often communicates this worldview in the form of story. Think about Genesis 1 and 2. We are given neither a systematic theological account of creation, nor are we given a scientific account. Genesis 1 and 2 tell the story of creation with God as the main character. Genesis 1 begins with "In the beginning" and then proceeds to tell the story of what God did in creation. We find out in this story that something very special occurs in the course of creation, namely, humans are created in the image of God (v. 27). God looks at what he made and declares it to be good throughout the narrative and ultimately "very good indeed" (v. 31).

This is an incredibly rich story and is foundational for much of the rest of Scripture. From the details of the story, we get, among other things, a proper view of the value of every single human being, the purpose of humans, the design of marriage, and what it is for humans to flourish. We are also set up for the fall of humanity in Genesis 3. Now, presumably, all of this could be stated in descriptive statements (and there are many commentaries and accounts of the theology of creation that do just that), but, in Genesis, the worldview is expressed in a story.

The Bible also includes poetry, historical epic, law code, wisdom literature, biography, and teaching letter. These are different forms of literature, but they each express the Christian worldview. In poetry and historical epic (like story), we are not straightforwardly told how to think (as teaching letters or law codes do), but they, in a way, paint pictures with imagery that point to the truths that underlie the poetry or narrative.

Theologians have the great task of attempting to capture an accurate picture of the Christian worldview in statements drawn from all parts and genres of Scripture. While Scripture perfectly expresses a Christian worldview, theologians will only ever produce fallible summaries and guides to understanding Scripture. As incredibly helpful as they can be, as Christians, we should derive our worldview directly from Scripture. Still, our derivations will only ever be fallible as well.

We can also see the Christian worldview expressed (again, fallibly) by other works of literature, such as Dante Alighieri's *The Divine Comedy*, John Bunyan's *The Pilgrim's Progress*, or Charles Dickens's *A Christmas Carol*. Or, more recently, there is C. S. Lewis's *The Chronicles of Narnia* or J. R. R. Tolkien's *The Lord of the Rings* series. Also, many movies explicitly express a Christian worldview, such as *The Passion of the Christ* or *The Case for Christ*. But there are many other movies that express aspects of a Christian worldview in less obvious ways, such as *Silence* or *The Book of Eli*.

This same point can be made about story in general. At some level, there is some worldview being expressed in any story. Again, the worldview expression can be very obvious or it can be rather subtle. Either way, it is there and it takes a critical mind to unearth the worldviews being expressed in the story one is consuming.

Third, Sire points out we can be *conscious of our worldviews or we can hold them subconsciously*. As we mentioned above, our worldviews are often assumed as we act in the world. We may see the world a certain way but don't have enough self-awareness to know how or why we see the world that way. Our worldview may be held subconsciously. And if we never reflect on our worldviews, we may never become conscious of them. But this isn't how it should be for a critical thinker. It is definitely possible for a worldview to be held consciously. We can be aware of the lens we have. In the example used above, you might feel strongly about the fact that the woods shouldn't be plowed under to build a new subdivision and not realize how your childhood experiences are informing this view. But you might be quite aware how you feel about the woods and quite reflective about how your growing-up experiences are informing your thoughts and decisions about the woods. You can even work hard to evaluate whether your view is proper and try to change it.

Fourth, Sire says that our worldviews are *about the basic constitution of reality, and that provides the foundations on which we live and move and have our being*. Our worldviews involve deep considerations and commitments about reality. The reason we often don't realize the specific worldviews we have is precisely because they are so fundamental. Again it is hard work to wonder about and reflect on the fundamental constitution of reality. Not everyone likes to chat about his or her worldview. This isn't exactly party talk. But like it or not, or whether we are conscious of it or not, we do see reality in certain fundamental ways. These ways dictate how we live and move and have our being. We will either hold our worldviews with intentionality on the basis of reflection and evaluation, or we will hold them unintentionally as an accident of our growing-up experience and our environment. Nonetheless, we have a worldview.

How Does One Get a Worldview?

We get our worldviews from a number of sources. We first get a worldview from the earliest childhood experiences. Even as adults we may still be affected by the context of where we grew up and how we were raised. This means our family situation, our schooling situation, and our cultural situation all have an effect on our worldviews. It happens to the best of us who set out to be different from our parents: one day we catch ourselves saying the very same things to our own kids and acting in similar ways. Or, when it comes to our school experience, if we grow up in a competitive system with high academic standards, it will impact how we approach life. It would likely be quite different from someone who grows up in a more community-based system that values exploration with one's peers.

Location matters. If we grow up in the United States, we'll likely have a different worldview than if we grow up in Western Europe, the Middle East, or in South America. But even within the United States, one's worldview can be shaped by the region in which we're raised. Living in rural Tuskegee, Alabama, is culturally quite different from urban Portland, Oregon. Even our specific community will shape, for better or worse, our worldview in numerous ways.

From the moment we come into this world and as we grow in our cognitive awareness, we consciously and subconsciously notice what's around us; we soak it up, and our hearts become oriented accordingly. We act like a dry sponge in a liquid in that we absorb what's around us by virtue of being in contact with it. Or perhaps the better analogy is the way trees and other plants naturally take on nutrients from the ground by a process of osmosis. We naturally absorb the ideas of the world around us. This is why our parents told us not to hang out with certain people in our school, and it is why they didn't allow us to listen to certain artists or watch certain shows and movies. The impact these things have on our way of thinking can be startling. This power is why Paul told us, "whatever is true, whatever is honorable, whatever is just, whatever is pure, whatever is lovely, whatever is commendable—if there is any moral excellence and if there is anything praiseworthy—dwell on these things" (Phil 4:8). Elsewhere, Paul said, "Do not be conformed to this age, but be transformed by the renewing of your mind" (Rom 12:2). We should dwell on the things of the Lord, in general, and biblical truths, in particular, precisely because these will have an effect on the way we think. In this, we will renew our minds, and it will shape our worldview to be more Christian.

Worldview Skepticism and the Principles of Logic

Before moving forward, we must face a serious challenge. Here's the question: If a worldview is an interpretive lens through which we see the world, can we evaluate our worldview to know that it is good or bad? Consider again someone who wears glasses and is looking at a wall that looks to be the color red. How does one know the wall is actually red? One may wonder whether the glasses are tinted, making a white wall only *look* red. How can the true color of the wall be verified? With glasses, one can remove them and perhaps see whether there is a red or white thing in view. But when it comes to a worldview, we can't exactly take our worldviews off for evaluation. It's not like we can simply step outside of our worldview to inspect its quality. This kind of worry can lead to a skeptical view we will call "worldview skepticism."[5] This view says we only have access to our worldview but not to the world itself. That is, we can never check to see whether the worldview lens is giving us an accurate view of reality. This is a challenge because if we are hopelessly stuck behind our worldviews, then it would be impossible to evaluate and think critically about our worldviews.

Are we hopelessly caught behind a worldview? Though we often do not realize how pervasive and subtle our worldviews are, the answer, I suggest, is no. We can in fact evaluate our worldviews and the worldviews of others. Though our worldview deeply affects how we see the world, it is important to keep in mind that our worldviews do not wholly produce or construct the world as we find it. Recall the example at the beginning of the chapter of the Christian and the atheist looking up at the night sky. The atheist sees the same basic facts of the world as the Christian, even if how he or she interprets these facts may be significantly different. Again, our worldviews inform *how* we see the world, not *what* is there to be seen. Thus, we can measure our worldviews by the facts of reality. It is a lens, but it is an interpretive lens, and the facts, at least to some degree, determine the interpretation.

Take the interpretation of Scripture, as an analogy. We can interpret every passage in the Bible in a variety of ways, and it may seem like we can read anything we want to into the text. But the text does plausibly constrain the interpretation, to a degree; it at least allows us to evaluate whether an interpretation is a good one. There are, for example, a variety of interpretations of the creation account in Genesis 1. But these interpretations need to make sense of the facts of the narrative. One can't plausibly interpret it as a Greek creation myth with procreating gods and goddesses. This, as they say, would do violence to the text. The point is many different interpretations can exist, and we can evaluate the interpretations on how well they explain the facts of account.

---

[5] This view is similar to postmodernism, which denies the fact that we can have objective knowledge of the world. The view is that all knowledge and truth is a matter of perspective. See Sire, *The Universe Next Door*, 214–77.

In the same way, there are many ways to view the world. But, as we shall see, not all worldviews are equally plausible given the facts of reality. For example, if a worldview denies the reality of, say, pain and suffering and thinks of these as mere illusions, then this is exceedingly implausible. If anything is clear, especially when we are going through it, it is the reality of pain and suffering. We would need extremely compelling reasons to believe that pain and suffering are mere illusions.

Among the facts of reality that we can use to evaluate our worldviews are the principles of logic and reason. I will argue that the logical principles themselves (as opposed to our beliefs about logic) are part of the facts of reality with which we are aware and are not part of the interpretive lens of our worldview—the basic principles of logic don't come to us from our culture or growing-up experience or our broader experiences as we get older. A person on one side of the world uses the same principles of logic as a person on the other side. It's not as though contradictory statements can be true in some countries and false in others. Contradictions are necessarily false no matter who is thinking about them. Mathematical facts are similar to this. This is not a matter of one's worldview. When two things are added to three things, they will necessarily equal five no matter where one is at in the world. This is not a cultural construct or a matter of interpretation. The basic facts of arithmetic and the principles of logic are pretheoretic in that we learn them as fundamental facts long before we learn how to think about them.

Now, systems of logic have been developed through the ages that are obviously theoretic. They come as well-worked-out theories of the great logicians who undoubtedly bring their worldview into the picture. What I am referring to is the awareness and use of the principles themselves (as opposed to the systems developed to describe the principles) that we become acquainted with at a relatively young age. We don't have to know the theories of logic to be aware of and make use of the principles of logic. In fact, you don't need to have a theory to grasp the logical principles, but you do need the logical principles to develop a theory of logic. In a similar way, we need logical principles to develop our worldviews (at least if they are to be logically consistent), not the other way around.

To see this, consider that for any child in any culture to begin to communicate thoughts and ideas, he or she must make use of the principles of logic. My son's first word, after pointing at a ball, was "Ball." If I had shaken my head and said to him, "Not a ball. Banana," he would have been quite confused indeed. However, he would not think that it is both a ball and not a ball (i.e., a banana). That is, he is not going to embrace a contradiction. He'd likely insist that it is in fact a ball. Even as a young child, he makes use of a logical principle called the principle of noncontradiction. This principle says that it can't be the case that a claim and its opposite (i.e., the negation of the claim) are both true at the same time and in the same sense.[6] My son, at this age, of course didn't know the name of this principle, nor could he have articulated it or even grasped a statement of this law of logic. But he definitely made use of the principle, and so do all of us from a very young age.

As we said above, as children, we begin to make sense of the world around us and form our worldviews. To do this, we must use the principles of logic. This is precisely what it means to make *sense* of the world. This isn't to say we always have a logical worldview. Still, there is an indisputable and unavoidable logic to it.

What about religious views that explicitly reject the principles of logic? Sometimes the principles of logic are called "Western" ways of seeing the world, while much Eastern religious thought sees reality as being, in some way, illusory and even contradictory. For example, a Zen master may direct the student of Zen Buddhism to reflect on the sound of one hand clapping, and this is supposed to lead to enlightenment. But, even though it seems to take, by definition, two hands to clap, the student is supposed to reflect on the sound of a one-handed clap. You might be scratching your head as to how that's possible, and that's the point. It is impossible—indeed, it is

[6] This is discussed at greater depth in chapter 4.

logically impossible. But thinking about this contradictory state of affairs is supposed to free the mind and lead to enlightenment.

Is this an embrace of a contradiction and a rejection of logic? No, a logic still is here. You cannot imagine one hand clapping (unless one goes the smart-aleck way of Bart Simpson, who famously slaps his fingers to his palm on the same hand) because it is not logically possible, and thus you can't reflect on the sound of it. There may be some value in the confounding effort of trying to reflect on a logically impossible state of affairs, but this does not therefore show logic is not a crucial part of the Zen Buddhist worldview. After all, the Zen master may direct the student to perform this exercise to free the student's mind, but this would constitute a logical reason. If reflecting on a contradiction did bring a kind of enlightenment, then this would be a good (i.e., logical) reason to engage in this meditative practice.

Also, when the Zen Buddhist spells out his beliefs, he will necessarily have to make use of the principles of logic if anyone is going to understand him. To assert, "you should reflect on the sound of one hand clapping," you implicitly make use of the principle of noncontradiction. The student would likely get an earful if the student said, "So you want me to *not* reflect on the sound of one hand clapping?" or "So you want me to reflect on the sound of two hands clapping?" The Zen master logically asserts something on the basis of the principle of noncontradiction.

The point is, one will have to use logic to deny it, and this is clearly problematic. You cannot make a coherent claim against the principles of logic without using the principles of logic. One will also not be able to live life without the principles of logic. In order to know what is food and avoid what is toxic and poisonous, he must use the principles of logic. Or what should I do at a crosswalk if I have the thought that there are and there are not oncoming cars? How could I ever get across? Or if the Eastern religious person wants to construct a building for religious practice, the builder shouldn't use contradictory plans, or the building may come down on his or her head. One can *say* they don't believe in logic, but talk is, as they say, cheap.

When my kids were little, they often played the "opposite game," but, in doing so, they ran squarely into the nature of logic. The opposite game was not so much a game as much as a way, all in good fun, to try to get out of something they were supposed to do. Suppose my daughter had committed to playing with her toys for only fifteen more minutes, and then she would straighten her room. When fifteen minutes were up, and we reminded her what she had committed to do, she said, with a mischievous smile, "I was playing the opposite game." The game (at least as I understood it) was that everything she says means the opposite. So if she said she would clean her room, because she was playing the opposite game, that meant she wouldn't clean her room.

Now, this is where my kids probably regret having to grow up with a philosophy professor dad. I often responded, "Okay, so you were *not* playing the opposite game." And she said, "No, I *was* playing the opposite game!" And I asked, "Okay, you were *not* playing the opposite game?" And this went on for a little while before she realized the futility of claiming she was playing the opposite game, since the opposite of this statement is that she was not playing the opposite game. The problem? If she was playing the opposite game, then she wasn't! But this made no sense, and that's the point. What she was bumping up against is the principle of noncontradiction. She couldn't claim to be playing the opposite game because if it's true, then she was not playing the opposite game, and round and round we go.

The point is that logic is unavoidable and universal. Thus, all worldviews are subject to the principles of logic. We become aware of and use the principles of logic whenever we are acting rationally, regardless of whether we say we deny them.

Using Logic to Evaluate Worldviews

So, that's good news: we are not doomed to hold our worldviews blindly. We can use logic and critical thinking as tools, along with the facts of the world, to evaluate our worldviews. Again, it takes some careful and reflective work, and it takes courage, but we can rationally evaluate our worldviews as well as the worldviews of others. We should reject our worldview, in whole or in part, when we come to see that it does not track with the facts of the world or that there is a more plausible way of understanding that aspect of the world.

What does this look like?

What this *doesn't* mean is that when a view sounds crazy or implausible, especially initially, it is therefore false. When we bump into someone who has a different worldview, it will almost always sound implausible—at least at first. In fact, pointing out that it sounds implausible far too often is the extent of how we critique other worldviews. We hear that someone believes there's no God or they believe in many gods and goddesses or they think we can achieve oneness with nature, and we dismissively roll our eyes. What we don't often realize is that the Christian worldview sounds implausible to those who do not hold to it too. The notions of a virgin birth, the doctrine of the Trinity, and a man rising from the dead sound outlandish to those who are unfamiliar with them. But you wouldn't want people to write off your Christian beliefs just because they sound implausible or weird at first exposure, so, similarly, we shouldn't write off the views of others. There are ways to critique worldviews, but merely pointing at them as sounding crazy is not one of them.

A second way worldviews should not be critiqued is from within another worldview perspective. For example, suppose we intend to critique pantheism, the idea that the world is God and God is the world, on the basis of the fact that it doesn't comport with the Christian view of the world. This isn't a genuine evaluation since we already know the pantheist does not hold to a Christian view. All this amounts to is pointing out the differences of the respective views. We haven't yet evaluated the views.

So, how does one evaluate a worldview?

In his classic book on worldviews, Ronald Nash offers tests or criteria for evaluating a worldview. Nash finds inspiration for the criteria from Gordon Clark, who says, "If one system can provide plausible solutions to many problems while another leaves too many questions unanswered, if one system tends less to skepticism and gives more meaning to life, if one worldview is consistent while others are self-contradictory, who can deny us, since we must choose, the right to choose the more promising first principle?"[7] Nash sees here three tests or criteria for evaluating a worldview.[8] There is the test of reason, the test of experience, and the test of practice. The first, the test of reason, evaluates the internal logical consistency of the worldview. Here we ask whether a worldview logically coheres, or is it, as Clark puts it, self-contradictory? The second, the test of experience, is where we evaluate a worldview in terms of how well it explains the facts of reality. We ask whether the worldview explains the world as we find it through our experiences. And, if it doesn't or if there is a better explanation, then this is good reason to think the worldview should be rejected in whole or in part. The third test, the test of practice, is an evaluation of its livability. Let's look at these each in more detail.

Logical Consistency

A worldview should be logically consistent. Its very claims should cohere in terms of their internal logic. Two claims are logically inconsistent when they can't both be true at the same time. The two claims may be both false, or one of them may be true while the other is false. But if two claims are logically inconsistent, they can't both be true. It's important to mention that when two claims are logically inconsistent, this doesn't necessarily tell us which claim is false, but we know at least one of them must be false. The following two ideas seem logically inconsistent:

---

[7] Ronald Nash, *Worldviews in Conflict: Choosing Christianity in a World of Ideas* (Grand Rapids: Zondervan, 1992), 54. See Gordon Clark, *A Christian View of Men and Things* (Grand Rapids: Eerdmans, 1952), 34.

[8] Nash, 55.

1. God is all loving.
2. God doesn't care about me when I suffer.

If God is all loving, then it seems to follow he must care about me when I suffer. Notice if that's right, then if 1 is true, then 2 must be false. And if 2 is true, then 1 must be false. They could both be false if God isn't all loving (as in he doesn't love everyone) but he does happen to care about me when I suffer. These look to be logically inconsistent because they can't both be true.

Consider another example:

1. God is all-powerful and all good, and gives all people health, wealth, and prosperity when they pray for it.
2. Many people in the world are suffering from sickness and poverty despite their prayers for relief.

There are many who believe that God aims to make us healthy, wealthy, and prosperous. This is sometimes called the "prosperity gospel." But it seems this view of God is inconsistent with the pervasive suffering in the world, even among those who pray to God for relief. If this is correct, then it looks like God is either not all powerful, not all good, or doesn't give us health, wealth, and prosperity when we pray for it. Both of the statements above, it seems, can't be true. This is a worldview in need of repair.

Note that it's possible for ideas to appear inconsistent when they are not. If someone believes that God exists and believes that God does not exist, this is a clear inconsistency because it is a flat contradiction. However, it's almost never this clear and straightforward. When we evaluate a worldview, it's important that we are able to show where there is an alleged inconsistency. But a view that initially looks logically inconsistent could be shown to be consistent. The person who thinks the view is consistent would need to show how the tension can be resolved.

For example, people will sometimes assert that the following ideas are logically inconsistent:

1. There is an all-powerful and all-good God.
2. There is evil, pain, and suffering in the world.

The thought is if God is all-powerful and all good, then there shouldn't be any evil, pain, or suffering in the world. But obviously evil, pain, and suffering are in the world, so there must not be an all-powerful and all-good God, given the (alleged) logical inconsistency. It would take us too far afield to properly address this tension here. However, for our purposes, it's important to see that these are not logically inconsistent as long as God has some justifying reason for allowing evil, pain, and suffering. If God has justifying reasons for allowing evil, pain, and suffering, then this resolves the alleged logical tension. Thus seeming inconsistency doesn't entail actual inconsistency. Perhaps a person who holds to the aforementioned prosperity gospel could argue his or her view is logically consistent with the pervasive suffering in the world. In other words, a person can rebut these charges, but to resolve the apparent tension, he or she would have to show the logical coherence.

Best Explanation

Not only do we want our worldview to be logically consistent, we also want it to make good sense of the world. When our worldview adequately explains the world as we find it, then we have good evidence for our worldview. This is a natural sense of "evidence" (further addressed in chap. 9). It's not the sort of evidence we get from running experiments in the lab. But we can evaluate how well the worldview makes sense of the world, especially compared to how well other worldviews explain the world.

When we do this, we consider how well the facts of the world justify the interpretive lens of our worldview. We can see this by returning to the analogy of judging whether our eyeglasses are giving us an accurate view of the world. Think about how an eye doctor determines a patient's prescription for improved sight. The eye doctor will run through different possible prescriptions to figure out which makes clear the letters or images on the screen. We want the lens that is a good fit in making clear what's before us. Likewise, we want the worldview that makes good sense of the world as we experience it. A good worldview well explains the facts of reality.

For example, a worldview should tell us how the universe came to exist. Not all worldviews explain this basic fact equally well. The claim that God created the world and designed it to be life-permitting plausibly explains how it all got here. But we can ask whether there is a better explanation. Perhaps an eternal universe is a better explanation. Perhaps a universe that originates in a big bang from quantum fluctuations explains the data the best. The point is that as we look at the data we can judge which of these theories best explains the facts as we find them.

Or if we think that every human has dignity and intrinsic value, then our worldview should explain this fact too. The Christian view explains this in virtue of the fact that humans are created in the image of God. As image bearers, we are endowed with an intrinsic dignity and value. If someone denies the existence of God, then it can be difficult to explain the dignity and intrinsic value of human beings. This is often seen as a problem for atheistic views. But if human dignity is a fact, then we can ask how well a worldview explains this fact.

What else must a worldview explain? Sire gives us eight questions each worldview ought to answer. Every worldview should weigh in on each of these areas, and we can evaluate them according to how well they explain these parts of the world. We are looking for the best explanation of reality.

1. What is prime reality—the really real? To this we might answer: God, or the gods, or the material cosmos. Our answer here is the most fundamental. It sets the boundaries for the answers that can consistently be given to the other six questions.
2. What is the nature of external reality, that is, the world around us? Here our answers point to whether we see the world as created or autonomous, as chaotic or orderly, as matter or spirit; or whether we emphasize our subjective, personal relationship to the world or its objectivity apart from us.

3. What is a human being? To this we might answer: a highly complex machine, a sleeping god, a person made in the image of God, or a naked ape.
4. What happens to a person at death? Here we might reply: personal extinction, or transformation to a higher state, or reincarnation, or departure to a shadowy existence on "the other side."
5. Why is it possible to know anything at all? Sample answers include the idea that we are made in the image of an all-knowing God or that consciousness and rationality developed under the contingencies of survival in a long process of evolution.
6. How do we know what is right and wrong? Again, perhaps we are made in the image of a God whose character is good, or right and wrong are determined by human choice alone or what feels good, or the notions simply developed under an impetus toward cultural or physical survival.
7. What is the meaning of human history? To this we might answer: to realize the purposes of God or the gods, to make a paradise on earth, to prepare a people for a life in community with a loving and holy God, and so forth.[9]

Livability

An eighth and final criterion for evaluating a worldview is its livability. This is not a direct test for the truth of a worldview. Rather, it tells us if the worldview is good and whether it leads to human flourishing. If a worldview tells us that the goal of humanity is to disconnect from reality and this turns out to be impossible, then this is an unlivable worldview. We obviously

[9] Sire, 22–23. In newer additions of Sire's *The Universe Next Door*, he gives eight questions each worldview should answer. For space considerations, I've only included the seven. His eighth question is "What personal, life-orienting core commitments are consistent with this worldview?"

wouldn't be able to flourish if the goal of life is unattainable. Again, even if a worldview is not livable, this doesn't necessarily mean it is false. Thinking about my personal checking account doesn't lead to my flourishing, but this of course does not change the grim reality of my checking account. But if two worldviews are internally consistent, explain the world equally well (i.e., the first two criteria are satisfied), but one of them is completely unlivable and the other leads to human flourishing, then the one that leads to human flourishing is of course preferable.

In addition to this, Sire makes the point that if we begin to think our worldview is not livable, this has the benefit of causing us to search it out and evaluate its truth in a way that we may not otherwise. He says:

> Subjective satisfaction is important, and it may be the lack of it that causes us to investigate our worldview in the first place. The vague, uneasy feeling we have that something doesn't fit causes us to seek satisfaction. Our worldview is not quite livable. We bury our doubt, but it rises to the surface. We mask our insecurity, but our mask falls off. We find, in fact, that it is only when we pursue our doubts and search for the truth that we begin to get real satisfaction.[10]

The thought is when a part of our worldview is not livable, it could be because it is not true. It, in a way, signals to us that we should perhaps take a second look. If our worldview turns out to make life completely hopeless, then we ought to make sure this is the right way to look at life. Again, just because an alternative worldview offers hope doesn't make it true, but this does provide motivation to take a careful look.

Evaluating a Christian Worldview

We close this chapter addressing a final concern. Does thinking that we can use the principles of logic and evidence to evaluate worldviews make logic

[10] Sire, 283.

an authority over our Christian worldviews? It is sometimes said that, as Christians, our ultimate authority is the Bible. Has what we've said made logic an authority over the Bible?

The answer to this question is a decisive no, at least as I've understood these issues. The Bible has authority because of its divine source. Full stop. This fact gives it its status as "divine revelation." No amount of reason or logic makes it any more or less authoritative. And just because one may not recognize it as divinely authoritative, it doesn't follow that it is not authoritative (denying the police officer's authority as he or she writes you a ticket also isn't going to work out well). Of course, it's true that we can either recognize or fail to recognize the authority the Bible has. But our recognition of its authority doesn't thereby make it authoritative. It has this already. For us to submit to its authority, however, we must come to a place where we do in fact recognize it as the divinely inspired Word of God. And logic and reason can be quite helpful on this journey.

Consider the following example: suppose Smith is standing before a complete library of the world's religious texts and has no prior knowledge of these texts. The Bible is there, as is the Quran, the Bhagavad Gita, the Book of Mormon, the Upanishads, and so on. Let's assume, for the sake of argument, that each of these claim, in effect, to be divinely authoritative. Standing there before all of these options, how could Smith decide which one is correct? It can't be the fact that the Bible claims to be divinely inspired. After all, they all make claims such as this. Smith must use the tools of logic and critical thinking to come to see that the Bible is divine revelation. Once he recognizes the Bible for what it really is, then Smith recognizes the authority it had all along. Logic and reason don't add or take away authority but they are tools for us to evaluate a source for whether it in fact has authority. Smith simply used these as tools on his journey toward these beliefs.

In closing, it is difficult to analyze and evaluate our worldviews when we are around only people who share our worldview. It would be like trying to analyze one's grammar or pronunciation of certain words when everyone seems to say them that way. I remind my Texas friends and colleagues that "y'all" is really not a word, but southerners who grew up saying "y'all" apparently cannot conceive of the violence they do to the two words "you" and "all." But if a person with a thick southern accent is dropped into a community in the Northeast, that person will likely become all too aware of the idiosyncrasies of people's pronunciations (as I became with my New Jersey accent).

Being overly isolated from other worldviews is a recipe for disaster, especially when a student has never evaluated her own Christian worldview. We eventually meet people who believe differently from us, whether it is on a college or university campus, in our community, or in the workplace. All of a sudden, when we bump into a worldview different from our own, it can be challenging and even traumatic. This is especially true if it is a setting where people know what they are talking about and they are hostile to a Christian worldview. Kids from a Christian background often feel lied to. They took mom, dad, and the youth pastor at their word that Christianity is obviously true. Now they are meeting people who are persuasively saying it is false.

Imagine a different scenario. Imagine that this Christian student has been encouraged from a young age to think carefully about her worldview. As she became a teenager, imagine her parents and youth pastor pressed her to ask deep and difficult questions about her Christian beliefs and find plausible answers. As she gets older, she's not simply assuming Christianity is true, but believes it on the basis of good evidence. By the time she rolls onto a secular campus or encounters someone who challenges her beliefs, she already holds her Christian worldview thoughtfully and rationally. She is not going to feel deceived; she doesn't hold her Christian worldview merely because mom, dad, and the youth pastor told her she should. She owns that worldview with confidence.

In both of these situations, the students have a Christian worldview. One has accepted it without strong reasons. The other has evaluated it carefully and can defend it with convincing reasons.

We don't want to be accidental Christians. That is, we don't want to be people who are Christians only because we have grown up in a Christian home or because we have gone along with group pressure. We should be Christians precisely because we think Christianity is true. But to get to this place requires the use of logic and critical thinking. As we mentioned in chapter 1, we are not called to be skeptics in this but to pursue a knowledge of God as we love him with all of our minds. Part of this pursuit is understanding our worldview in relation to other worldviews and evaluating them for truth.

The Argument from Reason

Humans, in general, have the capacity and the ability to reason. This ability can be diminished, for one reason or another, and even when it is not diminished, we don't reason perfectly in all situations. However, we do something quite different from animals. Animals clearly make decisions, but these decisions are largely driven by instincts and base desires. When I offer my dog, Ryder, his favorite treat, he will do many things to get the treat. He will, for example, spin in circles and (sometimes) roll over. What he never does, however, is reflect on whether it is rational for him to spin in circles or roll over to get a little treat. Dogs don't have this reflective or higher-order capacity to think about their thoughts or evaluate reasons, but humans do. We can consider ideas and determine their logical adequacy and rational plausibility. In short, humans are rational beings.

In the previous chapters, I laid out a case for why Christians should value reason and an intellectual life, as modeled by Jesus, that pursues and loves God with all of our minds. We also looked at the notion of a worldview and said a crucial part of the intellectual life is evaluating whether our worldview makes sense of the world as we find it. In this chapter, we ask whether the Christian worldview makes good sense of reason and logic itself, especially compared to atheistic worldviews. As odd as it may sound, we will give a reason for reason. I will argue that Christian theism makes good sense of reason itself, while atheistic worldviews do not.

There's some significant irony here. Atheists tend to extol the value of reason. In 2012, the "Reason Rally"—a large gathering of around 30,000 atheists, the irreligious, secularists, and humanists—was held on the National Mall in Washington, DC. This rally was a who's who of contemporary atheists and humanists. One of the primary purposes of the rally was to act as a "coming out" for American atheists to make their voices heard. The rally was framed around values of rationality, logic, science, and evidence. It was, after all, a rally for reason. This is indicative of how many atheists think about logic and reason.

Many atheists become atheists, especially those who "deconvert" from religious communities, precisely because they realized their former religious commitments were not based on good reason and evidence. Many of these understood faith to be an attitude that rejects or at least ignores reason and logic. And so, embracing reason and logic ran against the nature of their faith commitments. When reason becomes important (as it should), then one automatically has reason to lose this kind of (blind) faith. So, for many, it makes perfect sense for an atheist rally to be called a Reason Rally. Reason and logic are primary values for many atheists.

On the other hand, as we discussed in chapter 1, religious people aren't always the biggest advocates of reason. The religiously committed don't typically welcome intellectual challenges and emphasize a faith grounded in evidence. In fact, Christians, at times in the history of the church, have had an explicitly low view of reason. Tertullian, for example, often is given credit for the phrase *credo quia absurdum est* ("I believe because it is absurd").

Danish philosopher Søren Kierkegaard regarded faith as something of a blind leap in the darkness. For these thinkers, faith seemed to stand separate from or even contrary to reason.

Certainly, exceptions are on both sides, but atheists, on the whole, tend to emphasize reason and evidence more than Christians. The problem with this, however, is that reason and logic make good sense in a Christian worldview, or so I argue below, even if Christians tend to discount reason and logic. On the other hand, it's not at all clear that the atheist's worldview makes sense of logic and reason despite how these values are revered and emphasized. This is even more problematic once it is realized that if a worldview cannot make sense of reason, then it seems inconsistent to use logic and reason to support and argue for that worldview and against the worldviews of others. This becomes a kind of Achilles' heel for atheism and can provide an argument for the existence of God.

What Is Atheism?

One might think we should be able to define *atheism* without much trouble. Placing an *a* in front of *theism* means it is the denial of theism, which affirms the existence of God. This would seem to clearly imply atheism is the view that there is no God, but this definition has recently fallen into dispute. Instead, it's become popular among some atheists to say that atheism is the lack of belief in God. One might point out that there's a difference between saying, "I believe there is no God" (a belief) and saying, "I do not believe there is a God" (a lack of belief).

Why claim atheism is the mere lack of belief in God? Surprisingly, the primary reason seems to be so the atheist does not have to argue for the truth of atheism. Despite extolling the value of reason, this move seems designed to shrug off the burden of offering reasons for atheism. The theist claims God exists and thus must provide rational support for this claim, whereas the atheist only lacks a belief of God. Consider, for example, atheist George H. Smith's claim:

> The atheist is not obligated to answer arbitrary assertions, unproven assumptions and sloppy generalizations concerning the nature and consequences of the atheistic position. Atheism is the absence of a belief in a god, nothing more. If the theist wishes to draw monumental implications from this lack of belief, he must argue for his claims. . . . It is the atheist who demands proof from the theist, not vice-versa.[1]

The claim is that an atheist need offer no reasons for atheism since it is merely the absence of a belief. Theism, on the other hand, makes positive claims, and therefore those claims must be justified. Unfortunately, the way this often plays out in a discussion is the theist is stuck having to meet some (often extraordinarily high) burden of proof (i.e., the obligation to show one's belief meets the standards of rationality), while the atheist gets to sit back and poke holes in whatever the theist says. It automatically gives the atheist the rhetorical upper hand.

I don't think, however, this is the correct way to think about atheism. For one, I suspect the atheist does have beliefs about God's existence. A belief is simply assent to the truth of a statement or claim. There are some things for which I lack beliefs. About the politics of Lithuania in the 1980s, I lack beliefs. I don't know what form of government they had, much less what issues were being debated during that time. So, I lack all beliefs about Lithuanian politics in the 1980s. But most atheists are not like this. They have spent a lot of time thinking about whether there is a God, and I suspect they have concluded (i.e., formed the belief that) there is not. Even if it is just that atheists have not found the case for God compelling, it still seems that most have concluded and therefore believe that God does not exist.

Second, this has a tendency to shut down dialogue. It is much easier to shoot holes in a view than it is to defend a view. If you are engaged in

---

[1] George Smith, *Atheism: The Case Against God* (Amherst, NY: Prometheus, 2016), 27.

a formal debate (especially if there's prize money involved), then it makes sense to put yourself in the best possible position to win. However, if you and I are dialogue partners, both attempting to know the truth about these matters, then it seems infinitely better for each of us to lay out a case for our respective views, and then we can talk about it and learn from each other.

But even if atheists persist in thinking that atheism is the absence of a belief in God, I still think they have some work to do. Atheism may not need to be justified, but the atheist's worldview does need to be justified because the person who lacks a belief in God still has a worldview. There are various atheistic worldviews, but in each view, God does not exist. But even so, the worldview must explain the facts of reality, including the origin and design of the universe, and whatever else they think exists, such as morality, human rights, and so forth. That is, atheistic worldviews must make positive claims about the world, and those claims must be justified even if one thinks atheism is a mere lack of a belief in God. We then can compare how well atheistic worldviews explain the world relative to how well the Christian worldview explains things, and good dialogue can ensue.

The focus in this chapter is to ask whether atheistic worldviews can explain the existence of logic itself. I will argue that they cannot.

Logic and Worldview

Let's be very clear. The argument here is not that atheists lack reasons for their atheism. I've already said that atheists tend to revere logic and reason and that many atheists departed from their religious commitments precisely because they had reasons that ran against their religious beliefs. Many had doubts and asked questions but couldn't find satisfactory answers. Many atheists have a high view of logic and reason, and they often act quite rationally. Full stop. The argument in this chapter does not call that into question. The question is whether the atheistic worldview makes good sense of the principles of logic and reason themselves.

Whether God exists is, in fact, a massive game changer for how we see the world. It provides tremendous resources to explain various features of the world. If one thinks there is no God, then one has to explain the features of the world in some other way. For example, if there is no God, then one should explain why the world exists to start with. Many people agree that our universe began long ago in an event called the big bang. But what gave rise to the big bang? And why did a universe that is life permitting on at least one small planet develop rather than a universe that is not life permitting?

Notice, however, that if God exists, then the big bang can be explained by an exercise of the agency of God. He said, "Let there be . . . ," and—*bang!*—it was. Perhaps it was a bit more complex than that, but still, God's creative event offers a straightforward explanation of why a life-permitting world exists. The agency of God explains it for the Christian. If an atheistic worldview doesn't have the resources to explain this fundamental fact, then this is a problem for that atheistic worldview. The point is that positing God doesn't merely help the theist sleep better at night. God, as an explanatory thesis, makes terrific sense of many of the most fundamental worldview considerations, such as the regularity of nature, human meaning and purpose, and the existence of things like moral facts, moral obligations, human rights, human value, and beauty. Without positing God, each of these are rather difficult to explain.

Explaining Logic

Now, of all the things a worldview should explain, the principles of logic and reason are the most troublesome, at least for certain atheistic worldviews. Though the use of logic and reason is perfectly mundane, when we think about it worldviewishly, logical principles are rather strange things and can be difficult to locate in a worldview. Let me explain.

Let's first of all say what logic is. We'll have a lot more to say about this in the next chapter, but, for our purposes right now, we should understand logic as the standards by which we evaluate rational thought. When we form an argument for a claim, we lay out premises that rationally support a conclusion. Take these three statements, for example:

1. If I'm thinking thoughts, then I exist.
2. I'm thinking thoughts.
3. Therefore, I exist.

In one sense, all we have is a set of three statements, but look carefully at them. There's a logic to these claims, and it seems premises 1 and 2 clearly give us an excellent reason to believe premise 3, the conclusion. Why is an argument like this compelling for any person who understands the claims? It's because, as we reflect on this, we become aware of the logic of the argument and we can "see" (i.e., grasp with our minds) that it is a *good* argument. We can see that it satisfies the logical standards even if we are unable to articulate what those standards are.

Think about how extraordinary it is that we can see or grasp with our minds the logic of an argument like this. In the course of this book, you will learn the names of the logical principles involved with arguments and how they work. With this knowledge, you will better be able to spot and evaluate the logic of an argument. But even without knowing these things, you can, in a way, feel the force of the argument, and it's for this reason you can rationally believe the conclusion. As we saw in the previous chapter, Jesus didn't give us lessons in logic and critical thinking, but he did give extremely compelling arguments that convinced many because people appreciated their force.

Anytime you think through and evaluate ideas, you are using the principles of logic. This fact makes logical principles literally undeniable, or at least impossible to argue against. If you tried to say that logical principles do not exist, you would have to appeal to logical principles to make your case. And this clearly undercuts the case.

Even young children use and understand basic logical principles. In fact, a lot of our parenting is teaching kids to understand the consequences of their actions and ideas. We want our children to think, "If I play with matches in the house, very bad things will happen. Therefore, I shouldn't play with matches." There's some good logic here, and many children easily grasp this logic (hopefully before they light the living room on fire). We can all get better at evaluating the logic of arguments, which of course is the point of this book, so that we are able to consider the subtle points and logical moves some arguments make.

So everyone uses logic. We are able to grasp the logic of, at least, simple and clear arguments. But what is it we grasp when we grasp logical principles? What sort of thing is a logical standard?

The first thing to say is it is quite difficult to locate logical standards as a part of the natural world. These principles seem otherwordly from the start. I don't mean they are miraculous or just mysterious. I mean this in a literal sense: logical principles seem to be, by definition, beyond nature. Think of a tree. Things in the natural, physical world, such as trees, have certain natural, physical properties. A tree is a contingent thing, which means it exists, but it didn't have to exist, and for any living tree, there will be a time when it doesn't exist. When it comes to a particular tree, say, my large oak in the backyard, this beautiful tree of course exists, but it once didn't exist. And even though I'll likely be long gone, a sad day will come when it dies. My big oak tree didn't have to exist in the first place, but it does happen to currently exist. For all of these reasons, it is contingent. The tree also has physical properties such as a specific location (i.e., a precise place in our backyard), an ability to experience change (e.g., grows taller and thicker, loses leaves and branches, etc.), and certain current dimensions (e.g., around fifty feet tall, a three-foot diameter trunk at its widest, a certain number of branches, etc.). Though there is perhaps more to being a natural, physical thing, natural, physical things all seem to share these aspects: they are contingent things, they have a specific location, they experience change, and they have certain dimensions.

Logical principles are not like this at all. Logical principles are not contingent things. They don't come and go out of existence. They are what is known as "necessary." This means they don't merely happen to be the case.

There's literally no way they could fail to be the case. Indeed, we couldn't even conceive of something like a statement of the law of noncontradiction being false. It is necessarily, absolutely, and eternally true. Other examples of necessary truths are the truths of arithmetic. The claim 2+3=5 is necessarily true in the sense that it couldn't possibly be false. It is true now, it was true in the year 7500 BC, and it will be true in the year AD 7500 (no matter if we make it that far or not). It's true on Earth, Mars, and at the center of a neighboring star. It doesn't matter if every person has denied the claim of 2+3=5; it's still true. Logical principles are like this. They are necessarily and eternally the case.

And there are more differences still. Logical principles do not have a certain location, experience change, or have dimensions. Think about it. A person who occupies a certain location can be thinking about a logical principle, say, the principle of noncontradiction. But the principle of noncontradiction is not thereby located there; it doesn't, for example, pass out of existence when that person stops thinking about it. Even if there was no human being at all in the entire universe to think about logical principles, the logical principles would still exist.

The logical principles have one other aspect that is worth mentioning here. Insofar as these are standards, they are normative. A *normative principle* is one that is prescriptive. An example of a normative principle is a moral law. It tells us morally how we *should* act, not how we do, in fact, act. It doesn't merely describe the world; it is prescriptive. By contrast, something like a natural law, such as the law of gravity, is descriptive. It really only tells us how gravity, in fact, functions in the world. It describes how things behave in the world. It doesn't tell us how gravity (or even objects that are subject to gravity) *ought* to function when it is behaving. The distinction between descriptive and prescriptive statements is sometimes referred to as the is/ought distinction. Logical principles are normative in the fact that they tell us how we ought to reason to arrive at truth. We don't have to reason logically, but we rationally ought to.

With all this in mind, we can see how logical principles seem to be not of this world. They are eternal, absolute, unchanging, necessary, and normative. Nothing in the natural universe has these properties. Things with these properties seem necessarily beyond the natural world.

But now let's think about logical principles worldviewishly. Can one's worldview explain the existence of these extraordinary principles? Where, on one's worldview, can one situate the logical principles and rational standards?

The Argument from Reason

It is not uncommon for someone to deny the existence of some alleged feature of the world when it doesn't fit well with one's worldview. Arguably, the existence of extraterrestrial beings does not fit well within a Christian worldview. It would at least be odd if God created other rational beings in the universe. So, given that there is no good evidence and it sits ill with the Christian worldview, most Christians have denied the existence of extra-terrestrial beings.

For another example, plenty of philosophers see the problematic nature of the existence of moral facts for an atheistic worldview and therefore deny their existence. Some atheists will, of course, attempt to explain the existence of moral facts, but others take the bolder approach and deny their existence altogether. Perhaps we believe and act like there are moral facts, but this, they may say, is just how we have evolved. Michael Ruse and E. O. Wilson have expressed this view:

> Ethics as we understand it is an illusion fobbed off on us by our genes to get us to cooperate. It is without external grounding. . . . Morality, or more strictly our belief in morality, is merely an adaptation put in place to further our reproductive ends. . . . The way our biology enforces its ends is by making us think that there is an objective higher code, to which we are all subject.[2]

---

[2] Michael Ruse and E. O. Wilson, "The Evolution of Ethics," in James E. Huchingson, *Religion and the Natural Sciences: The Range of Engagement* (Eugene, OR: Wipf & Stock, 1993), 310–11.

I think Ruse and Wilson are wrong here because a view like this undercuts moral intuitions and moral behavior. For many philosophers, if we know anything, we know that certain things are morally wrong. It's obvious that torturing a child for fun is wrong, and we all know this. It's a problematic view, but it is a logically possible view. That is, it is a view that can be held with logical consistency even if it lacks plausibility when we take our moral intuitions seriously. But not so with denying logical principles.

Consider this argument:

1. Either logical principles exist or they don't.
2. It's not the case that they don't exist because this is self-defeating.
3. Therefore, logical principles exist.

Premise 1 is obviously true; it simply states the logical possibilities. Either there are logical principles or there are not.[3] It is necessarily true because there are no other options beyond either logical principles exist or they don't.

What about premise 2? Why is it self-defeating to say that logical principles do not exist? A claim is "self-defeating" when there is something about the claim itself or the assertion of the claim that provides its own defeater. Take, for example, someone who says in English, "I speak no English." Notice one is saying in English that one speaks *no* English. Speaking this phrase in English provides its own defeat because one just proved that one can speak at least a little English.

Suppose one says that logical principles do not exist. The problem is that if one means this claim is true and its negation false, then stating this is an implicit use of a logical principle (the principle of noncontradiction), and is therefore self-defeating. And it would be even worse if one argues for this position on the basis of logical principles. It would be like one is saying it is logically rational to believe that there is no logic or rationality. You couldn't consistently believe this.

---

[3] This is a statement of the principle of the excluded middle discussed in chapter 5. It is a necessarily true logical principle that says "either P or not P."

We can illustrate this with an imagined dialogue:

Logic denier: There is no such thing as logical principles.
Smith: Why should I believe this?
LD: Because it is logically rational to believe.
Smith: So you are saying the claim that there are no logical principles should be believed on the basis of logical principles?
LD: Yes, you got it!

The clear problem here is that one is using logical principles to form an argument against logical principles, which is obviously self-defeating. The claim is we cannot, in effect, *rationally* deny the existence of logical principles. To show this all we have to do is ask why we should believe that logical principles do not exist.[4]

If logical principles cannot be rationally denied without self-defeat, one's worldview must explain the logical principles. Because logical principles are otherworldly, it's not clear atheistic worldviews have the resources to explain logical principles. To see this, we will look at two prominent atheistic worldviews.

Naturalism

Many atheists hold to the atheistic worldview of metaphysical naturalism (naturalism, for short). We will understand naturalism, for our purposes, as the view that all things that exist are physical and composed of matter. There's the natural, physical world and that's it. Naturalism is almost always atheistic because it denies the existence of anything supernatural (i.e.,

[4] Of course, the medieval philosopher Avicenna had a more extreme recommendation for one who denies logical principles. Attributed to him is the statement "Anyone who denies the law of noncontradiction should be beaten and burned until he admits that to be beaten is not the same as not to be beaten, and to be burned is not the same as not to be burned" (Avicenna, *The Metaphysics* 1.8, 53.13–15).

anything beyond the natural world). The naturalist has, in a way, ruled out the existence of God or gods by ruling out anything that exists beyond the natural, material, physical world. But if what I've argued above is correct, it seems the naturalist has also ruled out the existence of logical principles, which undercuts the logical basis for the naturalist worldview itself.

C. S. Lewis put it this way:

> One absolutely central inconsistency ruins [naturalism]; . . . The whole picture professes to depend on inferences from observed facts. Unless inference is valid, the whole picture disappears. . . . [U]nless Reason is an absolute—all is in ruins. Yet those who ask me to believe this world picture also ask me to believe that Reason is simply the unforeseen and unintended by-product of mindless matter at one stage of its endless and aimless becoming. Here is flat contradiction. They ask me at the same moment to accept a conclusion and to discredit the only testimony on which that conclusion can be based.[5]

The idea is that naturalists may organize the Reason Rally, revere reason above all else, and strictly adhere to the dictates of reason. But the worldview claims that all that exists is natural and material. Logical inference (i.e., reasoning from premises to a conclusion) requires an appeal to the logical principles, and logical principles are not natural or material. If that's right, then any possible argument for naturalism is thereby undercut.

Lewis makes a similar point in *Miracles*:

> All possible knowledge, then, depends on the validity of reasoning. If the feeling of certainty which we express by words like *must be* and *therefore* and *since* is a real perception of how things outside our own minds really "must" be, well and good. But if this certainty is merely a feeling *in* our own minds and not a genuine insight into

[5] C. S. Lewis, "Is Theology Poetry," in *Screwtape Proposes a Toast and Other Pieces* (New York: HarperCollins, 1970), 54–55.

> realities beyond them—if it merely represents the way our minds happen to work—then we can have no knowledge. Unless human reasoning is valid no science can be true.[6]

Lewis's point is that we take our reasoning to lead us to actual knowledge of the world. But our reasoning couldn't accomplish that end unless we grasp (or, as Lewis puts it, perceive) real logical principles that exist outside of our minds. If what we take to be good reasoning is only a *feeling* of certainty or reasonability, and there are no mind-independent standards of reasons by which we can make proper inferences, then we are not rational. We would lack knowledge, as Lewis says, because there are no standards of reasoning that allow us to make rational inferences. If we believed truly, this would be random and accidental.

The problem here is the naturalist has nothing in his worldview to make sense of logic as mind-independent reality. Even if consciousness emerged in some natural or physical way from the brain, there may be genuine thought processes. But this doesn't give us rationality (i.e., reasonable thought processes). We would still need some objective logical standards by which these processes could be evaluated as reasonably good.[7] If there is nothing on the worldview of naturalism that makes sense of the logical principles and logical principles are denied, then the real problem arises. If naturalism denies the existence of logical principles, this is self-defeating. That is, the naturalist cannot appeal to rational standards to argue for the worldview without being logically inconsistent. Lewis goes on to quote J. B. S. Haldane, who cleverly says, "If my mental processes are determined wholly by the motions of atoms in my brain, I have no reason to suppose that my beliefs are true. . . . And hence I have no reason for supposing my brain to be

---

[6] C. S. Lewis, *Miracles*, in *The Complete C. S. Lewis Signature Classics* (New York: HarperCollins, 2002), 313, italics in original.

[7] This is not then the traditional mind/body problem but a problem of locating logical principles on naturalism.

composed of atoms."[8] Denying the existence of logical principles, on naturalism, means one has no reason to suppose naturalism is true.

The problem here is compounded if one also holds to determinism, as many naturalists do. If the world is only composed of atoms in motion (as Haldane puts it), then there seems to be no room for freedom of choice. Thus, for many naturalists one's feelings, desires, beliefs, and actions are nothing more than the deterministic preprograming of one's brain activity and chemistry. If beliefs are deterministically preprogrammed, it's hard to see these as rational. It seems beliefs would simply be the mere accident of deterministic natural forces. Without the freedom of choice to investigate, reflect on, or consider the evidence for one's beliefs, then it seems the beliefs will not be held rationally. And, just like before, the problem here is this undercuts the worldview itself. If naturalistic determinism is true and one takes it to be true, belief in naturalistic determinism is also a mere accident of natural forces. Given the view, one couldn't choose to consider the evidence to judge whether the belief is rational. Thus, if naturalistic determinism is true, beliefs are simply accidental, including the belief in naturalistic determinism.

Platonism

The second option for an atheistic worldview is to say that logical principles do in fact exist as eternal, necessary, and normative. On this view, the world is more than only natural, physical, material objects and processes (i.e., naturalism is false) even though there is no God or gods (i.e., atheism is true). We'll call this view atheistic Platonism (Platonism, for short), styled after the view of Plato. For our purposes, Platonism is the view that things like the principles of logic exist as necessary and eternal facts. Logical principles are not natural, physical objects. Instead they are what is known as abstract objects because they exist outside space and time.

---

[8] Lewis, *Miracles*, 15; quoted from J. B. S. Haldane, *Possible Worlds* (1927; repr., New Brunswick: Transaction, 2001).

We should note one could hold to a theistic form of Platonism, as many Christian philosophers have done throughout history. But one need not be a theist to hold to the basic form of Platonism I described earlier. Consider, for example, atheist philosopher Eric Wielenberg's work in ethics.[9] He defends a view called "moral Platonism," according to which moral facts exist as abstract objects. Given this, Wielenberg is clearly not a naturalist. He thinks moral facts exist outside of the natural, physical world. These things exist as abstract objects even though God does not exist. Likewise, one could explain logical principles by saying they are real, otherworldly, nonnatural things, but no God exists.

To be fair, this is not a popular view among atheists. By far, most atheists hold to some version of naturalism, but Platonism would be an available option, and some would argue it is a far more plausible worldview given the devastating problems we've seen with naturalism. The Platonist typically thinks naturalism is just too austere to explain the world as we find it and, thus, offers this view as a richer view to explain the world.

Platonism has the advantage of avoiding the self-defeating issues that plague naturalism. Nonnatural logical principles do in fact exist, on this option, but when we ask why they exist or on what basis they exist, the answer would have to be for no further reason than that they simply exist—that is, they are brute facts of reality. A "brute fact" has no explanation or further ground for its existence. If something exists brutely, then that's the end of the story in its explanation. It just exists. On this view, logical principles never came into existence, and they have no further ground. They exist brutely in a realm of infinitely many abstract objects.

From one vantage point, this is a principled view. If we know anything about the world, we know that things like logical principles exist. The person may also be convinced that God does not exist for various reasons. Rather than compromising on either of these convictions, the atheistic

[9] See Eric Wielenberg, *Robust Ethics: Metaphysics and Epistemology of Godless Normative Realism* (New York: Oxford University Press, 2014).

Platonist both affirms the existence of logical principles as abstract objects and denies the existence of God.

Now, one can object to this view by arguing against either of these convictions. One can, of course, argue that God does in fact exist by offering one of the many arguments for God's existence.[10] One can also rebut the arguments against the existence of God (e.g., the problem of evil). If it can be shown that there is good reason to believe that God does exist, then this is of course a problem for atheistic Platonism.

But one can also argue against the claim that logical principles exist as brute abstract facts. The issue is that Platonism's explanation of a realm of abstract objects seems hopelessly *ad hoc*. As will be discussed in chapter 12, a claim is ad hoc when it has nothing going for it other than the mere explanation of the facts. In other words, the claim has no independent reasons for thinking it is true. So, while one can believe that logical principles exist as abstract objects, one cannot explain why they exist without simply asserting them as brute facts, which is plainly ad hoc. Platonists have no independent reasons to think that logical principles exist as abstract objects; all they have is the fact that they are committed to the existence of the logical principles.

Imagine overnight the large tree in your yard fell. Suppose I posited that this event happened as a result of little fairies who used their magic to take the tree down. Does this explain why the tree fell? It actually does explain the facts, but it is hopelessly ad hoc. We have no independent reason to believe that fairies exist and that, if they did, they'd be interested in making the tree in your yard fall. Likewise, positing the existence of logical principles as brute facts explains reason and our ability to evaluate the logic of an argument. However, it has nothing more going for it than that. We are

---

[10] For some resources on the various arguments for God's existence, see Joshua Rasmussen, *How Reason Can Lead to God: A Philosopher's Bridge to Faith* (Downers Grove, IL: InterVarsity Press, 2019); Jerry L. Walls and Trent Dougherty, eds., *Two Dozen (or so) Arguments for God: The Plantinga Project* (New York: Oxford University Press, 2018); and Paul M. Gould, Travis Dickinson, and R. Keith Loftin, *Stand Firm: Apologetics and the Brilliance of the Gospel* (Nashville: B&H Academic, 2018).

given no independent reason to believe that these logical principles exist as brute abstract objects. That is, it is ad hoc.

It's also difficult to understand what it would be for a logical principle to exist as an abstract object. What is it for something like a logical principle to exist on its own outside space and time and govern the processes of rational thought? We are tempted to imagine a statement of the principle of noncontradiction floating in outer space somewhere. This is, of course, not the Platonist's view, but what are we supposed to imagine when we think of a logical principle as an abstract object? This is, in a way, an implausibly extravagant view. We would have to believe in an inconceivably large realm of timeless, spaceless objects that just exist on their own. It seems like a logical principle makes far better sense as a property of a rational mind. Given that the principles of logic are standards by which we evaluate arguments, it would have to be an ideal or perfect mind that transcends the universe. But this the atheist cannot countenance. If we wish to affirm logical principles as eternal, necessary, and normative but avoid the oddness and ad hocery of positing brute abstract principles, it looks like we'll have to posit an ideal and transcendent intelligence. But what could we be talking about here other than God?

Can atheists believe in logical principles? Yes, they can. Given what I've said above, atheists can believe in logical principles, and they can even be rationally astute in their beliefs. But the question here is whether there is an atheistic worldview that provides a good account of the logical principles. The two main representatives of an atheistic worldview fail to do so. Naturalism, the most popular atheistic view, lacks the resources to account for logical principles and seems to be forced to deny their existence, which is clearly self-defeating. Platonists can affirm logical principles but only as brute abstract objects, and this seems hopelessly ad hoc. The upshot here is that the existence of logical principles is a problem for atheistic views, at least the primary ones most atheists hold. If that's right, then we thereby have reason to believe that atheism is false and God exists. That is, these considerations give us a compelling argument for the existence of God:

1. If God does not exist, then either logical principles do not exist (naturalism) or they exist as brute abstract objects (Platonism).
2. It's not the case that logical principles do not exist because this is self-defeating.
3. It's not the case that they exist as brute abstract objects since this is ad hoc.
4. Therefore, God exists.

This of course assumes that the existence of God can explain the logical principles.

God Makes Good Sense of Reason

If God exists, then we do have an explanation for logical principles. The basic reason to affirm is that, on a Christian theistic view, a mind stands behind all of reality. There is a sense in which if logical principles are eternal, absolute, unchanging, and necessary, we don't have many worldview options for explaining them. The claim is that the Christian worldview posits the right kind of ultimate reality to explain the existence of these eternal principles, which is the divine mind itself.

God is not just another mind like you and me. The classical Christian view of God is that he is perfect, which means he is ideal in every good thing. As Anselm famously put it, God is that "than which nothing greater can be conceived."[11] Anselm's point is that God has all of his attributes perfectly and maximally. God is not only powerful, but he is perfectly and maximally powerful. God does not only know some truths; he knows *all* truths perfectly. God is not only moral, but he is perfect and ideal in his moral character. It is ultimately God's character that gives us the moral standard by which we should live. God is, in this way, the ground of morality.

[11] Anselm, *Proslogium; Monologium; An Appendix in Behalf of the Fool by Gaunilon; and Curs Deus Homo*, trans. Sidney Norton Deane, 2nd ed. (Chicago: Open Court, 1910), 8.

And in the same way, God is the ground of logic. God is not only rational, but he is perfect and ideal in his rationality. It is God himself who is the perfect standard of logic.

Unlike naturalism, the Christian view can posit the existence of objective logical principles. They are part of reality and explain why we can make inferences and evaluate arguments. And unlike Platonism, we can offer a plausible grounding for the logical principles that is not ad hoc. Rather than positing an infinite number of abstract objects, logical principles are grounded in a single object, namely, God. And we have a variety of independent reasons for believing that a perfect God exists. Christians have taken a great variety of things as reasons to believe that God exists. Again, these include the existence of a contingent universe, the fine tuning of the universe for human life, and moral facts and obligations.[12] Far from being ad hoc, the single thesis that God exists explains a great variety of reality and provides a proper grounding for that which we experience in reality.

Grounding logic this way has biblical support as well. Long before the argument from reason was formulated, the Bible pictures Jesus as the divine *logos*. John 1:1–3 says, "In the beginning was the Word, and the Word was with God, and the Word was God. He was with God in the beginning. All things were created through him, and apart from him not one thing was created that has been created." This is an incredible passage. What is easy to miss is that the Greek term, *arche*, translated here as "beginning" doesn't necessarily just mean a temporal beginning. It is far richer than that. It means the fundamental thing that is the source of all the rest of reality. John says that the fundamental part of reality was "the Word." This is the term *logos* from which we get the English word *logic*. Gordon Clark once put it this way: "The well-known prologue to John's Gospel may be paraphrased, 'In the beginning was Logic, and Logic was with God, and Logic was God . . . . In Logic was life and the life was the

---

[12] See Rasmussen, *How Reason Can Lead to God*, and Walls and Dougherty, *Two Dozen (or so) Arguments for God.*

light of men.'"[13] John 1 identifies the Word who became flesh and dwelt among us as Jesus Christ (vv. 14, 17). So John 1 is telling us that Christ is the logic of creation. Clark goes on, "Any translation of John 1:1 that obscures this emphasis on mind or reason is a bad translation . . . . In the beginning, then, was Logic."[14]

Clark's point is that Christ, as the logos, exemplifies and is the ground of logic. It is because of Christ that the world is intelligible and that there are logical standards for us to reason. Again, this is not to say one must believe or even know about Jesus Christ for him to be the ground of logic. It's just that Christ is the biblical explanation of the existence of logic itself whether one knows of Christ or not. Logic existed before and is thus not a part of the created world. It is a part of the divine mind. Christ is the logos. As Christians, we have a reason for reason.

Objections

Let's look briefly at two objections to seeing God as the ground of logic.

Objection 1: God Didn't Do a Very Good Job

This first objection emphasizes the fact that we can sometimes be really irrational. It says that if there is a God, he didn't do a very good job at creating us with the ability to reason. Why didn't he create us all as super geniuses who always believe truly?

No doubt, we don't always believe and act rationally. We routinely make mistakes in our reasoning, we get swayed by our emotions, and sometimes we believe because we simply want something to be the case. These mistakes often do not turn out well. Though we often know better (especially in hindsight), many times we are irrational in actual practice.

---

[13] Gordon Clark, *Logic* (Unicoi, TN: Trinity, 2004), 115.

[14] Clark, 116.

Why would the perfect God create us intellectually imperfect? Wouldn't the all-powerful God be able to do a better job?

It's clear that God could have made us without the ability to make intellectual mistakes. But he is certainly not obligated to do this so long as he has justifying reasons for creating us as he did. What are the justifying reasons? It's important to note that, on the Christian view, we live in a fallen world. God created a world that was very good indeed, but, as a result of human sin, we now live with the effects of the fall. Thus, some of our intellectual limitations are no doubt because of the fall, and they are not part of the original creation. This doesn't completely address the objection, but it does provide a theological backdrop for how to approach it.

God's goal for humanity is for us to trust and depend on God in submitting our wills to him. In light of the fall, we of course don't do this well. We often think we know best. Imagine how this would be compounded if we didn't have significant intellectual limitations, which often require us to be dependent on God. That is to say, our limitations produce in us the virtue of intellectual humility, which would be impossible if we were intellectually perfect. It's better (and a justifying good) that we depend on God more than we depend on our own intellects, especially in arrogance. This seems to be at least part of the lesson of the Tower of Babel in Gen 11:1–9. The people gather to build "a tower with its top in the sky" to, as they say, "make a name for" themselves (v. 4). God isn't against big buildings, of course, but he is against the arrogance that comes with this kind of achievement, and he therefore scattered humans by confusing their language. He, in a way, specifically limited their collective intelligence.

God doesn't want pure logic machines or super geniuses who can automatically reason to an optimal outcome any more than he wants moral robots who always do what they are told. His primary desire for us is to be dependent on him. He wants us to, in love, trust him and depend on him for our needs. The moment we think we know better than God is the moment we fail to be submitted to God's good and perfect will. Thus, given that God is after intellectual humility and trustful dependence, God is justified in creating us with intellectual limitations.

Objection 2: Which God?

Often it is pointed out that a great number of different conceptions of God have been advanced throughout the history of the world, and none of the above arguments entail the existence of the Christian God. The thought seems to be, at best, we have given reason to believe in a whole host of options and done nothing to show that the God of the Bible exists. Perhaps, as it is sometimes said, we should posit the great spaghetti monster instead of the Christian God. The thought is, if we are appealing to God, what's stopping us from appealing to any conception of God whatsoever, including fanciful ones?

The theist might respond by first pointing out that the aim here has not necessarily been to show that the Christian God exists and that all other conceptions are false. It's simply to show that grave difficulties result from explaining logic using atheistic worldviews. If that's right, then this implies some sort of theistic view. So even if we haven't ruled out all other conceptions of God and worldviews, we have shown that a God consistent with the God of the Bible plausibly exists on the basis of logic. This is no small feat because, if nothing else, it entails that atheism is false. So this is a win in the theist's favor, even if Christian theism has not yet been established.

But it is not clear that just any conception of God can stand as the ground of logic. Take, for example, the Mormon conception of God; he was once a man who achieved an elevated status. Thus, the Mormon God cannot be the ground of logic because logic preexisted the Mormon God's exalted state. Similar considerations apply to the Greek and Roman pantheons of gods. Though these gods were taken to be powerful beings, they were finite, often morally corrupt, and existed within the natural world. Perhaps most importantly, these gods often lacked knowledge and were sometimes fooled by humans (often with the help of other gods). These gods simply don't fit the bill for being the ground of logic. And, given these considerations, we can see the flying spaghetti monster is just silly and not even worth addressing.

What we need is a conception of God where God is transcendent, eternal, and a perfect and an ideal reasoner. It's true that this conception doesn't rule out all theistic worldviews. But it does narrow the field and provides reason to think this sort of God exists. And this sort of God is consistent with the Christian God.

Logic: The Basics of Critical Thinking

> Critical thinking is a desire to seek, patience to doubt, fondness to meditate, slowness to assert, readiness to consider, carefulness to dispose and set in order; and hatred for every kind of imposture.
>
> —Francis Bacon, philosopher

We turn now to a discussion of the basics of critical thinking. What is it? The short answer is "critical thinking" is when we think rationally about our ideas. More specifically, it is the thoughtful evaluation of ideas and the reasons we have for holding those ideas. Let's unpack this.

Critical: The word *critical* has a few meanings. It can be used to mean that one has a negative view of someone or someone's idea. Though critical thinking might involve disagreeing and having a negative view of an idea, this isn't exactly the sense we have in mind here. One can think critically about an idea one positively believes. The sense here has more to do with its root word, *criteria*. When one is critical, in this sense, one is believing something on the basis of good criteria, which, as we shall see, are the standards of logic. One is not thinking critically when one just accepts an idea without any good reason or evidence. But if one carefully considers the evidence for a claim, then one is being critical, in our sense.

Thoughtful: The idea here is that critical thinking requires, well, thinking. But it is a certain kind of thinking. Critical thinking is reflective thinking. We can and often do embrace ideas without thinking about them, especially, as we've seen, as we form our worldviews. In that case, it's an accident that we accept these views, and we hold these uncritically. In this case, we may not even realize we hold a view. Critical thought requires spending some time thinking about ideas.

Evaluation: There are lots of ideas out there, and many of them are false. Just think of the sheer number of ideas we encounter on social media. When we scroll through our feed, we are scrolling through idea after idea. These couldn't all be true, given that many views directly contradict one another. But it is not always easy to know which ideas are true and which are false. To be a critical thinker, one must evaluate the ideas according to the standards of logic and reason.

Reasons: Reasons, in the relevant sense, are anything that answer why I should believe a claim is true. A reason, if it is a good reason, is something that indicates the truth of a claim. If you make the claim "P is true" (where P is a placeholder that you could substitute for any claim), and I ask you why I should believe this, I'm asking for a reason to think P is true. Typically, when we ask for a reason, we are asking for a good or compelling reason—a fact that in fact indicates the truth of the claim. You may point to a variety of reasons for thinking that P is true, including more technical reasons. Or it may be something more mundane. Rationality comes in degrees (i.e., you can be extremely rational, moderately rational, or only somewhat rational), and so our job is rarely ever done when it comes to being rational in a belief. For most issues, we ought to continue thinking critically about them, evaluating the reasons for and against and, for some ideas, this may continue for the rest of our lives.

It is possible to have reasons for a belief and not be thinking critically about it. We can believe something for good reasons even if we haven't had time to reflect on the belief. Suppose I'm crossing a busy street, and I see an oncoming semitruck barreling toward me and I only have a few seconds to respond. In this case, I don't have to think critically about my belief here. I have REALLY good reasons to jump out of the way. Though this isn't critical thinking, given that there isn't time to reflect, we can reflect on a belief we have (when our lives are not immediately at stake) and consider whether it is, on the whole, rational. The process of reflectively evaluating a claim is the process of critical thinking.

You Already Use Logic

One of the primary ways to grow in our ability to think critically is to better understand and gain facility in using the principles of logic to evaluate ideas. It's important to see that you already use logic and have been using it since you were a child, even if you have never taken a course or read a book in the discipline.

Think through the following claims:

1. I have an exam tomorrow morning, so I'm going to study tonight.
2. There is a poison label on this bottle. Therefore, I should not let my child play with this bottle.
3. My gas tank gauge is sitting on empty, so I need to stop and get gas.
4. My hometown team is statistically better in every category than their opponent. Probably my hometown team is going to win tonight.
5. Jones believes that there is no such thing as a God or gods. Thus, Jones is an atheist.

Each of these is an "inference." With any inference, we reason through one or more statements and arrive at a conclusion. These seem obviously compelling, right? We think so because the logic in each of these inferences is solid, and it is fairly easy to "see" this, even if we lack technical training in logic. We make inferences similar to these every day of our lives. In doing so, we use logic.

Imagine a world where we couldn't consider a statement such as "there is a poison label on this bottle" and know that we *therefore* shouldn't let a child play with the bottle. If we couldn't make basic logical inferences like this, we wouldn't get very far in life. It's really quite extraordinary that we can all, in a way, feel the force of inferences that are clearly good. But we can also grow in our ability to recognize a good inference.

What Is Logic?

Just like good business, logic is all about relationships. But with logic, of course we are not talking about relationships with people. In logic, it is all about relationships between claims we make and the ideas we have. More precisely, logic is a set of principles that provide standards for evaluating the relationships between *statements*.

Statements

The basic building blocks for rational arguments are statements.[1] We will define a "statement" as a descriptive claim about the world that is either true or false.[2] A statement describes some aspect of the way the world is that is either accurate (true) or inaccurate (false). Here are a few statements:

"God exists."
"Granite is typically denser than marshmallows."
"Jesus had twelve disciples."
"Caesar crossed the Rubicon in 49 BC."

---

[1] What I'm calling statements are sometimes called "propositions."

[2] For our purposes, the world should be understood as including everything that exists in reality, including God.

Notice that each of these makes a descriptive claim about the world, and as such, they each make a claim that is either true or false. This is an essential feature of a statement. If a string of words does not have a truth value (i.e., it is neither true nor false), then it is not a statement.

Many different notions have been proposed for understanding the nature of truth. Most have not improved much on Aristotle's ancient analysis: "To say of what is that it is not, or of what is not that it is, is false, while to say of what is that it is, and of what is not that it is not, is true."[3] Aristotle is referring to two things: what we say and what is (i.e., reality). Truth is when these two things correspond or are appropriately matched up. What we claim is the case actually is the case. The content of what we say or claim is what we are calling the statement. Putting this together, truth is when a statement corresponds to reality. A statement can either correspond, which is a true statement, or it can fail to correspond, which is a false statement.

A helpful analogy may be to consider a painting. If I were to look at a painting of my house, there is a sense in which the painting corresponds to my actual house when it is a good representation of it. But if it is a painting with squiggles and a few random circles having nothing in common with my actual house, then the painting, in a sense, doesn't correspond to my house. This analogy will break down quickly, but this is similar to the correspondence of true statements. You have the statement, on one hand, that represents (or you might say, pictures) the world being some way, and you have the facts of the world, on the other hand. When these match up, then you have a true statement. When they don't, you have a false statement.

A statement can be true even if we do not *know* whether the statement is true. For example, it can be true that Caesar crossed the Rubicon in 49 BC, and someone does not know that it is true. One may not know who Caesar is or anything about his ascension to being the emperor of Rome.

[3] Aristotle, *Metaphysics,* 1011b25 (see chap. 1, n. 16).

But, if the statement corresponds to the way the world is (i.e., Caesar really did cross the Rubicon in 49 BC), whether you know it or not, then it is true. And if not, it is false.

Here are a few utterances that are not statements:

"Hooray!" (emotive response)
"Pass the salt." (command/request)
"Does God exist?" (question)
"If it rains just now" (fragment)

With each of these, we are not making a claim that's either true or false, and thus they are not statements. Look closely at each one. Notice that nothing is stated or claimed. They are not describing the world in some certain way that's either true or false. I may say, "Hooray!" after my favorite team scores, but this is only a response of emotion. It doesn't make sense to ask whether my emotive response was true or false because it's not descriptive. In the same way, if someone asks,"Does God exist?" this person is not describing the world. If I say, "My team is the best team in the league" or "Yes, God exists," now I've made statements that are either true or false. But with the emotive response and the question about God, no descriptive assertion is made.

Here are a few more statements:

"Unicorns exist."
"Grass is always and everywhere green."
"Congress is currently full of cleverly disguised robots secretly planted to destroy the country."
"2 + 3 = 14"
"It's morally permissible to torture people just for the fun of it."

These each make a claim about the world, and each is either true or false. However, this time they are all (arguably) false claims (you might be 50/50 on Congress). When we are talking about statements, they are all *either* true or false. Even if it is something that is obviously false, it is still a statement—just a false statement.

Three Principles of Logic

Understanding statements this way allows us to formulate three principles of logic (sometimes called "the three laws of logic" or "the three laws of thought") that govern the relationships of statements.

The first principle of logic is one we've already encountered: the *principle of noncontradiction*. This says that for any statement, that statement and its negation cannot *both* be true. A negation is when the exact opposite of the claim is made. The negation of the statement "God exists" would be "it's not the case that God exists" or, more simply, "God does not exist."

We can represent this principle like this:

> Principle of noncontradiction: for any P, it's not the case that P and not P.

If someone asserts P and not P, then this is a contradiction. P and not P cannot both be true. In fact, if a statement P is true, then it follows, on the basis of this principle, that not P is false. To illustrate, it can't be the case that "Smith's checking account is flush with cash" and "Smith's checking account is not flush with cash." If it turns out that "Smith's checking account is flush with cash" is true, then it's false that "Smith's checking account is not flush with cash." To think otherwise is to embrace a contradiction.

It is important to note that for these sentences—"Smith's checking account is flush with cash" and "Smith's checking account is not flush with cash"—to be considered contradictions, they must be understood in the same sense and be referring to the same moment in time. "Flush with cash" can mean a lot of different things to different people. Jeff Bezos, currently one of the richest people in the world, may not consider Smith's checking account to be flush with cash even though you or I may. So when we say it can't be the case that "Smith's checking account is flush with cash" and "Smith's checking account is not flush with cash," we have to mean the exact same thing in both sentences. Otherwise, there's no contradiction in saying, "Smith's checking account is flush with cash (on my standards)" and "Smith's checking account is not flush with cash (on Bezos's standards)." These statements are perfectly consistent but only because they have different meanings. Also, the statement has to refer to the exact same time. It could, for example, be the case that "Smith's checking account is flush with cash (on payday)" and "Smith's checking account is not flush with cash (after paying bills)." These wouldn't be contradictions if they are referring to different times. But if we say "Smith's checking account is flush with cash" and "Smith's checking account is not flush with cash," and we mean these terms in the same sense and we are referring to the same moment of time, then we have a clear contradiction.

The second principle of logic is the *principle of the excluded middle* (sometimes called the *principle of bivalence*). It says that for any statement, there are exactly two logical values, truth and falsity, and every statement, understood in a precise sense, is either true or false. This can be represented by the following:

Principle of the excluded middle: for any P, P or not P.

The point here is, for any statement, there are only two possibilities. The statement is either true or it is false. There is no third (or middle) option. It is one or the other. Either "Smith's checking account is flush with cash" or "Smith's checking account is not flush with cash." These options are exclusive. Only one of them can be true.

The third principle of logic is the *principle of identity*, which says that each thing is identical to itself. To represent it, we would have:

Principle of identity: x = x

Typically, we use "x" because, in a fundamental sense, identity holds between objects. The Eiffel Tower (as an object) is identical to itself. Smith is identical to Smith. But the principle of identity also applies to statements. For any statement P, P is identical to P (i.e., P = P). Now, I realize these may not sound profound; however, logical principles are supposed to be seemingly obvious. Often the way this principle is applied is that one will notice that identity holds between two statements where different words are being used to refer to something that is identical. So, for example, one may take there to be an identity between "God" and "the greatest conceivable being" in that, on the Christian view, these are identical.

One outworking of this principle is by seventeenth-century philosopher and mathematician Gottfried Leibniz. He developed a variety of principles of identity, but perhaps the most intuitive of these is the indiscernibility of identicals (or "Leibniz's Law," for short). This says:

> For any x and any y, if x is identical to y, then any property had by x is also had by y.

If one claims Smith committed the crime, one is making an identity claim. If Smith is the one who committed the crime, then, according to Leibniz's Law, any property had by Smith must also be had by the one who committed the crime. If we discover Smith has some property that the person who commits the crime does not have, then it follows that Smith is not the one who committed the crime. If Smith was at home at the time when the crime was committed and the one who committed the crime was across town, then it follows that Smith did not commit the crime. That is, he is not identical to the one who committed the crime.

In any case, these three laws are fundamental to all thought. We typically follow these principles when we form our thoughts and inferences, but occasionally we may have, for example, a subtle contradiction in our beliefs. Understanding these rather intuitive principles helps us to avoid logical incoherence.

Sentences Versus Statements

A statement is different from a mere sentence. A sentence is tied to language in a way that a statement is not. A sentence is really just a string of symbols on a page (or pixels on a computer screen or sounds from an utterance) that we use to express certain statements. So imagine that I write on a piece of paper the sentence "The grass is green." These symbols are grouped according to conventions of grammar to convey something. What does it convey? Most likely, when we read that sentence, we all had a thought come to mind about the stuff that grows out of the dirt in your yard, and we also thought of a certain color. Sentences are used to express statements that are the content of our thoughts and beliefs. And there's an indefinite number of ways to express a statement. The sentence *L'herbe est verte* expresses the same statement as the English sentence "The grass is green." This is an extraordinary fact about statements. The very same statement can be expressed in English, Spanish, or sign language, and it can be written in Latin, Braille, or hieroglyphics. It's all the same statement even if it is expressed through radically different modes of expression.

Suppose someone asks you, "Is the sentence 'grass is green' true or false?" To answer this, we need to know what one *means* when one says "grass is green." That is, we need to know what statement is being expressed in that sentence. It is certainly not the case that *all* grass is green. I currently have plenty of dead grass in my yard, which is brown, not green. If this is what is meant, then the statement is false. But, perhaps the person was asking about whether it is true that all *living* grass is green. Though it is the same sentence, it's a different statement. If this is what's being expressed, then this is still not quite true because there are species of grass that are not green when they are living, such as ornamental red grass. Or perhaps the person was asking about whether all living grass that is typically found in the yards of people living in the United States is green. Well, now, this might be true but only if this much more specific statement is in mind.

Notice what we did. The sentence had a number of different possible interpretations for the intended statement, and the truth value varied depending on what statement was in mind. Language is, in this way, messy and imprecise. Many words, at least in the English language, are ambiguous in that they have multiple meanings and our sentences are often vague. We have to look at the overall context of a sentence to figure out the intended statement. But since the truth value depends on what statement is being expressed, we can't evaluate a claim or argument without figuring out what statements are actually being made.

Jesus was often misunderstood. At one point in Jesus's ministry, he told the crowd, "Truly I tell you, unless you eat the flesh of the Son of Man and drink his blood, you do not have life in yourselves" (John 6:53). He then emphasized the need to eat his flesh and drink his blood. The disciples' response is great: "This teaching is hard. Who can accept it?" (v. 60). They were trying to figure how they could start snacking on Jesus! But of course Jesus was not instituting cannabalism here. What he was saying (i.e., the statements he was making) had to do with his sacrificial death on the cross and also alluded to the Communion meal (also known as the Eucharist or the Lord's Supper).

Arguments

A big part of critical thinking is making and evaluating arguments. An "argument" is a series of statements used to rationally support a certain conclusion. An argument, in this sense, is not the same as having or being in an argument with someone. We might hear someone say that Smith is in an *argument* with Jones, and they are upset with each other. What we mean in this case is Smith and Jones are having a dispute. Logical arguments are often made in disputes, but the dispute can often become emotionally driven, and, unfortunately, logical arguments tend to drop out of the picture.

In critical thinking, we are not talking about disputes but about logical arguments. An argument, in the logical sense, is composed of at least two statements where one of them gives us reason to believe the other. For this reason, a single statement cannot constitute an argument. The statements of an argument fall into two required categories of statements. First, there are premises. Though there are no limits to how many premises an argument may have, there must be at least one. The second category is the conclusion. Again, there must be at least one conclusion, but an argument can make multiple conclusions within a single multistage argument. Most of the arguments we will consider will have a single conclusion with relatively few premises. But we do not have an argument unless we have at least one premise and at least one conclusion.

"Premises," in a manner of speaking, argue for the conclusion. The premises are intended to give reasons for believing that the conclusion is true. The "conclusion" is the claim that one is intending to support. So here's the basic way it works. We make a claim (the conclusion) and then we support that claim with reasons (a single premise or many premises) for thinking it is true. If we do this, we've made an argument.

Again, there can be complex, multistage arguments with many premises leading to multiple conclusions. Arguments like this can become quite unwieldy. In teaching logic, we will often use a basic form of argument called a "syllogism," which is a simplified argument consisting of three numbered statements. The first two are the premises, and the third is the conclusion. Examples of arguments in syllogistic form are:

1. If it rained outside, then the streets are wet.
2. It rained outside.
3. Therefore, the streets are wet.

1. All college students love logic.
2. Joe is a college student.
3. Thus, Joe loves logic.

1. Jesus is either liar, lunatic, or Lord.
2. Jesus is not a liar or a lunatic.
3. Therefore, Jesus is Lord.

In each of these, statements numbered 1 and 2 are premises, and statements numbered 3 are conclusions. Typically, the conclusion will be signaled with what's sometimes called a conclusion indicator, such as "therefore," "hence," "so," or "thus." Notice that in each we are using the 1 and 2 statements to argue for or rationally support the 3 statement. What are our reasons for thinking the 3 statement is true? The 1 and 2 statements provide those reasons.

What's extremely beneficial about syllogisms is they clearly identify which statements are the premises and which are the conclusion. This helps make plain the logic of the argument. We can easily see what is being argued and then evaluate the argument accordingly.

Show Me the Argument

In the normal course of life, we rarely make arguments in syllogistic form. Instead, the arguments we make are, in a way, embedded or even sometimes disguised in the midst of other statements in the course of a discussion. Politicians are famous for this. Politicians will sometimes say a number of things without ever actually making a clear claim much less giving an actual argument.

In many cases, half the battle for evaluating an argument is figuring out exactly what the argument actually is. The arguments above are stated in syllogistic form, and this makes their logical structure wonderfully obvious. We know exactly what is being said and can move straightaway into evaluating the arguments. There's no question which statements are the premises and which are the conclusion. However, when we are having a discussion with someone or when someone is making a speech, the ideas are presented within a conversational flow and often include additional statements superfluous to the argument. People rarely make an argument as obvious and explicit as the syllogisms above. It can be even more frustrating when crucial premises are often unstated or implied.

An unstated premise is called an "enthymeme." Here's an example: "Humans are releasing large amounts of CO_2 and other gases into the atmosphere. And we have seen the global temperatures steadily rising year after year. So it's clear that humans are responsible for global warming." From what is stated, the syllogism is clear and would go something like this:

1. Humans are releasing large amounts of CO_2 and other gases into the atmosphere.
2. The global temperatures have steadily risen.
3. Therefore, humans are responsible for global warming.

Premise 1 and premise 2 look to be indisputable facts. We do release large amounts of CO_2 in the atmosphere when we burn things like wood, coal, natural gas, gasoline, and oil. We burn a lot of these items, and this causes massive amounts of CO_2 to be released. It is also clear, according to the experts, that the global temperatures have risen, on average, over the past century or more. But this isn't, as it stands, a good argument. The problem? A premise is missing. Looking closely at the argument, we notice nothing is connecting premise 1 with premise 2 to support the conclusion. When we hear these kinds of arguments, our minds often supply the missing premise and can see where things are going. However, in order to evaluate an argument, it is necessary to state explicitly what is implied. What is implied here is that the CO_2 humans release is causing the global temperatures to rise. So, by adding this premise to the argument, we see more clearly what's going on:

1. Humans are releasing large amounts of CO_2 and other gases into the atmosphere.
2. The global temperatures have steadily risen. [The CO_2 and other gases humans release are causing the rise in global temperatures.]
3. Therefore, humans are responsible for global warming.

But as it often happens, the implied premise here is controversial. Not everyone agrees that the primary cause of the rising temperatures is the human release of CO_2 as opposed to other natural causes. So, further evidence would need to be provided to support the conclusion.

It is your job, as a critical thinker, to find the argument in order to evaluate it. Here is a suggested strategy:

1. Find the conclusion. It is typically easiest to find a conclusion first before you find the premises of the argument. The conclusion may be stated first, and then reasons are given. Or it may be that the conclusion is given in dramatic fashion at the end with a conclusion indicator. It is easier to find the conclusion because it is the basic claim being made. When you boil it all down, what is the person ultimately claiming? This is the conclusion.
2. Find the premises. Once you have found the conclusion, you can then find the premises by determining which statements seem to support the conclusion. If a statement looks to support the truth of the conclusion, then it is a premise. Leaving all of the other statements aside, we look for what reasons the person ultimately offers. These are the premises.
3. Eliminate the extraneous statements and state any enthymemes. If a statement is irrelevant to the truth of the conclusion, then it can be eliminated. Ask yourself, Is this statement logically relevant? If there is a gap in the argument, then you may need to supply what is being left unstated.

Following this strategy helps you identify just what the argument is so that it can then be evaluated.

Standards of Evaluation

Logical Relevance

As critical thinkers, we want our arguments to be good. An argument is good when the premises provide good reasons for believing the argument's conclusion. But why can believing one thing (the premises) help you to know or rationally believe something else (the conclusion)? The answer has to do with the relation called "logical relevance," which is when the truth of one statement bears on the truth of another statement. Stated more precisely: for any two statements, A and B, A is logically relevant to B if in the case that A is true, B is to some degree likely to be true.[4] It's important to mention that the relation of logical relevance can hold in one direction but not the other. Or, as it is sometimes said, logical relevance is an asymmetrical relation. What this means is A can be logically relevant to B even if B is not logically relevant to A. If the statement "John is in the room" is true, then this is logically relevant to the truth of the statement "Someone is in the room." But "Someone is in the room" doesn't give us reason to think specifically that "John is in the room."

Consider the following two statements:

My gas tank gauge is sitting on empty.
I need to stop and get gas.

Notice that the first statement is logically relevant to the second. If the first is true, then this bears on the truth of the second. In fact, the first statement gives us a really good reason to believe that the second is true. It's the logical relevance that allows us to put these statements into an argument:

1. My gas tank gauge is sitting on empty.
2. Therefore, I need to stop and get gas.

It's premise 1 that makes a good case for the truth of the conclusion. Notice the following statements do not seem to have logical relevance:

My gas tank gauge is sitting on empty.
Grass is green.

Notice, this time, the first statement is not logically relevant to the second. We'll call this being logically irrelevant. Even if statement 1 is true, it does

---

[4] Two statements are also logically relevant if the truth of one gives us reason to think the other is false. We will be primarily concerned with statements that support the truth of other statements. This is the logical relevance that holds between premises and a conclusion in a good argument.

not bear on the truth of statement 2. That is, the truth of the first has no real relevance to whether the second is true or false. An argument can't be made for grass being green on the basis of my gas tank gauge being empty.

Though we will primarily be talking about statements that support the truth of other statements, a logically relevant statement can also falsify another statement. Here's an example:

> My gas tank gauge is sitting on empty.
> I should keep driving.

The first statement is clearly logically relevant to the second, but here it falsifies it. That is, it gives us reason to believe that the second statement is false.

In a good argument, logical relevance holds between the premises and the conclusion. This is to say that a good argument is one in which the premises, when true, provide reason to believe the conclusion is true. Sometimes the premises of an argument logically entail the conclusion, which is a robust logical relation. When premises "entail" a conclusion, the premises, if true, *guarantee* the truth of the conclusion.

In the following argument, the premise entails the conclusion:

1. Jones is in the next room.
2. Therefore, there is at least one person in the next room.

Notice how the truth of this premise literally guarantees the truth of the conclusion. If the premise is true (we are not necessarily committed to saying it is true when we say "*if* it is true"), then the conclusion must be true. There is no way for the premise to be true and the conclusion false, given the entailment. If the person named Jones is in the next room, then it is inconceivable that there is not at least one person in there. We see that, in the argument above, if premise 1 is true, then the conclusion is logically guaranteed to be true. In short, this premise entails this conclusion.

But not all good arguments involve premises that entail their conclusions. Premises (in a good argument) can also make a conclusion likely even if not guaranteed. Consider the following:

1. Smith's fingerprints are on the murder weapon.
2. Therefore, Smith (likely) committed the murder.[5]

Here it is easy to see that the premise does not entail or guarantee the conclusion. If the premise is in fact true, the conclusion could still be false. The reality is that if Smith's fingerprints are on a weapon used in a murder, then Smith is in trouble. But it is not guaranteed because there are many imaginable ways in which Smith's fingerprints ended up on the murder weapon where Smith is innocent of the crime. It could be the case that Smith's gun was stolen and used in the murder and his fingerprints were from prior use. Or it could be that Smith is being framed for the murder and his fingerprints were placed on the gun without his knowledge or without him using the gun.

Now, it's important to notice that though this premise does not entail the conclusion, it does give us at least some reason to believe that Smith is guilty of the murder. Again, Smith is likely in some serious trouble here given the fact that his fingerprints are on a weapon used in a murder. In most (though not all) cases, this occurs when one is guilty of the murder. So, all things being equal, the premise does give us reason to believe the conclusion, even though it falls short of entailment or a guarantee.

Again, premises could, of course, have nothing to do with each other. That is, they can be "logically irrelevant." Just because we have two or three statements, we don't necessarily have logical support. Have you ever caught children doing something they weren't supposed to do, and they start stringing statements together as an excuse for why they were doing it? They may

[5] This argument is probably best understood as being enthymematic. A further premise is needed to connect the fact that Smith's fingerprints are on the murder weapon and the conclusion that Smith committed the murder. We know that when someone's fingerprints are on a murder weapon, then that person recently handled the weapon. And so though this isn't explicitly stated here, we'll proceed as if this premise does provide support to believe the conclusion.

say all true things, but the problem is that they provide no reason whatsoever to believe the conclusion.

Deductive Standards

As we've seen, premises, when they are logically relevant in the sense outlined previously, can either entail the conclusion or make likely the conclusion. These give us two different standards by which we can evaluate arguments: deductive standards and nondeductive standards.[6]

Deductive Validity

It is time to name some of these things. The first standard we'll consider is called "deductive validity." If a premise (or premises) entails its conclusion, then the argument is "deductively valid" (or "valid," for short). An argument is deductively valid when it is set up so that the premises, if true, guarantee the truth of the conclusion. If it is a valid argument, then there is no possible way in which the premises could be true without the conclusion also being true.

Consider the following argument:

1. If it rained just now, then the streets are wet.
2. It rained just now.
3. Therefore, the streets are wet.

Ask yourself, Could these premises be true and the conclusion false? It seems that there is no way (you may have to stare at this for a few moments). If the conclusion is false (i.e., the streets are not wet), it will have to be because one or both of the premises are false. Either it did not rain just now (premise 2

---

[6] Many textbooks on logic and critical thinking make this distinction by talking about different forms of arguments. I think it is best to talk about these as standards of evaluation rather than different kinds of arguments. In my use of the terms, any argument will either pass or fail deductive standards.

is false) or the streets are dry even though it just rained (premise 1 is false). There is no other option. If both premises are true, then the conclusion must be true. This is because the premises entail the conclusion. Thus, the argument is deductively valid.

Or consider this argument:

1. If Jesus rose from the dead, then his claims are validated.
2. Jesus rose from the dead.
3. Therefore, his claims are validated.

Notice that if these premises are true, then this conclusion is guaranteed to be true. We would of course have to argue for each of the premises. But no matter if one is a Christian, is an atheist, or holds to a different religious tradition, this is clearly a valid argument.

If an argument is not valid (that is, if the premises do not entail the conclusion), then we say that it is "invalid." Again, this is a very strong standard. So, if it is even just possible that the premises are true and the conclusion is false, then the argument is invalid. Without the guarantee of entailment, the argument is invalid.

Consider the following argument, which is rearranged from above:

1. If it rained just now, then the streets are wet.
2. The streets are wet.
3. Therefore, it rained just now.

Now we ask the same question: Could these premises be true and the conclusion false? This time it is clear that they could. To see this, let us, for the sake of argument, just assume that premises 1 and 2 are true. With this assumption, can you now imagine some way in which the conclusion is false? Imagine that a water main broke and flooded the streets, and it did not rain. In that case, premise 2 would be true but not from rain. Premise 1 could still be true since it is a hypothetical claim. It says that *if* it rained just now, then the streets are wet. This could be true even if it didn't, as a matter of fact, rain just now. And yet, as we are imagining it, the conclusion is false—it didn't just rain. This shows that the argument is invalid. The premises do not entail the conclusion.

Or consider this parallel argument:

1. If you jumped into a lake just now, your hair is wet.
2. Your hair is wet.
3. Therefore, you jumped into a lake just now.

Even if premise 1 and premise 2 are true, it doesn't entail that you just jumped into a lake. It is true that *if* you jumped into a lake just now your hair will be wet. And let's say it is true that your hair is currently wet. But does that mean you just jumped into a lake? No, of course not. There could easily have been some other thing that caused your wet hair. You could have been caught in a rainstorm. You could have just taken a shower. Or you could have jumped into a river or been sprayed with a hose. In short, these premises do not entail their conclusion. The argument is, therefore, invalid.

Deductive Soundness

If I have a deductively valid argument, do I thereby have a good argument? No, not yet—at least, not necessarily. But we are, in a sense, on our way to a good argument. There are two deductive standards of which validity is only one. Notice that every time I have spoken about entailment and validity, I have mentioned an important clause: "if the premises are true." We should make special notice that this is a big "if." Statements like this are called hypothetical statements, and we have to be very careful to note what is being claimed. For a valid argument, the premises do not have to actually be true for us to imagine them to be true hypothetically. It just has to be the case that if they *were* true the conclusion *would* in that case necessarily be true. We can even do this when the premises are both clearly false. We can still imagine them to be true and ask whether they entail the conclusion. Now when the premises of a valid argument have false premises, then it is not of course, all things considered, a good argument. To be, all things considered, a good argument, it must both be valid and have true premises.

Consider the following argument:

1. If you know that 2 + 3= 5, then you know at least one math fact.
2. You know that 2 + 3= 5.
3. Therefore, you know at least one math fact.

This is a valid argument since the premises, if true, guarantee the truth of the conclusion. But we should also notice that this argument satisfies a further standard. For most of us, the premises are in fact true. We call this an argument that is "deductively sound." A deductively sound argument is one that is both valid and has true premises.

But what if the premises of a valid argument are not true? Consider this argument again:

1. If it rained just now, then the streets are wet.
2. It rained just now.
3. Therefore, the streets are wet.

Let's suppose you look out the window and see that premise 2 is false because it has been sunny all day. It is still a deductively valid argument, but it is not sound because of the false premise. In fact, an argument can be valid even if the premises are downright silly. The following is a deductively valid argument:

1. If the members of Congress are cleverly disguised robots designed to destroy our country, then there is a penguin in Antarctica with indigestion.
2. The members of Congress are cleverly disguised robots designed to destroy our country.
3. Therefore, there is a penguin in Antarctica with indigestion.

We may have our doubts about the intentions of the members of Congress at times, but clearly these premises are far-fetched and false. So this is not a deductively sound argument, even though it is valid. It's what we call an unsound argument.

Recall that deductive soundness requires two things. It must be valid, and it must have true premises.[7] If an argument is invalid, then it is unsound for that reason. But, even if it is valid, if just one of its premises is false, then the argument is unsound. To be sound it must satisfy both of these conditions. It must be valid in that the premises entail the conclusion, and it must have all true premises.

So, if I want to evaluate an argument according to deductive standards, I first of all ask whether the premises entail the truth of the conclusion (i.e., I ask whether it is valid). If the premises don't entail the conclusion, then the argument is invalid, and therefore unsound, for that reason. If it turns out that they do entail the conclusion (i.e., it is valid), I'm not done yet, because even silly arguments can be valid. I also need to figure out whether the premises are indeed true. If I do have a valid argument and if I do have true premises, then it is logically guaranteed that I have a true conclusion. I have a sound argument. There is no better argument than a deductively sound argument. It is pristine, since there is no logically conceivable way that the conclusion of a deductively sound argument can be false.

Here is a flow chart to summarize what we've said so far:

[7] We only have to say "true premises" instead of "true premises and a true conclusion"; if an argument is valid and it has true premises, then necessarily the conclusion is true. It goes without having to be stated.

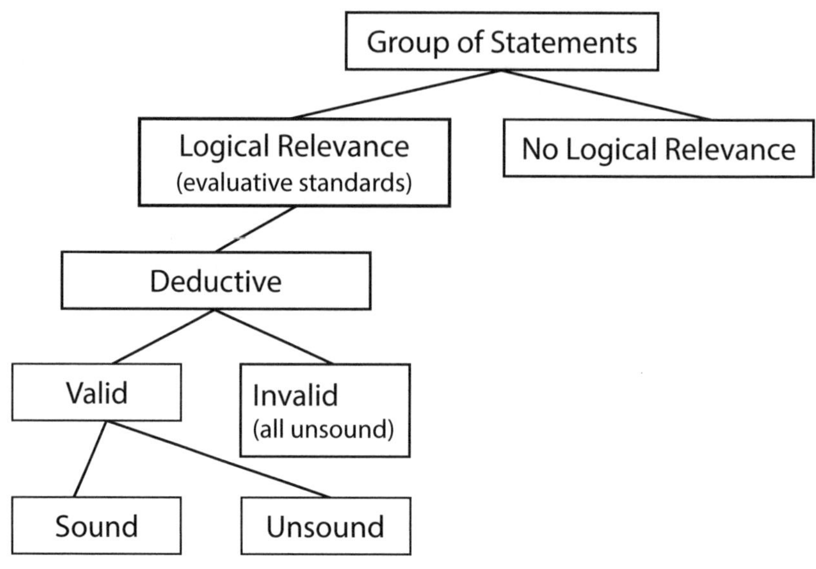

Nondeductive Standards

As was pointed out above, premises need not entail a conclusion for the argument to be a good one. When the premises of an argument make likely the truth of a conclusion, then this, too, is a good argument. We may not have a conclusion that is guaranteed to be true, but we do have a conclusion that is probably true. When an argument makes a conclusion very likely true, then it is rational to believe even if it is not guaranteed. Arguments of this sort satisfy what we'll call "nondeductive standards."[8] The distinction between deductive standards and nondeductive standards

---

[8] The distinction is often made between deduction and *induction*. I don't make the distinction this way since induction is a specific kind of argument (discussed in chap. 9) rather than a set of standards. Also, there are other arguments that achieve nondeductive standards that are not instances of induction, and using a different term to identify this standard of evaluation is preferable. For example, there are abductive arguments (or inferences to the best explanation) that are not, properly speaking, examples of induction. Again, I make the distinction between deductive

is that on deductive standards the premises must entail the conclusion, whereas on nondeductive standards the premises must only make likely the conclusion.

What does this look like? Consider a court case where Smith is on trial for murder. The legal case a prosecutor will make in a courtroom will typically be nondeductive. Suppose a number of compelling lines of evidence are against Smith. In this case we are rational in believing that Smith is guilty. That is, the evidence makes Smith's guilt likely. Even so, we could be wrong. Our belief (i.e., what we've concluded on the basis of the evidence) that Smith is guilty could be false. This is why court cases are often so contentious. Both sides present evidence, and the conclusions in a legal trial always involve what's likely the case. Nondeductively good arguments never guarantee truth. They only make a claim likely true though possibly false.

Even though a deductively good argument is preferable, in the above sense, much of our reasoning (like Smith's trial) will be on nondeductive grounds. We have very few guarantees of truth in life. We'll have to settle for what's probably the case and be open to new and better evidence.

Nondeductive Strength

There are also two standards of nondeductive reasoning.

The first standard is "nondeductive strength." When premises, if true, make likely the truth of the conclusion, this is a "nondeductively strong" argument (or simply strong, for short).

Here is the example we used above:

1. Smith's fingerprints are on the murder weapon.
2. Therefore, Smith committed the murder.

---

standards and nondeductive standards and think of induction as a particular form of argument that may achieve nondeductive standards.

This is a relatively strong argument because if the premise is true, then, unfortunately for Smith, there is reason to believe that he is the murderer. The good news for Smith, in this case, is the premise does not entail the conclusion. It only makes it somewhat likely. So it's quite possible the conclusion is false even if the premise is true. If the premises of an argument do not make likely the conclusion, then we would call this a weak argument.

It's important to point out that on this nondeductive standard, arguments can be stronger or weaker. This is unlike the standard of deductive validity. An argument is either valid or it isn't. It can't be more or less valid. But notice the argument above can be made even stronger in favor of Smith's guilt in the murder.

1. Smith's fingerprints are on the murder weapon.
2. Five people have testified under oath to seeing Smith commit the murder.
3. Therefore, Smith committed the murder.

Do premises 1 and 2 now entail the truth of the conclusion? No, because, although it's becoming much more unlikely, it is still quite possible that Smith is innocent of the murder. Can people testify that Smith committed the murder, and Smith still be innocent? Sure, it has happened many times. Witnesses can be extremely confident in what they thought they saw when, it turns out, they are mistaken. We should notice that this argument is stronger than the previous one, and it would be possible to make it even stronger if more evidence is discovered.

NONDEDUCTIVE COGENCY

As with deductive standards, having a nondeductively strong argument is not necessarily enough to have a good argument. The premises must also be true. We call this a nondeductively cogent argument. "Cogency" requires two things: the argument must be strong and the premises must be true.

Consider this argument once more:

1. Smith's fingerprints are on the murder weapon.
2. Therefore, Smith committed the murder.

Again, this seems to be a somewhat strong argument. If premise 1 is also true, then we have a nondeductively cogent argument. This is an argument that satisfies both nondeductive standards. What if it turned out that Smith's fingerprints were not on the murder weapon, but, with some more investigation, it is discovered that the fingerprint technician has a personal vendetta against Smith and fraudulently identified Smith's fingerprints. Even though premise 1, if it were true, makes likely the truth of the conclusion, we no longer have a reason to believe that Smith committed the murder since, as it turns out, premise 1 is not true—that is, it is a strong but uncogent argument.

This means we can also have silly, nondeductively strong arguments. Consider this argument, for example:

1. Cows can fly.
2. Therefore, you better not let your cows out of the barn, or they'll fly away.

This is, of course, a bad argument, but notice why: it's bad because the premise is false in that cows can't fly. But it is a strong argument because if premise 1 were true, then the conclusion would be made likely true. If cows could fly, then it seems you should be concerned about your cows flying away. But as it is, the premise is false, and thus it is a nondeductively uncogent argument.

Consider this argument Paul makes in 1 Corinthians 15:

1. The risen Jesus appeared to Cephas (1 Cor 15:5a).
2. The risen Jesus appeared to the Twelve (1 Cor 15:5b).
3. The risen Jesus appeared to over five hundred brothers and sisters at one time (1 Cor 15:6).
4. The risen Jesus appeared to James (1 Cor 15:7a).
5. The risen Jesus appeared to all the apostles (1 Cor 15:7b).
6. The risen Jesus appeared to Paul (1 Cor 15:8).
7. Therefore, Jesus rose from the dead.

Though these premises do not guarantee the conclusion, they do make it very likely true. That is, the argument is strong. First Corinthians 15 dates very early and so we seem to have good historical reason to believe the conclusion.

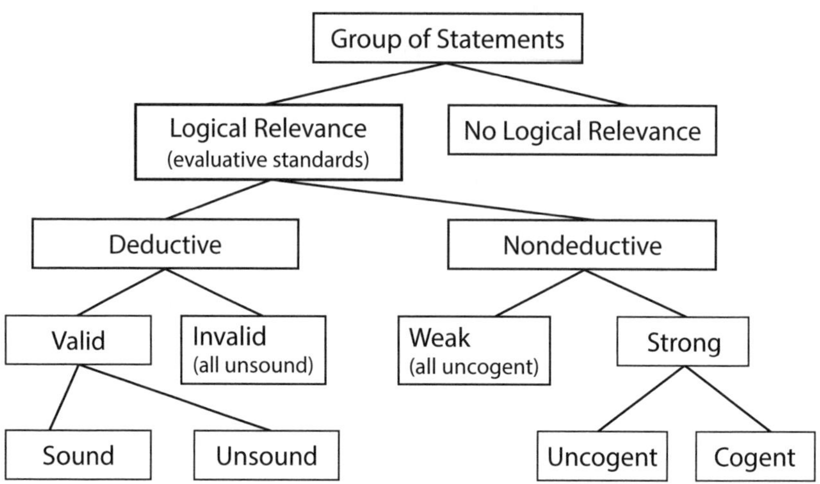

Conclusion

In this chapter, the aim was to introduce and give an overview of some of the basic concepts of logic. Some of this will likely feel confusing at first. It may even feel overwhelming, but we will continue to review these concepts in subsequent chapters and go deeper. Take your time with this material, and aim to gain a familiarity with the distinctions that are made.

Have you ever tried to play a game for the first time with people who are really good at the game? It can be overwhelming! What seems second nature for the other players can seem utterly confusing to you, and you might be tempted to quit in this situation. However, all you need to do is stick with it for a time, and you will likely gain the familiarity the other players have. It's not always fun in those beginning stages, but when you stick with it, there is often a big payoff. It's the same way with logic. If it feels confusing and overwhelming at this point, then you are normal. This is how it is for everyone at first. But stick with it, and gaining familiarity will pay off. What feels overwhelming and confusing at first will eventually make sense, and you'll be able to use these principles as you evaluate arguments and love God with all of your mind.

Deductive Standards of Logic

In the last chapter, we outlined two different sets of standards, deductive and nondeductive, by which we evaluate arguments. In this chapter, we will focus on the deductive standards of evaluation and go a bit deeper.

Let's begin with an illustration of the deductive standards of evaluation. Suppose we are electricians and have been hired to wire a house that is under construction. Our goal is that electricity will run from the main line on the street into the house, to all the light sockets, wall receptacles, and anything else that will need electricity. We spend the next few days running wires throughout the house. One of the most important things for an electrician to do is to make all the proper connections since a wire that doesn't properly connect is, of course, useless. But notice: it could be the case that we do a perfect job connecting all the electrical wires, yet none of the light sockets or receptacles have power. If the power isn't turned on at the street, the house will not have power even if all the wires are properly connected. So, to have a house with electricity, we need at least two things. We need to wire it properly, making all the connections, and we need to turn on the electricity, or the "juice."

Here's how this relates to logic. Just as a house must be wired properly, a deductively good argument must be set up properly. The validity of the argument is a matter of its structure and setup. Remember the validity of an argument has nothing to do with whether the premises or conclusion are true. A valid argument has only to do with it being structured such that the premises logically entail the conclusion. A house must be wired properly so that, when the juice is on, electricity flows to all the receptacles. A valid argument is one that is "wired properly"; if the premises are true, then the conclusion is necessarily true.

Let's look at this argument again:

1. If Congress members are all cleverly disguised robots designed to destroy the US, then there is a penguin in Antarctica with indigestion.
2. Congress members are all cleverly disguised robots designed to destroy the US.
3. Therefore, there is a penguin in Antarctica with indigestion.

Now, this is, of course, a bad argument. It's silly to think these premises give us good reason to believe the conclusion. It is, however, important to see that it is deductively valid. Remember how we defined deductive validity. The premises do not have to be true for the argument to be valid. But it must be the case that if they are true, the conclusion is guaranteed to be true. This is like a house that is wired properly but still lacks juice. The structure and the connections are there, but there is no electricity. In the same way, the argument could be set up properly such that if the premises are true, then the conclusion is true even if there is no truth. The logical structure and the connections are there, just without truth.

But there's another way a house may lack electricity. The electricity could be turned on, but suppose we failed to do a good job in wiring everything. Here there's juice, but the wiring is incorrect. If the connections are not all made, it doesn't matter whether the juice is turned on since the electricity can't flow to all of the receptacles. Similarly, an argument can be a bad argument where it does not have the proper logical structure even though it has all true statements.

Here's an example:

1. Topeka is the capital of the state of Kansas.
2. Granite is typically denser than marshmallows.
3. Therefore, Michael Jordan is one of the greatest basketball players to ever play in the NBA.

Notice each of these statements is true, and yet this is, of course, an obviously bad argument. But its failure has nothing to do with truth. It's a badly structured argument. The premises have no logical relevance to the conclusion. They give us no reason to believe the truth of the conclusion despite the fact that all the claims are clearly true.

Here's another example of an invalid argument that has true premises. This time it is a slightly more serious argument:

1. If Barack Obama is president of the United States, then Barack Obama is thirty-five years or older.
2. Barack Obama is thirty-five years or older.
3. Therefore, Barack Obama is president of the United States.

This argument has true premises. Our law requires that the president of the United States be thirty-five years or older, and Barack Obama currently satisfies this requirement. However, the conclusion is false. Obama is no longer the president of the United States, and given the Twenty-Second Amendment, he cannot serve a third term as president. So again, there is truth in the premises, but the argument is clearly invalid.

When it comes to houses, they must be wired properly, and the juice must be turned on. Likewise, when it comes to arguments and deductive standards, for an argument to be a deductively good argument (i.e., for it to be sound), it must be set up properly and have truth. That is, a sound argument must be valid, and it must have all true premises. This is a logically pristine argument. There is no possible way the conclusion can be false if the argument is deductively sound. Houses with good wiring and flowing electricity are pretty great too.

A Test for Validity

Many people understand the basic idea of deductive validity, but they may struggle to identify which arguments are valid and which are invalid. Here's a strategy for testing for validity:

1. Assume that the premises of the argument are true.
2. Ask, on the assumption of true premises, if the conclusion could be false. Here we are asking if there's any way, however weird or outlandish, for the premises to be true and yet the conclusion be false.
3. If it is possible that the premises are true and the conclusion is false, then it is an invalid argument. If not (i.e., the conclusion is always true whenever the premises are true), then it is valid.

The reason we can test for validity this way is if an argument is valid then it will be not be possible for the premises to be true and the conclusion false. We can test for this by imagining the premises being true (again, no matter how weird or outlandish they are) and trying to conceive of the conclusion being simultaneously false. Again: If it is possible, then it is invalid. If it is not, then it is valid.

Let's try it out with some of the arguments already given. Assume, for the sake of the test, the premises of the following argument are true:

1. If it rained just now, then the streets are wet.
2. It rained just now.

Now ask, if these premises are true, whether it is possible the following conclusion is false:

3. Therefore, the streets are wet.

Let's take this step-by-step. First, imagine that premise 2 is true. Imagine that you are currently standing outside, feeling raindrops hit the ground all around you. Next, imagine premise 1 is true. Imagine that if it just rained, then the streets are wet. This is easy to imagine because it is in fact true, at least in most situations. As long as someone doesn't live in an area where all of the streets are covered, then, by and large, if it rained, the streets would be wet. Now ask whether, if these two premises are true, it is possible that the streets are not wet (i.e., the conclusion is false). When we imagine the streets being dry, we should see that it must be because either it didn't rain just now (premise 1 is false) or because, even if it did rain, then the streets are not wet (premise 2 is false). In other words, the only way the conclusion could be false is if either premise 1 or 2 is false. But if they are assumed true, then the conclusion must be true. Given this, the argument is clearly valid.

Let's test another argument. Assume the following premises are true:

1. If Barack Obama is president of the United States, then Barack Obama is thirty-five years or older.
2. Barack Obama is thirty-five years or older.

Now ask whether the following could be false:

3. Therefore, Barack Obama is president of the United States.

Here it is easy to imagine true premises with a false conclusion because it is the case that the premises are actually true and the conclusion is actually false. Barack Obama is not currently the president of the United

States, and yet both premises are true. Thus, this argument is easily seen as invalid.

How about this one?

1. If you jumped into a lake just now, your hair is wet.
2. You hair is wet.
3. Therefore, you jumped into a lake just now.

Let's test this for validity. First, assume, for the sake of the test, that both premises are true. It's easy to do with premise 1 because it is so plausible. If you go into the lake, then it will have to be quite a rare situation for your hair to not get wet. Next, assume it is true your hair is in fact wet. Now, is there any possibility for these premises to be true and yet the conclusion be false? Yes! We can imagine any number of situations wherein your hair is wet from something other than jumping in the lake. Perhaps you recently showered or someone dumped a bucket of water over your head or it just rained or you jumped into a body of water that is not a lake. If any of these are true, then the conclusion is false even if the premises are true. Thus, it is an invalid argument.

Let's try one more:

1. Jesus is either liar, lunatic, or Lord.
2. Jesus is not a liar or a lunatic.
3. Therefore, Jesus is Lord.

Once more, we assume the two premises are true and ask whether the conclusion could be false. Notice that if the conclusion is false, then it would have to be because one or both premises are false. However, if we assume that they are true, that is, the options in premise 1 are all the available options (Jesus is either liar, lunatic, or Lord) and that the first two options (liar and lunatic) are ruled out, then it follows that Jesus is Lord. Many critics have argued that the premises here aren't true. But we are testing for validity, and this argument passes that test.

The Power of a Valid Argument

We of course want a valid argument *with* true premises. But it is important to note that we don't often know (especially with certainty) whether our premises are in fact true. While we can often put our arguments into a valid form, it can be difficult to decide whether the premises are true. We often have to settle for having premises that are plausibly true or that we have reason to believe are true. Much of the work we must do with a deductively valid argument is providing reason to think the premises themselves are in fact true.

But even with this, a deductively valid argument can still be quite helpful. Let's say you are looking at a valid argument and the conclusion of the argument is something with which you strongly disagree. Well, you cannot simply deny the conclusion of a deductively valid argument. To rationally deny the conclusion, you will have to deny at least one of the premises. But if you accept the premises of a valid argument as true, to be logically consistent you must accept the conclusion. This is what we'll call the *power* of a deductively valid argument: if one accepts the premises of a valid argument, then one *must* accept the conclusion. To deny the conclusion, you must deny one of the premises.

Take the following argument, for example:

1. If Jesus did not rise from the dead, then Christianity is false.
2. Jesus did not rise from the dead.
3. Therefore, Christianity is false.

If one is a Christian, then one will naturally be interested in denying this conclusion. But this is a deductively valid argument. That is, these premises entail the conclusion. So, the Christian theist cannot simply deny this conclusion without also denying one or more of the premises. If one accepts both of these premises, then one will have to accept the conclusion as well, given the validity.

Which premise should the Christian deny? Premise 1 is plausibly true. In fact, the apostle Paul expressed it in 1 Cor 15:17: "if Christ has not been raised, your faith is worthless." So the Christian, it seems, should accept premise 1. Thus, the Christian will have to deny premise 2. But here there's good news. There's a variety of evidence one can offer for the fact of Jesus's resurrection.[1] With this evidence, the Christian can quite rationally deny premise 2.

The power of a valid argument is seen when we present someone with an argument as well. When you can show someone the reasonability of your premises, and you show them the conclusion follows in a deductively valid way, then, to be rational, you've shown them they should accept the truth of the conclusion. They cannot reject the conclusion without denying one or more of the premises. And this can be powerful indeed!

Symbolization

When it comes to deductively valid arguments, we can symbolize the statements involved in the arguments. The reason we can symbolize the statements of a deductively valid argument is validity has only to do with the structure of the argument and not the actual truth of the statements. Thus, we can swap out the statements with symbols. We typically use a single capital letter to symbolize a statement. This is a great benefit for evaluating arguments because it makes plain the logical structure of the argument.

Here's an argument we have seen a number of times:

1. If it rained just now, then the streets are wet.
2. It rained just now.
3. Therefore, the streets are wet.

---

[1] See Michael Licona, *The Resurrection of Jesus: A New Historiographical Approach* (Downers Grove, IL: InterVarsity Press, 2010).

We also gave this argument:

1. If Congress members are all cleverly disguised robots designed to destroy the US, then there is a penguin in Antarctica with indigestion.
2. Congress members are all cleverly disguised robots designed to destroy the US.
3. Therefore, there is a penguin in Antarctica with indigestion.

What we should notice is that both of these arguments have the same form. That is, though the arguments make radically different claims, the arguments have the same structure. They are each instances of an argument form we call *modus ponens*.

We can symbolize each statement to see the form. In the two arguments above, each argument has a total of two statements. We'll assign each statement in the argument a capital letter:

It rained just now = P
The streets are wet = Q

P Q
1. If it rained just now, then the streets are wet.
P
2. It rained just now.
Q
3. Therefore, the streets are wet.

We can write this argument form like this:

1. If P, then Q
2. P
3. Therefore, Q

When we look at the other argument above, we see this same structure:

Congress members are all cleverly disguised robots = P
There is a penguin in Antarctica = Q

P
1. If Congress members are all cleverly disguised robots, then there is
Q
a penguin in Antarctica with indigestion.

P
2. Congress members are all cleverly disguised robots.

Q
3. Therefore, there is a penguin in Antarctica with indigestion.

By symbolizing, the structure is made quite clear, and we can see that it is also an instance of modus ponens.

We must follow a few rules whenever we symbolize arguments. The first rule is that we only symbolize *simple statements*. A simple statement says only one thing and cannot be reduced to any simpler statements. An example of a simple statement is "It rained just now." This says only one thing and it can't be reduced to any simpler statement. Notice the first premise in a modus ponens is a *complex statement*. The premise "If it rained just now, then the streets are wet" is composed of two simple statements: "it rained just now" and "the streets are wet." These simpler statements are then connected in a particular way (i.e., if it rained just now, then the streets are wet). The letters represent the simple statements embedded in the more complex statement. Connecting these simple statements are *logical connectives*, and, in this case, it is the *if/then conditional* (more about this momentarily). This gives us the symbolization of "if P, then Q."

The second rule of symbolizing is that whenever a statement gets a letter, the same letter may be used elsewhere in the argument but only for other instances of the very same statement. If it is a different statement, then it must get a different letter. We have to be careful here because two instances of the same linguistic sentence could have two different meanings, especially when used in different contexts. The example we used earlier was

"Smith's checking account is flush with cash." Depending on how much money someone is used to having, being "flush with cash" can mean many a lot of different things. Here's the rule: if we mean something different across instances of this sentence, even though it may be the same sentence, then it must get a different letter. Everywhere the same letter shows up in an argument must represent the exact same statement.

Again, consider the following two statements: "Smith's checking account is flush with cash (on a student's standard)" and "Smith's checking account is flush with cash (on Jeff Bezos's standards)." Though these may be the same sentence they are clearly different statements. Because there are different statements here, these each need a different letter. It would look something like this:

> Smith's checking account is flush with cash (on the standards of a typical college student) = P
> Smith's checking account is flush with cash (meaning on the standards of Jeff Bezos) = Q

Understanding this is important because language is often ambiguous; the same language can mean more than one thing. The word *bank* can mean a financial institution, the side of a river, a row of certain objects, or to bounce a basketball off of a backboard. It's all the same word but used to mean very different things.

The following argument has an ambiguity, and so we have to be careful how we symbolize it.

1. If a plant gets regular sunlight and plenty of water, then it will grow.
2. The (Ford motor) plant gets regular sunlight and has plenty of water.
3. Therefore, the (Ford motor) plant will grow.

The term *plant* in premise 1 means something different from the term *plant* in premise 2 and in the conclusion (as does the word *grow*). This has the appearance of being modus ponens, but it is not. The statement in premise

2 is completely different from the statement in premise 1. This difference is seen clearly when we symbolize the argument.

P Q

1. If a plant gets regular sunlight and plenty of water, then it will grow.

R

2. The (Ford motor) plant gets regular sunlight and has plenty of water.

S

3. Therefore, the (Ford motor) plant will grow.

Clearly, the following argument is not valid:

1. If P, then Q
2. R
3. Therefore, S

Symbolizing's third rule is, if two statements refer to two different times, then they must get different letters.

The Lakers won the NBA championship (in 2020).
The Lakers won the NBA championship (in 2019).

Again, even though the same basic sentence may be used to make these claims, these are not the same statements, and they must also get two different letters. The Lakers won the NBA championship in 2020, but they didn't even make the playoffs, much less win, in 2019. So these are clearly different statements, especially since one is true and the other is false. More importantly, for our purposes, they must get different letters. We symbolize these this way:

The Lakers won the NBA championship (in 2020) = P
The Lakers won the NBA championship (in 2019) = Q

The Common Argument Test for Validity

Following these rules, with an argument form such as modus ponens, you can plug literally any statement in for the P and the Q, and the resulting argument will always be deductively valid, given its form. It can be any crazy statements you want to plug in. As long as you follow the rules above, it will always be valid.

This gives another way to identify a valid argument: you can look for common valid argument forms. Whenever you recognize that an argument is an instance of, say, modus ponens, you can be sure that it is deductively valid. The same goes for other common argument forms. Again, the argument could have crazy and outlandish claims, but as long as it is in one of these forms, it is deductively valid.

Here are some other argument forms. Consider the following:

1. If it rained just now, then the streets are wet.
2. The streets are not wet.
3. Therefore, it did not rain just now.

This looks similar to modus ponens, but premise 2 and the conclusion deny the statements, which we represent with a "not." It has a deductively valid argument form, which can be symbolized in the following way:

P Q
1. If it rained just now, then the streets are wet.

Not Q
2. The streets are not wet.

Not P
3. Therefore, it did not rain just now.

This argument form is called *modus tollens* and has the following form:

1. If P, then Q
2. Not Q
3. Therefore, Not P

Modus tollens involves negations (i.e., when a statement is denied). Sometimes sentences with a negation will have a "not" explicitly at the front of the sentence, but at other times it is less obvious. A statement is negated so long as the statement contains a "not" or some other negating term. The following is an example of modus tollens, but it takes some rewording to see this:

1. If Bigfoot exists, then someone, at some point, would have seen it.
2. No one has ever seen Bigfoot.
3. Therefore, Bigfoot doesn't exist.

To symbolize the statements involved here, we make "Bigfoot exists" = P and "someone, at some point, would have seen it" = Q. Though premise 2 does not explicitly have the term *not*, if we symbolized it, we would make it Not Q because "No one has ever seen Bigfoot" is logically equivalent to the negation of "someone, at some point, would have seen it." We could reword it as "It is not the case that someone, at some point, has seen Bigfoot" with no loss of meaning. Thus, when we symbolize this argument we see that it is an instance of modus tollens:

P Q
1. If Bigfoot exists, then someone, at some point, would have seen it.

Not Q
2. No one has ever seen Bigfoot.

Not P
3. Therefore, Bigfoot doesn't exist.

Here are some other common argument forms that are always valid:

Disjunctive syllogism
1. Either P or Q[2]
2. Not P
3. Therefore, Q

---

[2] In order for this to be a valid argument, this statement must be understood as an exclusive disjunction, such that the disjunctive statement exhausts all possibilities. See the discussion of exclusive versus inclusive disjunctions later in this chapter.

Hypothetical syllogism

1. If P, then Q
2. If Q, then R
3. Therefore, if P, then R

Dilemma syllogism

1. If P, then Q or R
2. Not Q
3. Not R
4. Therefore, not P

Universal syllogism

1. All S are P.
2. X is an S.
3. Therefore, X is a P.

The common argument form test for validity can be really handy, but it is definitely limited in its application. Many more deductively valid arguments exist beyond these forms. With these, you will have to utilize the test for validity we discussed above.

Common Invalid Argument Forms

There are also argument forms that look like the common valid argument forms but are actually invalid. Consider this invalid argument we discussed above:

1. If it rained just now, then the streets are wet.
2. The streets are wet.
3. Therefore, it rained just now.

We might be tempted to think this argument is an instance of modus ponens, but is it? Look at it carefully. It is not an instance of modus ponens. If we symbolize the argument, we get the following:

P Q
1. If it rained just now, then the streets are wet.

Q
2. The streets are wet.

P
3. Therefore, it rained just now.

So it would have this form:

1. If P, then Q
2. Q
3. Therefore, P

This error is called "affirming the consequent." With it symbolized, we can see this argument is not the same as modus ponens. The first premise is the same, but then it asserts Q (instead of P) and concludes, therefore, P (instead of Q). But from the fact that "If P, then Q" and "Q," it doesn't follow that P is true. By being familiar with this form, we can know that arguments in this form are always invalid.

Other common invalid argument forms include:

Denying the antecedent
1. If P, then Q
2. Not P
3. Therefore, not Q

Affirming the disjunct
1. P or Q
2. P
3. Therefore, not Q

Complex Statements and Connectives

Conjunction

As was mentioned earlier, a simple statement is one in which the statement says only one thing and cannot be reduced to any simpler statements. For example:

Grass is green.

It is a simple statement in that it makes a single claim about the world that is either true or false. And it cannot be broken down into any simpler statements. If we were to symbolize this statement, it would get one single letter.

P
Grass is green.

We can use any letter to represent a statement.

Not all statements are simple. Consider the following:

Grass is green and snow is white.

This is a complex statement because it is a statement composed of two simpler statements. It, in effect, says two things. It asserts both that "grass is green" and "snow is white" at the same time. The simple statements are *connected* in a certain way. Notice these two simple statements are asserted as true at the same time and are connected by the word *and*. In logic, we call this complex statement a "conjunction," and we call the simpler statements that comprise the conjunction its "conjuncts." For a conjunction to be true, it must be the case that both conjuncts are true at the same time. If only one of the conjuncts is false, then the entire conjunction is false. When we assert a conjunction, we are, in effect, asserting both conjuncts are true. So, if one conjunct is false, then the conjunction itself is false.

This complex statement can be symbolized in the following way:

P and Q
Grass is green and snow is white.

Although a conjunction always asserts the truth of at least two simple statements at the same time, it could assert the truth of more than two.

Grass is green, snow is white, and the sky is blue.

Here all three of these conjuncts are asserted as true together. If any one of them is false, then, once again, the whole conjunction is false.

We should also note that it is most common for a conjunction to be written with the word *and* connecting the simpler statements, but it doesn't have to. For example, the following are all conjunctions because they all assert the truth of two simpler statements:

Grass is green, but snow is white.
Grass is green; however, snow is white.

Or the sentence could be stated where we may not see discrete conjuncts, at first. We may have to, so to speak, clean up the statement, so the conjuncts are more obvious.

Grass and dollar bills are green.

This is equivalent to saying "Grass is green, and dollar bills are green" and would likewise be symbolized as "P and Q."

Disjunction

Sometimes we make a statement in which we are asserting not that two simple statements are true but only that one or the other is true. For example:

Grass is green or snow is white.

This complex statement is called a "disjunction," and each simple statement is a "disjunct." For a disjunction to be true, just one of the disjuncts must be true. The statement above is saying that either grass is green or snow is white. But when we say this, it only takes one of those statements being true for the whole disjunction to be true. The disjunction is false just in the case that both disjuncts are false.

This can be represented symbolically as:

P or Q

When it comes to a disjunction, sometimes when we say something in the form of P or Q we mean one or the other is true and it can't be the case that both are true. Other times, we mean one or the other and possibly both are true. Suppose I were to say,

> According to Jesus, you will serve either God or money. (from Matt 6:24)

Notice here that Jesus said either one of the disjuncts are true, but not both. Jesus said that you can't serve both God and money. It is one or the other. In this instance, "P or Q" is what we call an "exclusive disjunction" (sometimes called the "exclusive-or").

However, suppose I were to say:

> Either Jones or Smith committed the crime.

Notice here both disjuncts could turn out to be true. Jones and Smith could have collaborated together in committing the crime. What we mean when we say "P or Q" here is that either one of these disjuncts is true, or they are both true. This we will call an "inclusive disjunction" (or the "inclusive-or"). Unless we note otherwise, we will be primarily concerned with inclusive disjunctions.

Negation

If a statement is negated, then this, too, is a complex statement because it is not merely asserting a simple statement. A negation asserts the opposite of the simple statement. When a statement is negated, the opposite truth value is asserted. That is, negating a statement, in a way, flips the truth value. If P is true, then Not P is false, and vice versa.

As was mentioned above, the statement need not have an "it's not the case that . . ." in front of the statement for it to be a negation. All it takes is a negating term somewhere in the sentence. Some examples of negated statements are:

> Bigfoot does not exist.
> No one has ever seen God.
> It hasn't rained.

Logical connectives always have a scope. The scope of a connective is simply what statements it joins together. The scope is obvious when it comes to a conjunction with just two conjuncts (i.e., P and Q). The scope of the conjunction here is both P and Q. But when we get more complicated, the scope has to be defined using parentheses. This is especially true with negations. If I say, "It is not the case that Bigfoot exists and grass is green," this could either mean:

> it is not the case that Bigfoot exists, and it is not the case that grass is green;

or,

> it is not the case that Bigfoot exists, and it is the case that grass is green.

It all depends on whether the scope of the negation is meant to include the statement "grass is green." If it was the first, we would symbolize it as "Not (P and Q)" using the parentheses to show the negation includes Q. But if it was the second, it would be "Not P and Q" where the scope of the negation only includes P.

Even though your grammar teachers likely warned you against such things, there can also be multiple negatives. The following statement has two negatives:

It's not the case that Bigfoot doesn't exist.

This would be symbolized as the following:

Not (Not P)

It's worth noting that this complex statement is logically equivalent to P.

The Conditional

Next, we have the conditional.

If grass is green, then snow is white.

The conditional is symbolized like this:

If P, then Q

The statement that follows the "if," in this case the P, is called the "antecedent." And the statement that follows the "then," in this case Q, is called the "consequent." We must be careful with the conditional because a variety of things could be intended with a phrase of this form. For example, we could mean this in a causal sense. We could mean that if P is the case, then this causes Q to be the case. Though this is a natural way to read this conditional, for our purposes, unless otherwise qualified, we will be talking primarily about the material conditional. All a material conditional says is if P is true, then Q is also true. But if P is not true, then Q can be either true or false and the conditional is still true, but it's true otherwise. Now, this might strike us as a bit counterintuitive, but what this means is that if it's a true material conditional, the one thing it can't be is a true antecedent and a false consequent.

The Biconditional

The final complex statement that we will look at is the biconditional. An example of a biconditional is:

Grass is green if and only if snow is white.

This is symbolized in the following way:

P iff Q

This is read as "P if and only if Q." The meaning of a biconditional is logically equivalent to a conjunction of two material conditionals. "P iff Q" is equivalent to "(If P, then Q) and (if Q, then P)." Notice that we use the parentheses to denote the scope of each conditional—each conditional is a conjunct of the larger conjunction in that they are both being asserted as true together.

The biconditional is unique among the complex statements outlined above since it is a combination of complex statements. Just as we can make complex statements out of simple statements, we can take those and make even more complex statements. There's really no limit to how complex a statement can be. For this reason, we don't typically name these more complex statements.

For example, we may have the following:

(P and Q) or (R and S)

This is a disjunction, but notice the disjuncts are each conjunctions. What this means is that the main connective in this statement is the disjunction—whereas it has two minor connectives that both happen to be conjunctions. The difference between a main and minor connective is a difference of scope. The minor connective will join two statements but only as a part of the larger statement. The scope of the major connective extends to the whole statement. In the statement above, the connective of the first conjunction, "and," only joins the P and the Q but really has nothing to do with the other statements (i.e., R and S). It is, in this sense, minor. The "or," however, is the major connective because it comprises the entire complex statement. Again, we use parentheses around the conjuncts to show that the scope of that connective only includes what's within the parentheses.

The "or" outside of the parentheses tells us that the statement is ultimately a (complicated) disjunction.

Consider the following:

If P, then [if (Q and R), then (S or T)]

Because of the complexity here, we've had to use both parentheses and brackets to clarify the scope of statements. Here the main connective is the conditional, followed by a rather complicated consequent. It is actually made up of another conditional that has a conjunction for an antecedent and a disjunction for a consequent. This may be a bit too much like alphabet soup, but stare at these long enough and you'll see the structure of these statements.

Conclusion

Working with deductive standards of logic is quite a precise science and certainly tedious at times. It is easy to lose the forest for the trees, as they say. We can get so focused on getting our symbols set up properly that we forget we are talking about actual arguments. It is immensely helpful for thinking critically about the world to understand the nature of deductive logic. Admittedly, it is not always exciting. But this is because we are focused on a deep level of rational thought. We are looking at the structure of deductive logic. If God is the ground of logic, as we argued in chapter 4, we therefore have a theological reason to know the depth of rational and logical thought. We are, in a sense, knowing God in a deep way by virtue of knowing deductive logic.

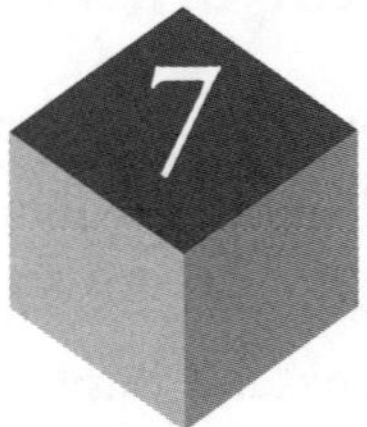

Truth Tables

All statements are bivalent. This means that for every statement there are exactly two truth values. It is always either true or false. Given this fact about statements, we can represent the truth values for P in a table:

P
T
F

We call this a "truth table," which is a diagram that displays all the possible combinations of truth values of a statement or a series of statements. The top row is the statement letter and the two rows below this present all possible truth values for the statement. Truth tables are useful for displaying the logical possibilities, and seeing these possibilities helps us understand the complex statements we've described above. It will also give us yet another way to test for validity. The table above shows the logical possibilities for the simple statement P, and there are only two: it can be either true or false. That's it. There are no other logical possibilities. So far, so good!

Simple Statements Represented

When, however, we have more than one statement involved, it gets more complicated. We have more logical possibilities of truth values, and so we must represent that in our truth table. To represent the logical possibilities of two simple statements, it looks like this:

P	Q
T	T
F	T
T	F
F	F

Notice that if we have two statement letters, then there twice as many possibilities of combinations for the truth values. They can both be true, P can be false and Q true, P can be true and Q false, or both could be false. Every time we add a new letter, we must expand the table so that we can represent all the different logical possibilities. The more statement letters you have, the more possible combinations of truth values. How do you know how many rows you will need? If you have one statement, then you need two rows. If there are two statements, then you need four rows. If you have three statements, you need eight rows, and so on.[1]

Following this, if we are going to make a truth table for P, Q, and R, we need eight rows.

[1] What's happening is that the necessary number of rows is always determined by two to the power of the number of simple statements (2^x). So if there are two simple statements, then you will have 2^2, which equals four rows. If you have three, you will have 2^3, which equals eight rows, and four will be 2^4 equaling sixteen.

P	Q	R

Now we need to complete this table with Ts and Fs. But we need to make sure we get all possibilities represented with no repeats. Though we can accomplish this in more than one way, I suggest an easy strategy that will ensure all logical possibilities are represented. In the first column, we alternate Ts and Fs. From here, we double this for each column. Thus, in the second column put the Ts and Fs down as pairs. The third column gets sets of four. If there is a fourth, we list them in sets of eight, and so on. If we follow this method, we will have every possible combination represented.

P	Q	R
T	T	T
F	T	T
T	F	T
F	F	T
T	T	F
F	T	F
T	F	F
F	F	F

Once you get good at this, you can fill out a longer truth table quickly. As you look at each row, notice that each combination of Ts and Fs are represented without any row repeating.

Here is a truth table for four simple statements. Notice that in the first column the Ts and Fs alternate, and in the second they are in pairs. Then in the third, there are sets of four, and, in the last, they are in sets of eight:

P	Q	R	S
T	T	T	T
F	T	T	T
T	F	T	T
F	F	T	T
T	T	F	T
F	T	F	T
T	F	F	T
F	F	F	T
T	T	T	F
F	T	T	F
T	F	T	F
F	F	T	F
T	T	F	F
F	T	F	F
T	F	F	F
F	F	F	F

By following these conventions, every possible combination of truth values is represented on the truth table. You could do this for as many statements as you want, but the tables get exponentially larger because each new statement always results in more logical combinations of truth values. With too many statement letters, the table can become too long and unwieldy to be practical.

Now that we understand how to lay out all of the logical possibilities of simple statements, we can look at how to display the logical possibilities of complex statements.

Complex Statements Represented

We'll begin with the truth table for "Not P." Recall that this is a complex statement because it is a negation of the simple statement P. When representing complex statements, in order to keep everything straight, we will make something of a key of every letter that shows up in the more complex statements. This will be a great aid to plug in those values to the more complex statements on each row of the truth table. The key will be kept to the left of the table. These set the truth values of those letters for every instance across a particular row. For the negation, we only have one letter, P, and so we'll only need two rows. We'll then include a column for P, which is our key, and a column for Not P:

P	Not P

Next we begin to fill in the values for P using our strategy given previously. Since it is only one statement letter, we only get two possible values:

P	Not P
T	
F	

The key sets the value for the particular row and then, in light of these values, we work out whatever the truth value is for the complex statement as we work our way across the table. So then we fill in the column under Not P given the values of the statement letters in the key of that particular row. Remember that when we have a negation of a statement, this always flips the truth value. If the statement P is true, then Not P is false and vice versa. So to represent those possibilities, we write out the table this way:

P	Not P
T	F
F	T

The column under "Not P" gives us the logical possibilities of this complex statement given the values of "P" in the left-hand column.

Let us now look at some of our other complex statements and how to represent them on a truth table. Consider the conjunction "P and Q." Again, the first thing we do is display our key comprising each letter in the conjunction and their logical possibilities. Since we now have two simple statements, we need four rows and we fill it in according to our strategy to make sure we represent all possibilities. We also include a column for the complex statement:

P	Q	P and Q
T	T	
F	T	
T	F	
F	F	

We should recall that if someone asserts a conjunction (P and Q), then both conjuncts are asserted as true together. So the conjunction itself is true only if both conjuncts are true, and it is false otherwise. If one conjunct is false or both conjuncts are false, then the conjunction is false. So, we fill out the truth value for each row in light of the values set by the key:

P	Q	P and Q
T	T	T
F	T	F
T	F	F
F	F	F

As we see, there is only one logical possibility for a conjunction to be true (i.e., the first row). That is, both conjuncts must be true, and it is false otherwise.

When it comes to a disjunction, the story is quite different. Since a disjunction says either of the disjuncts is true, all it takes is one of the disjuncts to be true for the disjunction to be true. Since we are assuming the inclusive disjunction, it is also true when both disjuncts are true. This gives us the following truth table:

P	**Q**	**P or Q**
T	T	T
F	T	T
T	F	T
F	F	F

The disjunction has three logically possible ways to be true and only one logical possibility to be false. It's only false when both disjuncts are false, and it is true otherwise.

When it comes to the conditional, we should recall that we are assuming the material conditional; this means if P is true, then Q is also true. Remember that the only way for a material conditional to be false is if the antecedent is true and the consequent is false. Following all of our rules and strategies gives us:

P	**Q**	**If P, then Q**
T	T	T
F	T	T
T	F	F
F	F	T

As we can see, the only row on the truth table that gets a false for the conditional is the row where P is true and Q is false. Again, as we discussed in the last chapter, it may seem a bit counterintuitive, but the conditional is true otherwise.

When it comes to the biconditional, things are a bit more complicated because the biconditional is a conjunction of two conditionals. Remember that "P iff Q" is equivalent to "(If P, then Q) and (If Q, then P)." Notice that since we are only dealing with two simple statements (the P and the Q), we still only need four rows on the table, but we'll need more columns. As we've said, the main connective of this complex statement is a conjunction. In order to find the truth value of the main connective, we'll need to first find the truth values of the minor connectives, which, in this case, are the two conditionals. So one way to do this is to lay it out with columns for the truth values of each of its minor connectives and then a column for the truth values of its major connective. It would look like the following:

P	**Q**	**If P, then Q**	**If Q, then P**	**(If P, then Q) and (If Q, then P)**
T	T			
F	T			
T	F			
F	F			

We bring the values across to the two conditionals first.

P	**Q**	**If P, then Q**	**If Q, then P**	**(If P, then Q) and (If Q, then P)**
T	T	T	T	
F	T	T	F	
T	F	F	T	
F	F	T	T	

But now we are looking at a conjunction. We need both conjuncts to be true for the conjunction to be true. Carrying the values across to the final column gives us the following:

P	Q	If P, then Q	If Q, then P	(If P, then Q) and (If Q, then P)
T	T	T	T	T
F	T	T	F	F
T	F	F	T	F
F	F	T	T	T

We can save a little time (and space) by writing in the values under one column. As before, we start with the truth values of the minor connectives before we look for the main connective. A convention to keep things clear is to write your Ts and Fs smaller under each minor connective than under the main connective. Again the main connective here is the conjunction, and the minor connectives are both conditionals.

P	Q	(If P, then Q) and (If Q, then P)
T	T	T T
F	T	T F
T	F	F T
F	F	T T

P	Q	(If P, then Q) and (If Q, then P)
T	T	T T T
F	T	T F F
T	F	F F T
F	F	T T T

The truth values under the "and" (which has a slightly larger font) display the truth values for the biconditional since it is the main connective. We can summarize this with the following truth table:

P	Q	P iff Q
T	T	T
F	T	F
T	F	F
F	F	T

Using the same conventions, we are able to display the logical possibilities of even more complex statements. Take the following complex statement: If P, then [if (Q or R), then (Not S)]. Just as before, we display the logical possibilities in our key for each letter in this complex statement. Because there are four letters, we'll need sixteen rows. We follow our strategy for laying out all logical possibilities:

P	Q	R	S	If P, then [if (Q or R), then (Not S)]
T	T	T	T	
F	T	T	T	
T	F	T	T	
F	F	T	T	
T	T	F	T	
F	T	F	T	
T	F	F	T	
F	F	F	T	
T	T	T	F	
F	T	T	F	
T	F	T	F	
F	F	T	F	
T	T	F	F	
F	T	F	F	

T	F	F	F	
F	F	F	F	

We then fill in the truth values for each minor connective, starting with the innermost parentheses. We write these small to denote that they are the minor connectives.

P	**Q**	**R**	**S**	**If P, then [if (Q or R), then (Not S)]**
T	T	T	T	T F
F	T	T	T	T F
T	F	T	T	T F
F	F	T	T	T F
T	T	F	T	T F
F	T	F	T	T F
T	F	F	T	F F
F	F	F	T	F F
T	T	T	F	T T
F	T	T	F	T T
T	F	T	F	T T
F	F	T	F	T T
T	T	F	F	T T
F	T	F	F	T T
T	F	F	F	F T
F	F	F	F	F T

We then fill in the truth values of the next connective with slightly larger Ts and Fs. This is the conditional that is within the brackets:

P	**Q**	**R**	**S**	**P, then [if (Q or R), then (Not S)]**
T	T	T	T	T F F
F	T	T	T	T F F
T	F	T	T	T F F

F	F	T	T	T F F
T	T	F	T	T F F
F	T	F	T	T F F
T	F	F	T	F T F
F	F	F	T	F T F
T	T	T	F	T T T
F	T	T	F	T T T
T	F	T	F	T T T
F	F	T	F	T T T
T	T	F	F	T T T
F	T	F	F	T T T
T	F	F	F	F T T
F	F	F	F	F T T

And finally, we fill in the major connective for this complex statement, and this gives us the possible truth values.

P	Q	R	S	If P, then [if (Q or R), then (Not S)]
T	T	T	T	F T F F
F	T	T	T	T T F F
T	F	T	T	F T F F
F	F	T	T	T T F F
T	T	F	T	F T F F
F	T	F	T	T T F F
T	F	F	T	T F T F
F	F	F	T	T F T F
T	T	T	F	T T T T
F	T	T	F	T T T T
T	F	T	F	T T T T
F	F	T	F	T T T T
T	T	F	F	T T T T

F	T	F	F	T T T T
T	F	F	F	T F T T
F	F	F	F	T F T T

Beyond simply representing the truth values of a statement, we can also use truth tables to show whether a statement is contradictory or tautologous. We have a "contradiction" when a statement and its negation are both asserted. Contradictions are necessarily false in the sense that it doesn't matter whether the statement is true or false because every row of the truth table will be false. That is, there is no possible way a contradiction is true. Fs will be all the way down. For example, "P and Not P" is an obvious contradiction. Here's the table for that:

P	**P and Not P**
T	F F
F	F T

No matter whether P is true or false, "P and Not P" is necessarily false. The truth values under the main connective (i.e., the "and") are all false.

Here is another example of a bit more complicated contradiction: If (P or not P), then (Q and not Q). When we represent this statement on a truth table, we get this:

P	**Q**	**If (P or not P), then (Q and not Q)**
T	T	T F F F F
F	T	T T F F F
T	F	T F F F T
F	F	T T F F T

As we see here, this statement is a contradiction because it is necessarily false under the main connective. No matter what statements you plugged in for the Ps and Qs, it will always be false.

A statement is a tautology when the statement is necessarily true. A tautology will have no line under the main connective that is false. Ts will be all the way down. "If (P or Not P), then Q" is a tautology, and it is represented like this:

P	Q	If (P or Not P), then Q
T	T	F F T
F	T	F T T
T	F	F F T
F	F	F T T

This is a tautology because every line on the truth table under the main connective is true. This is equivalent to saying that this statement is necessarily true, again, no matter what simple statements we plug in to the Ps and Qs. Even on the last line of the table, where both letters are false, the statement itself is true.

Using Truth Tables to Test for Validity

Truth tables can be used to test for validity because, as we've said many times, a valid argument is one in which it is not possible for the premises to be true and the conclusion false. We said we can test for validity by seeing whether it is even just possible that the premises of an argument are true and the conclusion false. If it is, then the argument is invalid. If it isn't possible, then the argument is valid. Thus, we have everything we need with truth tables to display each statement from an argument to see whether it is possible for the premises to be true and the conclusion false. That is, we can test for its validity by displaying all possible truth value combinations. Again, a truth table is a way to display the logical possibilities of each statement of an argument. So, if it is possible for the premises to be true and the conclusion false, we would see this on a truth table.

Take, for example, an argument form such as modus ponens. Though we already know modus ponens is valid, we can show its validity on a truth table. We do this by giving each statement of modus ponens its own column. Again, we have two simple statements involved with modus ponens, and so we have four rows of logical possibilities:

P	**Q**	**1. If P, then Q**	**2. P**	**3. Therefore, Q**
T	T			
F	T			
T	F			
F	F			

When we carry the truth values across the table, we get the following:

P	**Q**	**1. If P, then Q**	**2. P**	**3. Therefore, Q**
T	T	T	T	T
F	T	T	F	T
T	F	F	T	F
F	F	T	F	F

Look carefully at each row of the truth table. What we are looking for is any row that has true premises and a false conclusion. We do not find this in the above table because modus ponens is necessarily valid—it's modus ponens, after all. If invalid, we would see a row where the premises are both true and the conclusion false. But this table shows that it is impossible for the premises to be true and the conclusion to be false.

However, consider this argument:

P	**Q**	**1. If P, then Q**	**2. Q**	**3. Therefore, P**
T	T			
F	T			
T	F			
F	F			

When we fill in all of the values, we do in fact have a line in the truth table where both premises are true and the conclusion false.

P	Q	1. If P, then Q	2. Q	3. Therefore, P
T	T	T	T	T
F	T	T	T	F
T	F	F	F	T
F	F	T	F	F

This means that this argument form is invalid. It is logically possible for both premises to be true and the conclusion false. These results are not surprising since we've encountered both of these argument forms before.

How about an argument where it is less obvious? Take the following as an example:

1. If (P and Q), then R
2. If P, then Q
3. P
4. Therefore, R

This is not a common argument form, and I, for one, cannot tell from a glance whether it is valid or invalid. So we can make a truth table for the argument and easily see whether it is valid or invalid.

The first step is to notice that we have three simple statements, and so we need to have eight rows. We also need a column for each premise and the conclusion.

P	Q	R	1. If (P and Q), then R	2. If P, then Q	3. P	4. Therefore, R
T	T	T				
F	T	T				

T	F	T				
F	F	T				
T	T	F				
F	T	F				
T	F	F				
F	F	F				

We now fill in the truth values as before. To simplify things we'll put the truth values only for the main connective.

P	**Q**	**R**	**1. If (P and Q), then R**	**2. If P, then Q**	**3. P**	**4. Therefore, R**
T	T	T	T T	T	T	T
F	T	T	F T	T	F	T
T	F	T	F T	F	T	T
F	F	T	F T	T	F	T
T	T	F	T F	T	T	F
F	T	F	F T	T	F	F
T	F	F	F T	F	T	F
F	F	F	F T	T	F	F

What we see is there are no rows of this truth table where the premises are all true and the conclusion false. In fact, the only row in which all the premises are true is the first row. But in this row, the conclusion is true. So this is a valid argument form.

Consider the following argument:

1. If P, then Q
2. If Q, then R
3. Not P
4. Therefore, Not R

P	Q	R	1. If P, then Q	2. If Q, then R	3. Not P	4. Therefore, not R
T	T	T	T	T	F	F
F	T	T	T	T	T	F
T	F	T	F	T	F	F
F	F	T	T	T	T	F
T	T	F	T	F	F	T
F	T	F	T	F	T	T
T	F	F	F	T	F	T
F	F	F	T	T	T	T

The second and fourth rows show that it is logically possible to have all true premises and yet a false conclusion. Thus, this argument is clearly invalid.

Conclusion

We have covered a considerable amount of content in the last two chapters. It may be difficult to believe, but we've only covered the small tip of a huge iceberg of deductive logic. These are the basic concepts that figure into a number of the very advanced systems of logic.

You may be wondering at this point what this has to do with Jesus. Let's not forget where we've been. We were challenged to an intellectual faith where we, most importantly, love and pursue God with all of our minds. We saw the way in which Jesus exemplified the use of careful logic and that the Christian worldview makes good sense of logic. And in the past two chapters, we've taken a dive into logic. Again, this can be confusing and sometimes tedious material. But we simply won't be able to be adept at logic and critical thinking (i.e., we won't have an intellectual faith) without gaining facility with these concepts. In short, to be like Jesus intellectually, we must be able to use logical arguments like he did. Mastering these concepts will set you well on your way.

Categorical Logic

A big part of understanding our world is categorizing the things we find in it. As we discover things, we give them names, notice commonalities, and thereby categorize them into groups. We do this, as kids, with our toys, but we really never stop. We do this as adults with the world as we understand it in deeper and more mature ways.

Not only do we name and categorize things; we relate categories together. We realize, for example, that the category "humans" falls within the broader category of "things that will one day die." Thinking about statements like these, and the principles that govern them, brings us to an important area of logic called "categorical logic" that has its roots in ancient Greek thought. Though categorical logic has many unique features, it is a form of deductive logic. That is, as we will see, we will use deductive standards to evaluate the arguments of categorical logic.

Sweeping Categorical Claims

Sometimes we make sweeping claims about the world. We may, at some point, realize our mortality and say that, unless God intervenes, all of us humans will one day die.[1] All of our days are indeed numbered. To make the statement "all humans will one day die" is to say something about every human being.

Consider the same thing said differently. To say that all humans will one day die is to say something about the category of human things. It is not specifically to say something about the category of giraffes or any other kind of animal, even if a similar thing can be said about them.

But this sweeping statement also makes reference to another category besides the human category. It says something about the category of things that will one day die. For short, we can call this "the category of mortal things." Of course, many other things are in this category. It includes giraffes, trees, canaries, mosquitoes, and the rest of biological life. Everything that will one day die is in the category of mortal things.

The statement "all humans will one day die" is an example of a *categorical statement.* Notice this statement relates the categories of humans and mortal things together. A categorical statement says something about the relationship between at least two categories of things. In the statement we've been considering, it says the entire category of human things (i.e., all humans) are within the larger category of mortal things. All humans are among the things that will one day die.

Here are other categorical statements that have the same categorical form:

All Texans are nice.

All pizza is delicious.

---

[1] For the ease of reference, we will continue to use the phrase "all humans will one day die," making the assumption that this is only the case if God does not intervene.

Sometimes the categorical form is not obvious given how it is worded. Scripture, at times, makes big and sweeping categorical claims. Take these, for example:

"For all have sinned" (Rom 3:23).
"The LORD is righteous in all his ways" (Ps 145:17).

We can put Rom 3:23 into categorical form because the verse is logically equivalent to saying "All humans are sinners"—the entire category of humans is within the category of sinners. But is this true? Are all human beings sinners? Is this what Paul is saying in Rom 3:23? Surely not, because Paul clearly believed Jesus was both human (see Phil 2:7; Rom 5:17) and one "who did not know sin" (2 Cor. 5:21). So, Paul surely doesn't mean that all humans are sinful since Jesus was a human who did not sin. This highlights how difficult it can be to specify a category properly. When we understand the overall context of Romans 3, we see that it is referring to the category of humans affected by the fall. Thus, the categorical statement (with proper theology) is:

All humans affected by the fall are sinners.

How do we put the Psalm 145 passage into this categorical form? It looks something like this:

All the ways of the Lord are righteous.

This statement relates the ways of the Lord with righteousness. That is, everything that falls under the category of being a way of the Lord will also fall under the category of being righteous.

There is another kind of sweeping categorical statement where the relationship between categories is different. In the example above, there was a relationship of *inclusion*. The category of humans was included within the category of mortals. However, it could be a relationship of *exclusion*. Take the following for examples:

No students enjoy logic at first.
No people live on Mars.

The first example says that the category of students is not within the category of those who initially enjoy logic. If this is true, every individual in the student category will *not* be in the category of those who initially enjoy logic. That is, students are excluded from the category of those who enjoy logic from the start.

We should recall from chapter 5 that a defining feature of a statement is that it is either true or false. This is certainly the case with categorical statements. Some of the statements we have discussed so far are true, and some are almost certainly false. For example, the statements "All Texans are nice" or "No students enjoy logic at first" are false, even if many students don't enjoy logic at first and even if almost all Texans are nice. There are students who actually do really enjoy logic from the very beginning, and there are Texans who are having a perpetual bad day and are not, on the whole, nice.

Again, sweeping categorical claims make big claims about the world. They are saying either that every single thing in that category falls within a certain other category or that no single thing falls within the category. There's a sense in which sweeping claims are quite bold because all it takes is one single counterexample to show it is false. A counterexample is an instance of something designed to disprove a claim. A grumpy Texan is a counterexample to the claim "All Texans are nice." That is, if there is only one grumpy Texan, then it is, strictly speaking, false that *all* Texans are nice. If there is just one student who enjoys logic from the start, then it is, strictly speaking, false that no students enjoy logic at first.

But it is also clear that sweeping claims can be true. As we mentioned above, according to Psalm 145, God is maximally righteous and morally perfect in all aspects. All of his ways fall into the category of being righteous. There are no exceptions; every single one of God's ways are morally perfect. This comes out of the nature of God's perfect moral character. Paul, in the broader context of Romans 3, wrote that all humans affected by the fall are sinful in all of our deeds. According to Paul, this is what makes us in need of God's righteousness that is expressed in Jesus Christ's life and ministry. There are literally no exceptions to these sweeping claims.

In casual conversations we often do not speak in precise terms. So, when someone says, "All Texans are nice," he or she may just mean that many of them are nice. Or perhaps they mean that all the Texans they have met have been nice. In casual conversation it's often not necessary to get overly precise about what is being asserted. However, in logic and critical thinking, our goal is to get as clear as possible.

Particular Categorical Statements

Not all categorical statements are sweeping. In fact, some of them make a claim about a specific example, a sort of representative of a category or a subset of the category. Like the sweeping statements above, particular categorical statements relate two categories together. This representative or subset of a category is related to another category of things.

Take, for example, the statement "Some Texans are grumpy." This is a categorical statement since it relates together the categories of Texans, by virtue of there being some Texans that fall within the category of grumpy things. But rather than making a sweeping claim about *all* Texans, we have related together a particular (or perhaps a group of particulars) of the category of Texans with the category of grumpy things. By "some," we mean "at least one." So, what we have said is that "at least one thing in the category of Texans is included in the category of grumpy things." It could be the case that many or most or even all but one Texan are not grumpy. But if at least one Texan is grumpy, then this categorical statement is true.

Other examples include:

Some of the disciples doubted (see Matt 28:17).
Some people are vegetarians.

Just like with the sweeping categorical statements above, there is more than one particular categorical statements. All the particular statements we've discussed so far have expressed the inclusion of a particular from one category, or subset, in another category. But there are particular categorical statements that exclude the particular from another category.

Take the following, for example:

Some ravens are not black.

What's being said is at least one thing in the "raven" category is not in the "being black" category. This statement leaves open the possibility that there may be some ravens that *are* black. All we can really say from this is that one or more ravens are not black. Here are a couple of other particular categorical statements of exclusion:

There is at least one human who did not sin.
Some students do not own a car.

On the first statement, we are saying at least one individual in the category of humans does not fall within the category of sinners. This is, of course, Jesus. The second statement says that there is at least one individual in the student category that is not in the car owners category.

Particular categorical statements are easily made true since it only takes at least one categorical instance. If we say, "Some ravens are black," this statement is true so long as there is at least one black raven. Or if we say, "Some ravens are not black," here again it only takes one nonblack raven to make this true. Because of this, they are not as easily shown to be false. With the sweeping categorical statements, all it took was one counterexample for the statement to be false. If we say, "All ravens are black," then one nonblack raven makes this false. However, the statement "Some ravens are black" is not shown false by one example of a nonblack raven or even many examples of nonblack ravens. For this statement to be false, it would have to be the case that there are no ravens at all that are black. Though it is possible, it would be quite difficult indeed to ever show this to be the case. To know this with confidence, we would have to explore every square foot of the universe where ravens could possibly reside and inspect them for their color. The point is that particular categorical claims are, in a way, not as bold as sweeping categorical claims.

Symbolizing Categorical Statements

Categorical statements can be symbolized into what we'll call "standard categorical form" (or standard form, for short). Just as before, symbolizing categorical statements allows us to see more clearly the logic of categorical arguments. We can symbolize each of the statements we outlined above with the following:

1. All S are P.
2. No S are P.
3. Some S are P.
4. Some S are not P.

We use Ss and Ps for a particular reason. The S refers to the subject, and the P refers to the predicate. Categorical statements relate a category in the subject of the sentence with a category in the predicate. The first two statements are sweeping (also called "universal") statements. They attempt to say something about all of reality. By contrast, the second two statements say something about particular things or a particular subset of things. The first and the third statements make positive or affirmative statements, whereas the second and fourth are negations. These are given the following names:

1. Universal affirmative: All S are P.
2. Universal negative: No S are P.
3. Particular affirmative: Some S are P.
4. Particular negative: Some S are not P.

Contradictories

Categorical logic goes all the way back to, at least, the philosopher Aristotle (384–322 BC). He pointed out that these statements stand in certain logical relationships with each other. Notice that a statement of the form "All S are P" and a corresponding statement in the form of "Some S are not P" cannot both be true and they cannot both be false. Consider the following instances of these categorical statements:

> All humans will one day die.
> Some (at least one) humans will not one day die.

If the statement "All humans will one day die" is true, then the statement "Some humans do not die" must be false. In other words, these cannot both be true. But we should also notice that they can't both be false either. If it's false that "All humans will one day die," then it is true "Some humans will not one day die." One of these must be true and the other false.

These are examples of what we call "contradictories." When it comes to contradictories, one of these must be true and the other false. To affirm both of these (i.e., to affirm the conjunction of these two statements) is to affirm a contradiction. We have talked about the principle of noncontradiction, which says that a statement and its negation cannot both be true. This is essentially the same thing.

What's important to see is that saying, "Some S are not P" is logically equivalent to saying it's not the case that "All S are P." If I say, "Some humans will not one day die," then this is equivalent to saying it is not the case "All humans will one day die." So, if we negate "All S are P," we can substitute in "Some S are not P" without any loss of meaning. Consider the following:

> Some humans will not one day die = Not (All humans will one day die)
> All humans will one day die = Not (Some humans will not one day die)

With contradictories, they can't both be true, but they can't both be false either. It is either the case that "all humans will one day die" or that "some humans will not one day die."

It is not only "All S are P" and "Some S are not P" that are contradictories. The categorical statement forms "No S are P" and "Some S are P" are also contradictories. If we stare at these, we can see that if "No S are P," then it can't be the case that "Some S are P," and vice versa. That is, "No S are P" and "Some S are P" cannot both be true, and they cannot both be false.

Here are some examples of these contradictories:

No humans will one day die.
Some (at least one) humans will one day die.

These cannot, logically speaking, both be true, and they cannot both be false. Necessarily, one of these must be true, and one must be false. That is, if it is true that "no humans will ever die," then it is false that "some humans will one day die." But if it is true that "some humans will one day die," then it is false that "no humans will one day" die. Again, we can see this given that the negation of one is logically equivalent to the other:

No humans will one day die = Not (Some humans will one day die)
Some humans will one day die = Not (No humans will one day die)

Contraries

There are other relationships between the four categorical statements in standard form. Some are what we call "contraries." These are, in a sense, similar to contradictories in that they can't both be true. But they are different because it is possible that they are both false. Let's first consider some examples that are not categorical statements:

Only one God exists, and it is the Christian God.
Only one God exists, and it is the Muslim God.

On the Christian view, God is a trinity, whereas on the Muslim view, God is a strict unity. So, it couldn't be that God is both a trinity and a strict unity. It could be that one or the other is true, but unlike a contradiction, logically speaking, these could both be false if, say, polytheism turned out to be true.

To see the difference here, the following is an example of a contradiction:

Only one God exists, and it is the Christian God.
It's not the case that only one God exists and it is the Christian God.

Again, logically speaking, one or the other of these pairs of statements must be true. Given that they are contradictories, they can't both be true, and they can't both be false. Contraries, on the other hand, can't both be true, but they can both be false. This is the basic difference between contraries and contradictories.

The statements in standard categorical form that together are contraries are:

"All S are P" and "No S are P."

As contraries, these can't both be true. If "All S are P" is true, then of course it can't be the case that "No S are P." But they could both be false. For both of these to be false, it would have to be the case that simultaneously "Some S are P" and "Some S are not P" are true.

Consider these examples:

All humans will one day die.
No humans will ever die.

First of all, it's clear these can't both be true. If "all humans will one day die," then it is false that "no humans will ever die." However, they can both be false, but this is only the case if both of the following are simultaneously true:

Some humans will one day die.
Some humans will not die.

If these particular statements are true, then both of the sweeping claims are false. If some humans will die and some will not, then it's false that all humans die and it is also false that no humans die.

Subcontraries

Now, there's a relationship between the forms "Some S are P" and "Some S are not P." These are called "subcontraries," which means, in a way, the opposite of what it is to be contraries. Here they can both be true, but they cannot both be false. Consider these examples:

> Some giraffes live in zoos.
> Some giraffes do not live in zoos.

Notice that both of these are in fact true, as long as at least one giraffe lives in a zoo and at least one giraffe lives out in the wild (i.e., not at a zoo). But they can't both be false.

If giraffes tragically went extinct, then the second statement would be true, namely, a giraffe does not live in any zoo (because they don't live anywhere given their extinction).

If, again quite tragically, giraffes became an endangered species where there are no longer any giraffes in the wild, then the first statement would be true. The only giraffes that exist would be in zoos.

The point is that with subcontraries, it can't be the case that both of these statements are false. If one of the subcontraries turns out to be false, then the other is true.

Subalterns

There is one relationship left to describe, and this is the relationship between what are called "subalterns." "All S are P" and "Some S are P" are subalterns. This means that if "All S are P" is true, then it follows that "Some S are P" is true. And if "Some S are P" is false, then it follows that "All S are P" is false. If "all humans will one day die" is true, then it follows that "some humans will one day die" is true. Or if "some humans will one day die" is false, then "all humans will one day die" is false.

All the previous relationships have included the phrase "and vice versa" since the previous relationships held in both directions. If a statement P is a contradictory of Q, then it follows that Q is a contradictory of P. By contrast, subalterns only go in one direction. If "All S are P" is true, then this entails "Some S are P" is true. But it is not the case that if "Some S are P," then necessarily "All S are P" is true. It's possible, but it is not a matter of entailment. The other example of subalterns is "No S are P" and "Some S are not P." If it is the case that "No S are P," then it follows necessarily that "Some S is not P" but not vice versa.

The following diagram takes all of what we just described and elegantly depicts it in what has classically been called the "Square of Opposition":

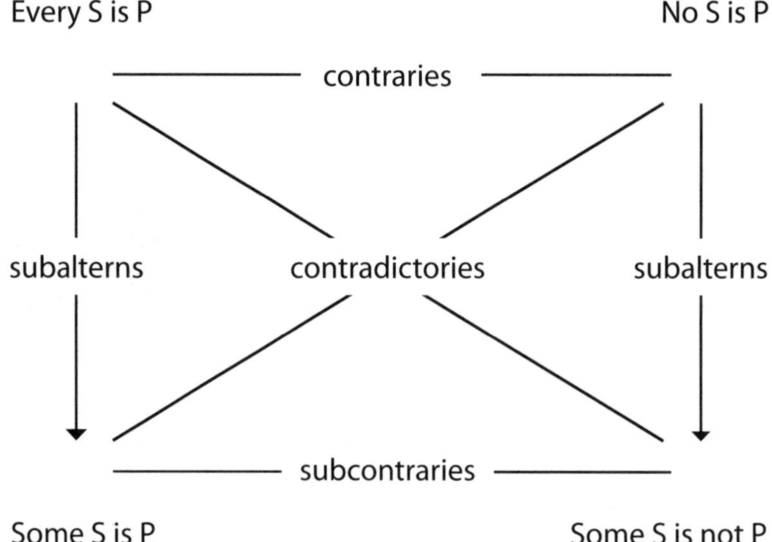

Diagramming Categorical Logic

When categorical statements are put into standard form, it allows us to see the logic of the statement more clearly. We can go one step further and display the statements in a Venn diagram, named after the nineteenth-century philosopher and mathematician John Venn. The diagram is a way to show the relationship between categories. Each circle of the Venn diagram represents a category. We should notice that each circle has a portion that overlaps and a portion that does not. With this we are able to represent each of the four categorical statements.

Universal Affirmative

Here's how this goes:

All S are P

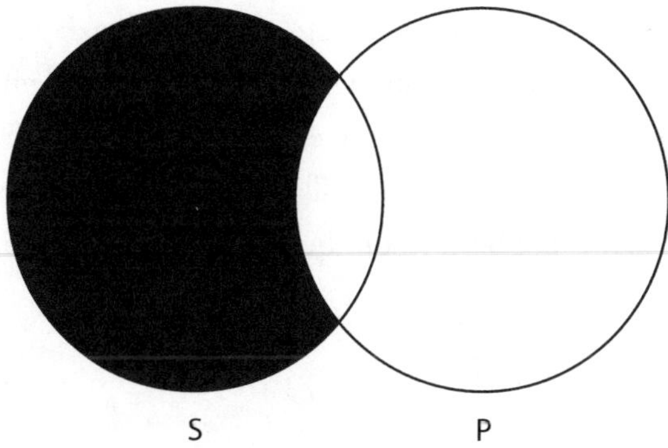

The blacked-out portion of the S circle means there are no things in that region of the diagram. In a way, we've pushed everything that is S into the category of P things. The black area has, in a sense, been cut out of existence. So for this diagram, there are no S things that are not also a P thing. The only part of the S circle that is not blacked out is the thin football-shaped region, which constitutes the overlap between the S category and the P category. This is why with this diagram we are able to say "All S are P." The only place where there are Ss is in the overlap, making every single S thing also a P thing.

But notice it is not only the overlap portion that is not blacked out. The rest of the category of P things (not in the overlap) are P things that are not S things. We don't know from this statement alone whether there are P things that are not S things, but there could be.

Let's illustrate this with an example.

All humans will one day die.

Let's break this statement into its two categories:

S = humans
P = beings that will one day die

To say all humans will one day die is to say that everything in the human category is within the category of beings that will one day die. But notice many other beings besides humans will one day die. Dogs will one day die. Giraffes will one day die. Trees will one day die, and so on. Everything else that is in the category of beings that will one day die would be in the region of the P circle that is not blacked out but is not in the overlap.

Universal Negative

Consider the diagram for the universal negative:

No S are P

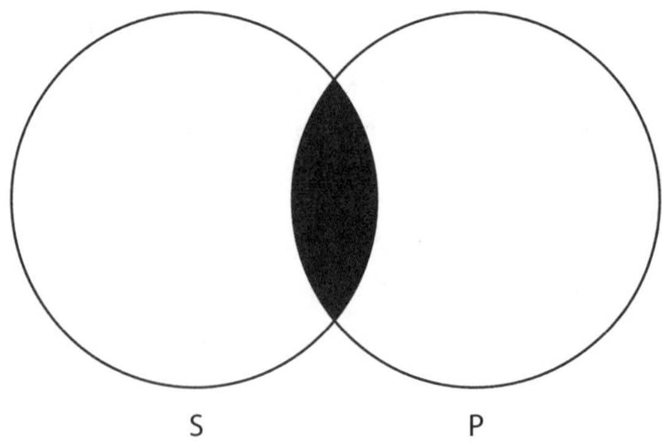

Here the blacked-out portion of the diagram is the overlap between S things and P things. Remember, if it is blacked out, this means there is nothing in that area. There are no S things that are P things, and there are no P things that are S things. Everything in the category of S things and P things stays separate. For example:

> No self-respecting Republican would vote for a middle-class tax increase.

If we break this down into its two categories, we get:

> S = self-respecting Republicans
> P = individuals who vote for middle-class tax increases

If we put all of the self-respecting Republicans in the S circle and all the voters for tax increases in the P circle, then, to represent the logic of this statement, we would black out the overlap since there are no S things that are P things.

Particular Affirmative

When it comes to the particular affirmative, "Some S are P," we cannot simply shade an entire area because all it says is that at least one S thing is a P thing. In other words, it is not making a sweeping (or universal) claim like the first two. Instead, we need a convention for representing when there is at least one thing in that category. When it comes to diagramming particular statements, our convention will be to include an "X" in an area of the Venn diagram to denote that there's at least one thing in that area. There can be at least one thing in either the overlap or in either of the areas where they do not overlap.

So, "Some S are P" is represented like this:

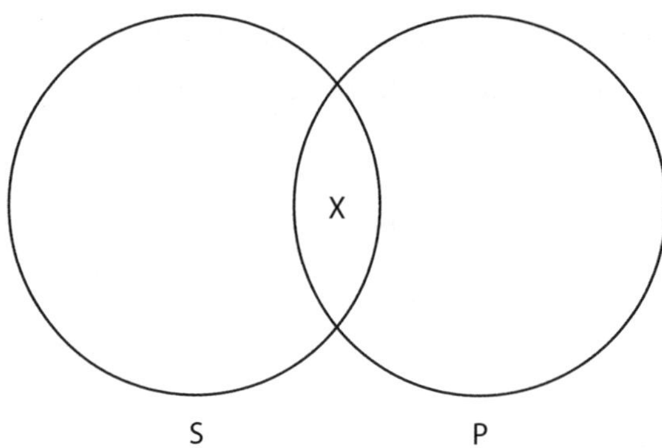

We don't know much else about these categories. There may or may not be individuals in the non-overlapping sections of either S or P. All we know is that there is at least one S thing that is also a P thing.

Particular Negation

Following the same convention, "Some S are not P" is diagrammed in the following way:

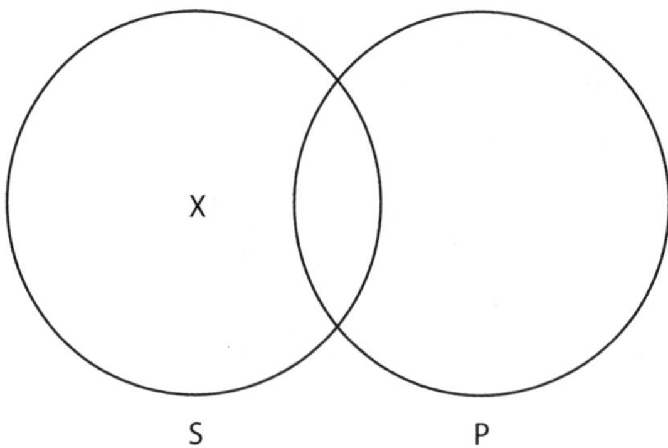

Here there is at least one S thing this not a P thing. We don't know from this statement whether there is anything in the P circle or in the overlap. All we know is that at least one S thing is not a P thing, and that's represented in the diagram.

Representing Two Categorical Statements

We can also represent two categorical statements using Venn diagrams. We can represent two statements with three circles, so long as one category is in common with the two statements. Let's consider the following two categorical statements:

All humans are mortals.
All coffee fanatics are humans.

Let's look at these statements represented by themselves first. We represent each category with its own circle.

All humans are mortals:

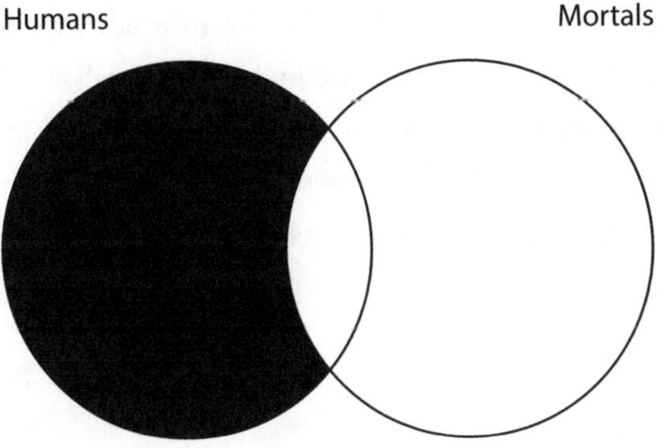

All coffee fanatics are humans:

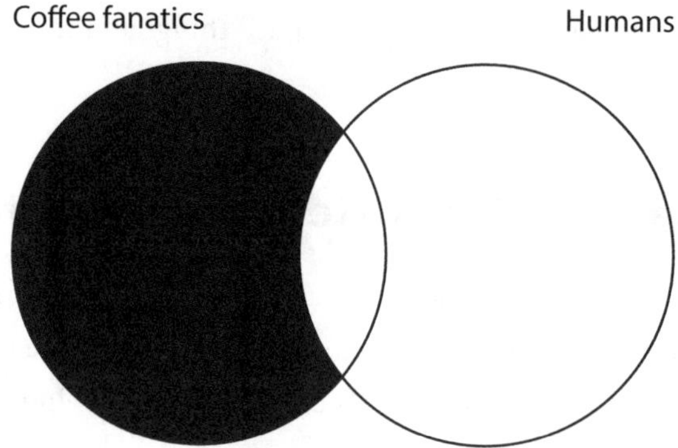

As we see, all humans are pushed into the mortals category in the first diagram, and all coffee fanatics are pushed into the human category in the second.

Remember that in a typical categorical statement we have two categories related together represented by the two circles of the Venn diagram. We have the two categorical statements above, but they have a category in common—the category of being human. So, in total, we have three categories being related in these sentences: humans, mortals, and coffee fanatics. To represent these two categorical statements by Venn diagram, we will need three overlapping circles that represent the three categories. Each of the circles overlap with each of the other circles, and there is the middle portion where all three overlap.

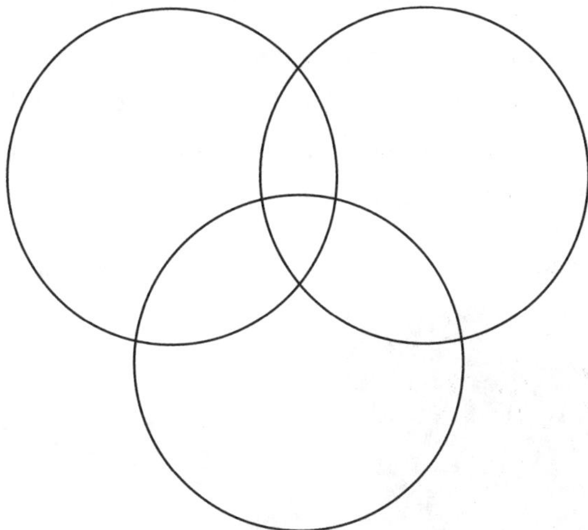

We can put the Venn diagrams above together in the following way to represent these sentences together:

All humans are mortals.
All coffee fanatics are humans.

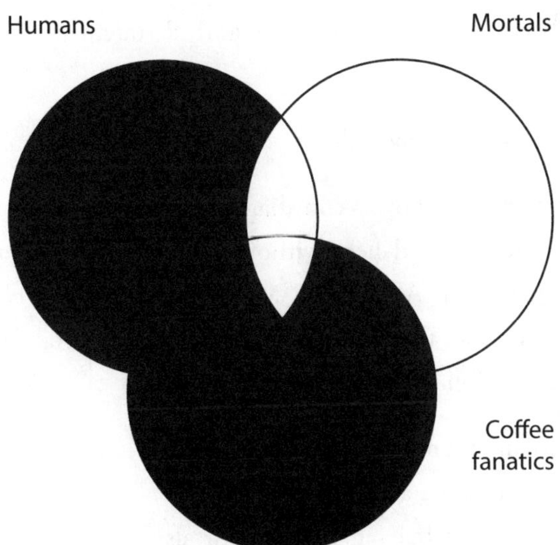

What's important to notice here is that there are certain implications of these two statements, and we can see these implications automatically represented within this Venn diagram. We should notice, given these two statements, that there is nothing in the category of coffee fanatics that doesn't overlap with the mortals category.

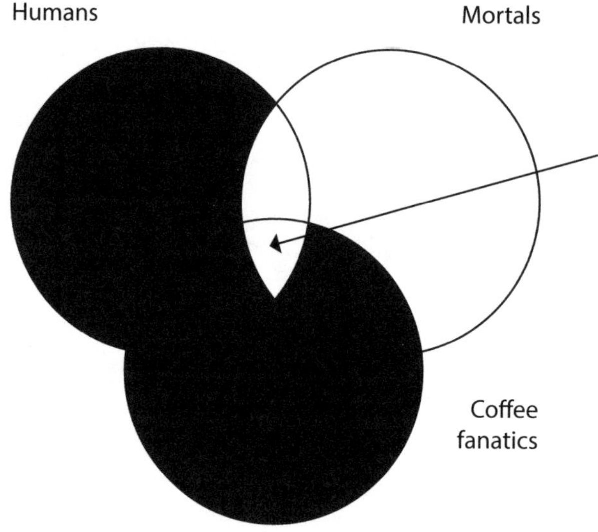

What this means is, from these two categorical statements, we can derive the following:

> All coffee fanatics are mortals.

You should stare at the above Venn diagram until you see how this statement is already represented here without having to add anything. What this means is that from "All humans are mortals" and "All coffee fanatics are humans," it follows that "All coffee fanatics are mortals." This can be formulated into the following syllogism:

1. All humans are mortals.
2. All coffee fanatics are humans.
3. Therefore, all coffee fanatics are mortals.

This becomes extremely useful because we can use a Venn diagram like this to test whether an argument of categorical statements is deductively valid. We do this by looking to see whether representing the two premises above the conclusion is already represented, without doing anything further. The reason this works comes back, once again, to the definition of deductive validity: an argument is deductively valid when the truth of the premises guarantees the truth of the conclusion. When two categorical statements are represented by a Venn diagram, if the argument is deductively valid, then we should be able to find the conclusion in the diagram without doing anything further. If we can, then this means the premises guarantee the truth of the conclusion.

Look again at the Venn diagram representing "All humans are mortal" and "All coffee fanatics are humans." Do you also see that "All coffee fanatics are mortals"? For the conclusion to already be represented, there shouldn't be any coffee fanatics who are not also in the mortal category. This is indeed the case, and so this means this argument is valid.

Let's try another:

1. All college students love logic.
2. Some college students are insomniacs.
3. Therefore, some insomniacs love logic.

When representing a combination of universal and particular statements, a good strategy is to do the universal statements first. This helps us to know where to put our X to represent the particular statement. If a region of the diagram is already blacked out, then that region is closed off for where to put the X.

Let's start with our universal statement in premise 1. It gives us the following:

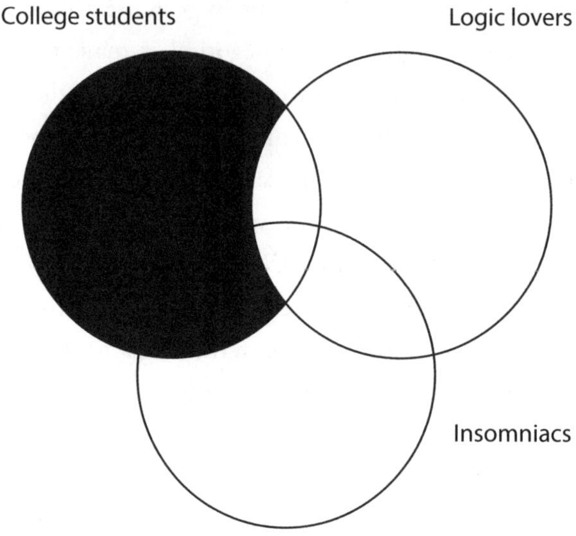

And now we want to represent the statement "Some college students are insomniacs." There's only one place left to put the X because the statement "All college students are logic lovers" blacked out any non-logic-loving college students. So this forces the X to go into the overlap between college students and logic lovers. It looks like this:

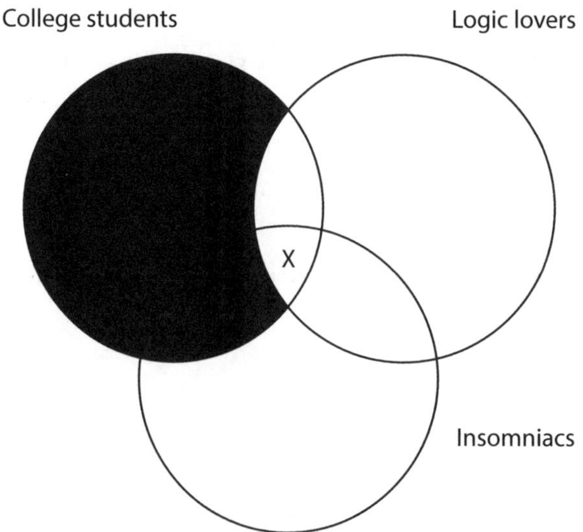

Now we ask, without having to do anything else, do we see the statement "Some insomniacs love logic"? Yes, we do because the X falls within both the category of insomniacs and the category of logic lovers. That is, there is at least one insomniac who loves logic. This shows that the argument is deductively valid.

Let's look at a similar argument (but be careful to notice the difference):

1. All college students love logic.
2. Some insomniacs love logic.
3. Therefore, some college students are insomniacs.

Because it has both universal and particular statements, we start with representing the universal statement. Given premise 1, we push all of the college students into the logic-lover category:

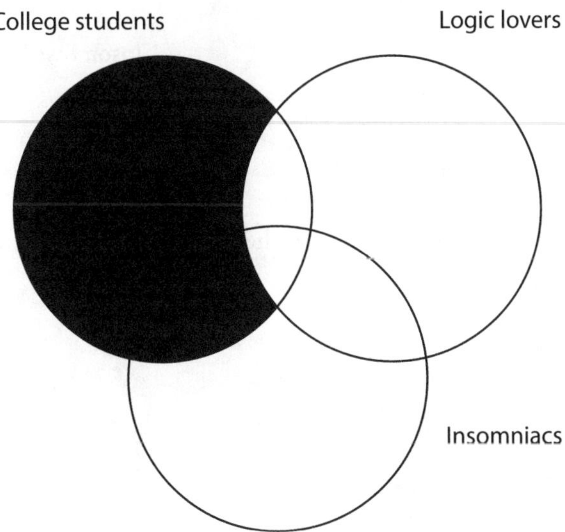

But now we must represent "Some insomniacs love logic." This time we are not forced into a single region on the Venn diagram. Notice that there are two open regions that relate insomniacs and logic lovers. From these statements alone, we don't know whether any insomniacs who are logic lovers are also college students. That is, it could be that the X goes into the overlap of all three, or it could be that it goes into the overlap of only the insomniacs category and the logic-lovers category.

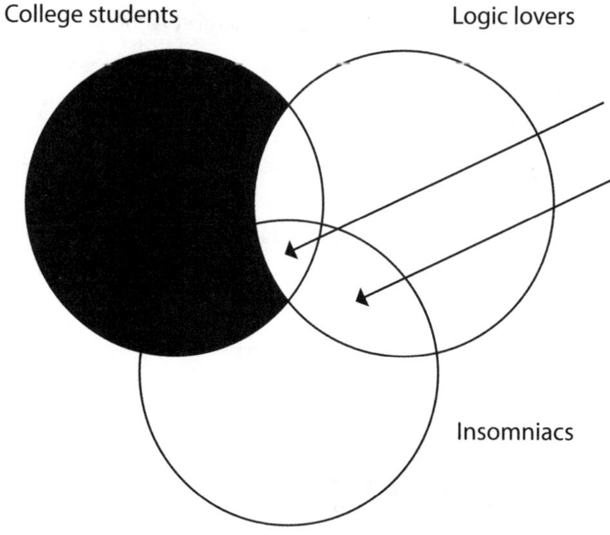

So, our convention is to put the X on the line between these two regions in the following way:

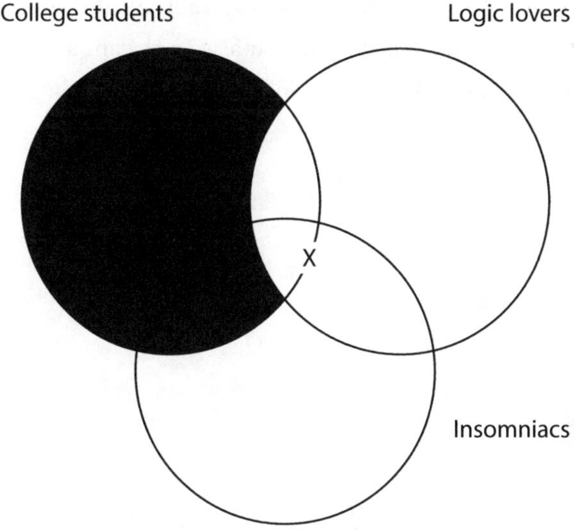

When we ask whether we see the conclusion—"Some college students are insomniacs"—represented in the diagram, the answer is no. The reason is, again, that we don't know whether there is an individual who is both a college student and an insomniac. From the diagram of this argument, we see that it is possible no college student is an insomniac. That is, the statement "Some college students are insomniacs" may be true, but it is not entailed by the premise statements. And this means the argument is invalid.

Conclusion

Categorical statements are quite common. We encounter them in Bible study and theology, and we encounter them in everyday life. Relating categories together should feel familiar. We make sweeping and particular categorical claims all the time. We may not be familiar with evaluating categorical claims with a careful use of logic. But there are clear logical relationships that hold between the different forms of categorical statements the Square of Opposition represents. Though Aristotle (or perhaps someone earlier than him) discovered these facts, they are facts of God's world. These facts and how they hang together are, in a way, elegant and beautiful and point to the elegance and beauty of God himself.

Nondeductive Standards of Logic

The character Sherlock Holmes, originally created by Sir Arthur Conan Doyle, made even more popular by numerous movies and television series, is often described as being involved with the "science of deduction." The irony here is Sherlock Holmes is rarely reasoning deductively as he conducts his investigations. Instead, normally, he's actually reasoning nondeductively. As an investigator he, with an incredible and unmatched wit and cleverness, notices small bits of evidence and is able to work out with a *high probability* who the likely suspect is—and he's almost always right. But this is textbook (as we will see) nondeductive reasoning.

We should see two things with the example of Sherlock Holmes's style of reasoning. First, Holmes is not using deductive reasoning because he is dealing in probabilities. As he examines a crime scene with a dead body, for example, he may notice a certain kind of dirt on the victim's shoes, the subtlest of details about how the victim is dressed, how the body is arranged in the room, seemingly unrelated objects in the room, or what is in the victim's pockets and reaches a conclusion that's almost always right. Second, we should notice he's normally right because he reaches the conclusion that has a high probability of being right given nondeductive standards. This may not be as pristine as deductive reasoning, but he's obviously extremely rational in coming to his conclusions. After all, he's Sherlock Holmes! So basing our claims on nondeductive reasoning is a very valuable source of rational thought.

In the past few chapters, we have been focusing on deductive standards, and especially the deductive standard of validity. We turn now to look more in depth at nondeductive standards of logic.[1]

Just to remind ourselves, the nondeductive standards for a good argument are strength and cogency. A strong argument is one where the premises may not entail the truth of the conclusion, but they do make it likely (or probably true). That is, the premises of a strong argument, when true, make the conclusion to some degree likely. That is, the premises of a strong argument give us good reason to believe the conclusion. A weak argument is one in which the premises, even if true, do not make the conclusion likely to be true. With a weak argument, the premises do not give us good reason to think the conclusion is true. A *cogent* argument requires two things. The argument must both be strong, and all of the premises must be true.

Strength

Let's begin with an example of a weak argument:

[1] In a footnote in chapter 5, I pointed out that many textbooks call these inductive arguments. I don't use this language because we are primarily dealing with different kinds of standards of logic and not different kinds of arguments. Also, I prefer the term *nondeductive* versus *inductive* because an inductive argument is one kind of nondeductive argument, but there are others. For example, we will see that a very common nondeductive way of reasoning is explanatory arguments. This is called "abductive reasoning," or sometimes "inferring to the best explanation."

1. All the ravens Smith has personally seen are black.
2. Therefore, all the living ravens in the world are black.

This is a weak argument because all the ravens Smith has seen are likely an extremely small subset of the total ravens that exist in the world. Smith doesn't have a good reason to think that the conclusion is likely true, given his or her experience of ravens.

Let's consider the argument we saw in chapter 5:

1. Smith's fingerprints are on the murder weapon.
2. Therefore, Smith is guilty of murder.[2]

Let's assume premise 1 is true. Smith's fingerprints are on the murder weapon. Though there are many things going on in the background of a case like this, most people know what it means when someone's fingerprints are found on a murder weapon. And we know it is not good. Smith is likely in a great deal of trouble—that is, premise 1 gives us reason to believe that the conclusion is true. It is, to some degree, a strong argument. Now, if Smith's defense lawyer can show some innocent reason Smith's fingerprints are on the murder weapon, then, even though the premise is true, the conclusion would not be rational to believe. However, without this other evidence, it seems quite likely that Smith is guilty of the murder. In most cases, when a person's fingerprints are on a murder weapon, it is because he is guilty of murder.

On deductive standards, an argument is either valid or invalid. Validity does not admit of degrees. An argument is either valid or it's invalid with no other options. Strength, on the other hand, comes in degrees. The premises

[2] If we are careful here, we must say more than only "Smith's fingerprints are on the murder weapon." This is enthymematic in that we have a rough idea what it means when fingerprints are found on a murder weapon. We know that fingerprints are uniquely identified with their owner. In other words, we know when a person's fingerprints are on the weapon. We also know that when someone's fingerprints are on an item it means that person likely recently handled it. Given this, it raises the likelihood of Smith being guilty of the crime given that he probably handled a weapon that was used to commit murder.

of an argument can make the conclusion very likely, moderately likely, or only somewhat likely. This is because we are talking about likelihoods and probabilities, and something can be more or less probable.

The following argument is much stronger than the one above:

1. Smith's fingerprints are on the murder weapon.
2. Five people testified to seeing Smith commit the murder.
3. Smith's DNA was found at the scene of the crime.
4. Smith confessed to committing the murder.
5. Therefore, Smith is guilty of murder.

Smith is in very serious trouble in this case. It is going to be extremely difficult for Smith's defense lawyer to counter, or explain, these lines of evidence. But that's the point: it's *almost* certain the defense lawyer can't do this, but it is still possible. Just ask yourself: Is it still possible that the premises are true and the conclusion false? Yes, it is. Though it is highly unlikely, it could be the case the premises are all true yet the conclusion is false. To see this, consider, first, that Smith could own the weapon, and that's why his fingerprints were there. Second, people mis-see things. It is possible that five people think they witnessed Smith commit the murder, but it wasn't in fact Smith. Furthermore, perhaps Smith was at the scene of the crime for some other reason just before the murder was committed, and so his DNA is there. Smith could even have confessed to the murder having not committed it. Would this be odd? Yes, extremely odd, but these odd scenarios have all happened many times in the past. Even more importantly, we can imagine each of these scenarios being true, and this is all it takes to see that the premises could be true while the conclusion is false.

What we are pointing out is that despite how rational it would be to conclude that Smith is guilty, given the premises, the argument is not valid. That is, the argument fails on deductive standards. But that's not an altogether bad thing. In this case it fails the test for validity, but it is still an extremely strong argument. Again, Smith is in big trouble here. He's most likely going to jail and no one is going to be worried that the argument is invalid. The jury will reason on the basis of the likelihood of Smith's guilt because of the evidence presented. This is how virtually all court cases are decided, it is how Sherlock Holmes solves cases, and it is how we often reason, as well, in everyday matters.

A common question with nondeductive reasoning is how we determine strength. It is often a matter of our intuitions.[3] Now, this can seem somewhat subjective and a matter of opinion. Someone might think an argument is quite strong, while others might think it is weak. Some people will think a premise makes a conclusion compelling, and others find the same argument less so. For this reason, nondeductive reasoning is, in a way, looser and a bit messier than deductive reasoning. There is no easy way to solve this issue when it comes to nondeductive reasoning. There will be disagreement, especially in the details.

While this can be a challenge, the fact that people disagree should push us toward an attitude of intellectual humility. We need to be careful we are not guilty of privileging certain arguments only because their conclusions are in agreement with our own views. The fact that people see the issues differently from you shows us that we do not have the corner on the market of truth. This will help us listen and be more thoughtful in evaluating our views.

Also, though there is disagreement about many of the important issues, we can often find broad agreement with others about our principles of critical thinking. There is actually quite broad agreement about what, in general, constitutes a strong case even if there is disagreement about which view is ultimately stronger. For example, almost everyone agrees if five eyewitnesses all offered independent testimony that agreed it was Smith who committed the crime, then this is strong evidence for Smith's guilt. We might disagree about the details of the case (and perhaps the truth of the premises), but almost no one will say having five independent eyewitnesses is of little evidential value.

---

[3] In chapter 10, I'll argue that we often decide strength in terms of what theory is the best explanation on the basis of abductive theoretical principles.

Cogency

Like valid arguments are not necessarily deductively good arguments, an argument can be strong and still be a bad argument. This happens when the premises do make likely the conclusion (i.e., it's strong) but one or more of the premises turn out to be false. Is the argument about Smith's guilt a good argument? Here it is again:

1. Smith's fingerprints are on the murder weapon.
2. Five people testified to seeing Smith commit the murder.
3. Smith's DNA was found at the scene of the crime.
4. Smith confessed to committing the murder.
5. Therefore, Smith is guilty of murder.

It is a very strong argument, but is it cogent? Well, we really can't say since the argument was made up for the sake of illustration for the purposes of this book. But if this were real, again, Smith should probably be worried about his future. But what if each of the premises turned out to be false? Let's say there was a clerical error, and someone else's fingerprints were on the murder weapon. The five people actually testified that Jones was at the scene of the crime. And so on down the list. Smith now has nothing to worry about because, though this is a strong argument—in that the premises make the conclusion likely—it is a bad argument given that the premises are false. It is what we called "uncogent" and, for this reason, may be rejected.

Cogency requires an argument to be both strong and have true premises. Said somewhat differently, a cogent argument is one where all the premises are true and these premises make likely the truth of the conclusion. With a cogent argument, we have a conclusion that is likely true and thus rational to believe.

Everyday Reasoning

Much of our everyday reasoning is nondeductive. We are typically not as good as Sherlock Holmes, but we get around our world fairly well primarily by virtue of our probabilistic judgments. We don't usually have deductive grounds for our beliefs about the world because many of our everyday judgments are based on observation. We use our five senses and our intuitions to navigate the world. We observe facts and often make judgments based on what we think probably occurred.

Let's assume you wake up and find puddles on the ground, your driveway is wet, and water is dripping off of your roof. You would likely conclude that it rained overnight and you would almost certainly be right. It would be truly unusual, but someone with a hose could have watered down your house, driveway, and yard in the early hours of the day. In this case, it would look like it rained, but it didn't. Again, this is very unlikely, and that's the point. Your grounds for believing that it rained (assuming you have no reason to think someone went wild with the garden hose) are nondeductively strong in that they make likely the conclusion.

This also will be the case for any beliefs we base off of someone's testimony (either in person or from a book, website, or video). If someone reports some facts, then we often have good reasons for believing those things. Let's say your roommate reports to you that it is raining outside. All things being equal, you have a reason to believe it is raining outside. But clearly this only makes the conclusion likely and therefore rational to believe it's raining outside. For any number of reasons, your roommate could report it's raining outside when it is not. Or consider when an informational website reports certain facts having happened at certain times. Now, we have to be very careful here because of the phenomenon of fake news. Let's say it is wsj.com. If the *Wall Street Journal* reports certain historical facts, then this gives us nondeductively strong reasons to believe them since it is a highly reputable website. But the *Journal* com can get it wrong; it's just, again, unlikely.

The point is we can still be extremely rational when our belief is based on nondeductive grounds. There's no shame in having beliefs that are highly likely to be true. It's possible we are wrong, and this should, again, lead to intellectual humility, but we can still be quite rational as we follow the evidence where it leads.

Common Nondeductive Argument Forms

There are many common forms of nondeductive arguments, but there is a difference here from common valid arguments. Recall that deductive validity only has to do with the form or structure of the argument. This is why we could outline a variety of forms of arguments that were always valid no matter what statements are substituted for the symbol. For an argument to be valid, it doesn't matter what the argument is claiming. All that matters is that the argument has the appropriate form. Nondeductive arguments don't work like this because they deal in what is probably the case, and what is probably the case has much to do with the way the world is rather than just the structure of the argument.

Take the argument we've been looking at:

1. Smith's fingerprints are on the murder weapon.
2. Five people testified to seeing Smith commit the murder.
3. Smith's DNA was found at the scene of the crime.
4. Smith confessed to committing the murder.
5. Therefore, Smith is guilty of murder.

We said this is an exceedingly strong argument, but what form of argument does this have? It would be something like

1. P
2. Q
3. R
4. S
5. Therefore, T

When we symbolize the argument, it just looks like we've strung four random statements together in favor of a fifth. This argument also has that form:

1. Jesus loves me.
2. Wednesdays are earlier in the week than Fridays.
3. The cheetah is the fastest land animal.

4. The *Titanic* sank on April 15, 1912.
5. Therefore, donuts are tasty.

Though donut lovers will agree that the conclusion is true, no one should think that the premises offer any support at all for the conclusion despite the fact it is in the same form as the argument above.

The point is the strict form or structure of the argument is considerably less important for determining whether an argument is nondeductively strong. But there are still common ways we reason nondeductively. We won't be able to simply symbolize these arguments to see their logical structure; however, what we can do is look at common forms of nondeductive reasoning and suggest what makes these kinds of arguments stronger.

Enumerative Induction

A classic form of nondeductive reasoning is the *enumerative inductive* argument (sometimes called *inductive generalization*). With an enumerative induction, one starts with (or enumerates) particular statements and then, from this, infers a generalization. The premises give a sampling of particular instances from which the conclusion makes a generalized claim.

Here's the general form of that argument:

1. S1 has property p.
2. S2 has p.
3. S3 has p.

. . .

n. Sn has p (where "n" refers to whatever number of examples would be included in the series).

Therefore, Ss, in general, have p.

For example:

1. Raven 1 is black.
2. Raven 2 is black.

3. Raven 3 is black.
4. Therefore, all ravens are black.

Now, this is a rather weak argument. The sampling of three instances certainly does not give one strong reason to generalize about all ravens because there are countless ravens in the world. With only three instances of ravens being black, it could easily be that a great variety of ravens is in the world with many different color combinations. Or, perhaps not—perhaps only black ravens are in the world. But our sample size of three ravens doesn't warrant the inference to *all* ravens. For all we know, our sample is representative of a small region but does not well represent the population at large.

What this example highlights is that an enumerative induction gets stronger the more particular instances are enumerated. This is because the more particular instances means there is less of a gap between the set of instances and the generalized statement. For example, let's say 1 million ravens are in the world. If one has enumerated three ravens being black, then there is a huge (and unwarranted) leap to saying all ravens are black. But if one enumerates ten thousand black ravens, then this is a stronger enumerative induction. It probably still doesn't warrant the claim that all ravens are black, but the point is that the more particulars that are enumerated, the stronger the argument.

Or the argument can be made stronger if the conclusion is made more modest. To say that "all ravens are black" is going to take an extremely large amount of enumerated particulars for it to be made likely. Notice again that all it would take for this statement to be false is if there was one nonblack raven in the world. But we can change the conclusion of the argument and close this gap between particulars and the generalization with the following conclusion:

4.* Therefore, almost all ravens are black.

Or

4.** Therefore, a majority of ravens are black.

Or

4.*** Therefore, many ravens are black.

The more we moderate or walk back our claim, the less particular examples are needed to justify the claim. A relatively small number of ravens being black perhaps would be strong support for 4.***. This is an important point for being a critical thinker. We often confidently overstate our conclusions, but our evidence often doesn't support the overstated claim. When we are more modest in our claims, we are actually more rational because we are more likely to stay within what's supported by the evidence.

We also have ways of increasing the quality of our enumerated samples. We can increase the size of the sample, but we can also vary the sample. We can, for example, look at ravens in different parts of the world. And if we have quite a large and varied sample size—say, by the regions of the world—and all of these particular ravens are black all over, then this seems to be strong reason to believe that a majority of ravens are black.

This gives us two strategies for making enumerative inductions stronger:

1. Close the gap between particular instances and the generalized conclusion either by increasing the number of particular instances or making a modest generalized claim.
2. Enumerate varied examples that make the generalization likely more accurate.

Statistical Reasoning

Studies show that statistics are made up on the spot 75 percent of the time. Do you believe that? Well, I just made it up on the spot, so I wouldn't suggest putting much stock in it!

An argument form that's closely related to enumerative induction is statistical reasoning. People love to throw around statistics, and, for better or worse, we often find claims convincing when based on statistics. If someone can back up their claim with some stat, it often seems to add considerable strength to the claims being made. But like all forms of reasoning, we must be careful. Statistics can be used to say a lot of different things.

What, first of all, is a statistical argument? A statistical argument is simply one that employs statistical data to support a claim. It is often used to make a claim about a person or thing within a group on the basis of the group's statistical data. Here is an example of this sort of statistical argument (again made up for the purpose of illustration):

1. At the University of Christianity, 99 percent of students believe that the Bible is true in everything it asserts.
2. Jones is a student at the University of Christianity.
3. Therefore, Jones believes the Bible is true in everything it asserts.

This is a strong argument. In fact, it has a 99 percent chance of being true.

Though there are a number of ways in which statistics can fit into the arguments we make, here is one form of argument from statistics:

1. p is X percent true of group A.
2. S is in group A.
3. Therefore, p is true of S.

The first thing that makes for a good statistical argument of this form is when the statistic cited is greater than 50 percent. If it isn't, then we obviously don't have a strong argument. If only 10 percent of people are left-handed, then it is, by definition, not likely that a randomly selected person is left-handed. It is far more likely that the person is right-handed. The higher the percentage, the more likely the conclusion is.

We should keep in mind, however, that sometimes it can still be worth believing something when something is less than 50 percent likely. For example, let's say it is 40 percent likely a ship, the *Jolly Roger*, will sink if it goes out to the open seas. Even though, strictly speaking, it is more likely the *Jolly Roger* makes the voyage successfully (i.e., 60 percent likely), most of us won't like those odds. The reason for this is 40 percent is still quite high, especially when we are talking about something as extreme as sinking in the open seas. Even though it is not likely, we may believe that result is worth avoiding.

The second thing that makes for a good statistical argument is good statistics. A statistical argument is only as good as the statistics it references. Statistics are often obtained by doing a survey or poll with a subset or what's known as a sample of a population. For the statistic to be representative, the sample should be as large as possible and as random as possible. If the sample group is too small, then it may not accurately represent the diversity of the group. Or if the sample is not completely random, then again it may not represent the whole. If, for example, only men were polled for a statistic of how many people would be voting for a political candidate, then the statistic is biased and likely not representative of the overall target population group. And if this is the case, then the statistical argument is, for this reason, not a strong argument.

Argument from Expert Testimony

Many of us can do a lot of different things moderately well, but there are also people who are genuine experts on certain topics. Let's say you wanted to know the date the Declaration of Independence was signed. If you asked a professor of early American history, she would likely tell you that even though the declaration was adopted on July 4, 1776, it was not signed until August 2, 1776. Given the claims by this expert, this would seem to give you a strong reason to believe that the date the declaration was signed was August 2, 1776. Or, your doctor tells you that you have an infection in your throat; because he is the expert, this is strong reason to believe that this is so. It's certainly stronger than if I try to tell you that you have an infection of the throat.

It's easy to see why an appeal to the claims of these individuals constitutes strong grounds. It's precisely because they are experts that their testimony raises the probability of a claim being true. The professor of early American history and the medical doctor have had years of education and years of experience, and because of this, we have good reason to believe what they say on these questions. Here's the argument we may make:

1. A professor of early American history says the Declaration of Independence was first signed on August 2, 1776.
2. Therefore, the Declaration of Independence was first signed on August 2, 1776.

There are other ways in which we can appeal to expert testimony for answers to our questions. Many of us do not have easy access to an expert such as a professor of early American history, and so we turn to books or the internet. Published resources are, in some ways, even stronger grounds because if something is published, then it has been researched and presumably fact-checked by others. Academic resources ought to go through the process of being peer-reviewed. The peer-review process is where other scholars and experts critique and offer feedback on the claims that are made. Not every book, of course, goes through a peer-review process, and even fewer websites go through this process. But for the ones that do, on the basis of expert testimony, we are provided with a wonderful source of information. If we wanted to figure out when the Declaration was first signed, most of us would probably turn to the internet to find this information because it is more expeditious. Again, we should be looking at reputable information-based websites—such as Britannica.com or History.com—for this kind of historical information and should avoid sites such as Wikipedia, given that many of its articles are not peer reviewed. It is important to know the process a website uses in confirming the reliability of its content. Many websites are opinion based (the *Daily Caller* or the *New York Times* Op-Ed), and some are even satirical (the *Onion* or the *Babylon Bee*). These are not intending to present straight facts. Opinion-based websites present someone's interpretation and evaluation of the facts, which can be helpful for us as we form our own views, but we shouldn't take what someone on one of these sites says as settled facts.

Though we'll give a more-filled-out version of this argument form below, as a first stab, we can state "arguments from expert testimony" the following way:

1. S, who is an expert in the relevant area, says p is true.
2. Therefore, p is true.

Now, we need to be careful here because there is also a fallacy of *appealing to authority* (we will look at this in detail in chapter 12). What happens is that a person fallaciously appeals to an authority or expert to justify a claim. Consider the following argument:

1. Richard Dawkins says that foxes are part of the *Canidae* family.
2. Therefore, foxes are part of the *Canidae* family.

Contrast this argument to the following, which is fallacious:

1. Richard Dawkins says God does not exist.
2. Therefore, God does not exist.

Immediately, we should notice that in the first argument Richard Dawkins is being used as an authority within the area of his expertise, while in the second argument, he is not. An expert can only be used to legitimately weigh in on the specific area in which the person is truly an expert. Just because someone is an authority in one area, say, science, it doesn't follow he or she is an authority on philosophical matters or claims about God. Richard Dawkins is, by all accounts, a world-class, Oxford University–trained zoologist and evolutionary biologist. He certainly has the right to weigh in on philosophical and religious matters, but he is not working in his area of expertise. This would be similar to me, as a philosopher, attempting to weigh in on some issue in zoology or evolutionary biology.

Second, an authority's claim doesn't give us strong reason to believe something controversial even if it is within that person's area of expertise. That is, one can't merely appeal to an expert if there is wide disagreement among other experts. The professor of early American history can tell us the date of the signing of the Declaration of Independence because this is not a controversial issue. Richard Dawkins can tell us about where the fox falls in the taxonomy of canines because this is a well-agreed-upon fact. But there are many live issues where there is not a consensus among the experts. In this kind of case, an expert's say-so doesn't settle the issue. However, when someone is a true expert and weighing in on his or her area of expertise on an issue where it's relatively noncontroversial, then we have a strong reason to think the claim is true.

A final thing to keep in mind with arguments from expert testimony is, for it to be a strong argument, we need to have reason to think a person actually is an expert. It is not always easy to know whether someone is a genuine expert or whether he or she only claims to be. Having advanced degrees in a discipline is generally a good indicator that someone is an expert, but it doesn't always make a person an expert in every facet of that discipline. And there are of course plenty of people who are experts despite the fact they do not have a degree. So it is not always easy to tell, but one way or another we should have reason to believe someone actually is an expert before we base our beliefs on his or her testimony.

This gives us a more-filled-out version of the form of an argument from authority:

1. S states that p is true.
2. S is an expert in the area of p.
3. p is not a controversial issue.
4. Therefore, p is true.

With all of this, it may turn out we get bad information, but this once again highlights the risk with any nondeductively strong argument. An argument based on expert testimony will never guarantee the truth of its conclusion. No matter how much of an expert the person is and no matter how uncontroversial the conclusion is, it will still be possible the conclusion is false. However, when it meets the above criteria, support from an expert can make a claim reasonable to believe.

Argument from Analogy

When one thing is like another thing in a specific respect, there is an analogy between these two things. Of course, the two analogous things do not have to be alike in all respects. In fact, we often compare two things that are rather different in most respects but may share some specific feature. Analogies are often used to explain a complex concept that is relevantly similar (or analogous to) something simpler. For example, the Bible often compares a believer's relationship with God to the relationship between a parent and child. That is, there is an analogy between the God/human relationship and the parent/child relationship. Given the bigness of God, it can be difficult to understand the God/human relationship. But everyone has some familiarity with the parent/child relationship, and thinking about this relationship helps explain the more complex relationship between God and humans. This of course doesn't mean the relationships are exactly the same in every way. Indeed, as they say, every analogy breaks down at some point.

Seeing analogies is extremely helpful for understanding our world. By spotting an analogy, we can often infer something further. This gives us the argument form called "argument from analogy." In an argument from analogy, we notice certain shared attributes between two individuals or things, and, from this, we infer a further attribute.

Consider the following argument from analogy that Jesus made in Matt 7:9–11: "Who among you, if his son asks him for bread, will give him a stone? Or if he asks for a fish, will give him a snake? If you then, who are evil, know how to give good gifts to your children, how much more will your Father in heaven give good things to those who ask him." Jesus's point was that if a son asks his parent for food, the parent is not going to give him things that are not food. That's not what a good parent does. By analogy, God will give good things to those who ask him. This does not mean God is the ultimate Santa Claus and will simply give us what we ask for. To see this, it is important that we understand the analogy. Any loving parent will do what it takes to provide for the basic needs of his or her child, but the parent won't needlessly spoil the child. Notice Jesus didn't picture the son asking for anything extravagant. The child was presumably hungry and asked for food. And any capable parent will do whatever they can to provide for their child's hunger needs. By analogy, God is loving and desires to meet our fundamental needs as well. Here's Jesus's argument:

1. The parent/child relationship and the God/human relationship share the attribute of being parental and loving.
2. In the parent/child relationship, the parent will provide good things for a child's needs.
3. Therefore, in the God/human relationship, God will provide good things for our needs.

We can put the argument from analogy in a more general form:

1. S1 and S2 share the attributes a_1, a_2, . . . a_n.
2. S1 also has the further attribute of x.
3. Therefore, S2 has the further attribute of x.

In an argument from analogy, we notice certain shared attributes, a_1, a_2, . . . $a_{n,}$ between two individuals or things, S1 and S2, and then infer that since S1 has some further attribute, x, then S2 also has x.

Let's look at another example of argument from analogy. Imagine you have an acquaintance named Jones, and Jones graduated from the university with a history degree. You also know that Jones displays considerable historical knowledge. You can throw her questions about random historical facts, and she very often knows the answer. You also know that Jones has a framed university degree hanging in her office. You then meet Smith, who has similar historical knowledge and also has a framed university degree hanging in his office. From this, it seems reasonable to infer that Smith also has had a university education in history.

Here's that argument:

1. Jones and Smith both have considerable historical knowledge and have framed university degrees hanging in their offices.
2. Jones graduated from a university with a history degree.
3. Therefore, Smith also graduated from a university with a history degree.

How strong is this argument? Well, though it's not especially strong, these premises do lend some support to the conclusion. We are given some reason for thinking Smith graduated from a university with a history degree. But it could easily be that Smith did graduate from a university but not with a history degree. It could just be that Smith became a history buff in his spare time. If either of these is true, then the conclusion is false.

When evaluating an argument from analogy, two things should be kept in mind. First, the analogy can't be pushed too far in making an inference. As mentioned above, analogies are going to break down at some point. The God/human relationship is like the parent/child relationship in some important ways. But the analogy between God's relationship to us and a child's relationship to his or her parents falls short quickly. There should be some logical connection between the fact inferred and the analogy. Because God's love for humans is analogous to the love a parent has for a child, we can reasonably infer that God will provide our fundamental needs in a way analogous to the parent/child. But it doesn't give us reason to believe that we are biologically related to God. In the Jones and Smith example, the fact that both have considerable historical knowledge and framed diplomas does give us some reason to think that, like Jones, Smith was a history major. But it certainly doesn't tell us, for example, that Smith and Jones went to the same university or at the same time. These inferences are a logical jump from the analogy.

Secondly, an argument from analogy gets stronger the stronger the analogy is. So if Jones and Smith are both high school history teachers, are part of a society for history majors, and both express familiarity with leading historical scholars, then the inference becomes much stronger. It becomes even more likely that Smith has a history degree from a university.

Conclusion

People reason nondeductively in many more ways. We've given a sampling of some of the more common and important ways in which this is done. In addition to this, we have identified what factors make these forms of reasoning strong inferences. In the next chapter, we'll dig a bit deeper into nondeductive reasoning as we focus on scientific reasoning and a form of reasoning called inference to the best explanation.

Science and Inference to the Best Explanation

Let's say you are sitting on your front porch enjoying a breezy afternoon, and suddenly, with a good wind gust, a tree in your front yard falls to the ground. Being naturally curious, you wonder why this happened. You may investigate a bit and will likely make a judgment about how to explain it. When we encounter curious things and events in the world, it is natural for us to attempt to explain what we observe. We may consider a variety of possible explanations and come to what we consider the best explanation.

When we reason like this, we are reasoning abductively. Abductive reasoning, sometimes called "inference to the best explanation," is a form of nondeductive reasoning that looks for the best explanation, in terms of possessing theoretical virtues, over alternative explanations. A "theoretical virtue" is an aspect of an explanation (or theory) that makes it more likely to be true over competing hypotheses. This form of reasoning is clearly nondeductive because a theory is only ever the *best* explanation in the sense that it is strongest among all alternative theories on offer. The theoretical virtues never guarantee the conclusion; they just explain it better than the rivals.

Let's consider the fallen tree again. How shall we explain this curious event? We should first note that our background knowledge will certainly figure in to how we explain what we've seen. We know things about trees, wind gusts, termites, gravity, and so forth, and these things will inform the explanation of what we think happened. Given our background knowledge and what we find in our investigation, we may conclude that the best explanation for the tree suddenly falling is that it was seriously rotted out and the wind gust blew it over. Other explanations are possible, but these, let us assume, are not going to seem as good as this one. We could have thought the best explanation was that termites had eaten the tree so that the wind blew it over. But suppose no evidence exists for this. Or we could have thought it was an elaborate practical joke by friends who sawed almost all the way through the tree the night before. They currently are hiding in the bushes pulling a thin, unseen wire, and this, along with the wind gust, toppled the tree. Or we could believe something even more elaborate than this. Perhaps the best explanation is that the gods are angry with us and they invisibly pushed the tree over to make a point. But let's say, as we consider the facts before us, these explanations are not nearly as good as that the tree had rotted out and happened to fall because of the wind. Could we be wrong? Once again, of course we could. But in a case like this, it seems we have quite a plausible explanation.

Often, theorizing in science also is abductive in nature. In science, when one posits and tests a hypothesis, one is looking for the best explanation of the scientific data. Before spelling out the process of abductive reasoning, let's take a closer look at scientific reasoning, as this is a prime example of this form of reasoning.

Scientific Reasoning

In today's culture, science is held in a high regard,[1] but science is often thought to be hostile to Christian faith. There's little doubt that science has been a tremendous tool for discovering facts about our world, enabling unbelievable technological advance and providing significant improvement of our quality of life. So it is very important, as Christians, that we understand scientific reasoning.

What is scientific reasoning? We might say that scientific reasoning is reasoning on the basis of facts discovered through our scientific inquiries. Now, this is not the most helpful definition because we need to know what makes an inquiry scientific. Or, more simply, we need an answer to the question, What is science? This is a big question and one for which there are a variety of views. For our purposes, we can say that "science" is a method of inquiry that endeavors to explain the natural world, which is the world of physical and material things. Science doesn't tell us about nonnatural (e.g., supernatural) reality—such as souls, mental states, concepts, logical principles, moral principles, and so on. None of these are physical or material. So, like all methods of inquiry, science has its limits. For example, it can tell us a lot about human bodies (as natural entities), but it doesn't tell us what it is to be human. This is a philosophical matter. Science also can't tell us what is morally right or wrong for humans to do. It can't tell us what our dignity and worth is or what our rights are as human beings. Science is

[1] Sometimes science is seen as the *only* good way in which we know things. This view is called *scientism*, and it is a deeply flawed view. Scientism itself is not a scientific view; it is a philosophical view. There are no scientific means to support scientism itself. We can use science to show all the good things science brings us. But to say it is the only good way in which we know things will require philosophical reasoning, which by its own criteria is supposed to be reasoning that's no good. So its own criteria cannot support this view. In short, it is self-refuting.

silent on all of these issues because they are not, I suggest, issues within the domain of the natural world.

It's for this reason that science cannot ultimately tell us whether God exists. Again, science can be helpful in the sense that it can tell us about the features of the natural world, and this data is relevant to developing arguments for or against the existence of God. Given the fact that God, whether he exists or not, is a supernatural entity, scientific considerations cannot be the final word on whether God exists.

Neil deGrasse Tyson, an astrophysicist and science popularizer, was once asked, "Do you believe in God?" He said:

> The more I look at the universe, the less convinced I am that there is something benevolent going on. . . . I look at disasters that afflict Earth, and life on Earth: volcanoes, hurricanes, tornadoes, earthquakes, disease, pestilence, congenital birth defects. You look at this list of ways that life is made miserable on Earth by natural causes, and I just ask, "How do you deal with that?" So philosophers rose up and said, "If there is a God, God is either not all powerful or not all good." I have no problem if, as we probe the origins of things, we bump into the bearded man. If that shows up, we good to go! Okay? Not a problem. There's just no evidence of it.[2]

It's important to see what Tyson says here. He's looking at the pain and suffering of the world and saying that it doesn't look like it is a world created and sustained by God. This is of course not an intellectual struggle unique to Tyson. But Tyson thinks it's at least possible we'll "bump into the bearded man." I'm sure Tyson doesn't mean that he is literally looking to bump into a bearded guy somewhere along the way. He's no doubt

[2] Martha Teichner, "Neil deGrasse Tyson, Our Joyful Guide to the Stars," *CBS Sunday Morning*, April 30, 2017.

being colloquial and hyperbolic. However, he seems to think that if there is a God, we'll find him somewhere in the universe by science. But this puts God in the wrong category. Of course we don't bump into a God of this sort, bearded or not. God is not a physical or natural thing within the universe to be discovered by science.

So, science has limits, but it is still extremely important, and it is therefore vital we understand how scientific reasoning works. Scientific reasoning is a prime example of nondeductive reasoning. We almost never have scientific conclusions where the premises guarantee the conclusion. We arrive at scientific knowledge by trial and error. Scientists use experiments and exercises that produce data. They then look for ways the data is pointing them to a conclusion.

A scientific inquiry often begins with posing a question. Remember, science is all about discovering how things work in the natural world. So the question might be: How does lightning work? What causes metal to rust? Why does an airplane wing generate lift when it is in motion? Can the seed of a cornstalk be genetically modified to produce certain desirable traits in the corn crop? One formulates a hypothesis that is intended to answer the question. The hypothesis is the proposed explanation for the issue at hand. At this point, the scientist is making something of an educated guess that is based on prior data and knowledge and then will devise a way to test the hypothesis for its accuracy. The scientist will run experiments predicting what should be seen if the hypothesis is the accurate explanation. If the hypothesis ends up being borne out by the data, then the scientist should accept the hypothesis. If it is not, then it's time to go back and formulate a better hypothesis and then test this new hypothesis in the same way.

Built into the methodology is a search for the best explanation. Sometimes this abductive approach is pictured as a special methodology of scientists. This is of course not true. We often reason according to abductive principles when we reason about the world. In the example of the fallen tree earlier, how did we know the best explanation was that the tree had rotted out and that the other possible explanations were no good? In short, how do we infer to the best explanation?

How to Reason Abductively

To understand inference to the best explanation, we should first note that we are looking for explanations of some phenomena. The phenomenon might be anything, for example, the arrangement of the universe, planetary motion, a dead body, missing keys, a dead car engine, or the feeling of depression. When we encounter a phenomenon, we begin to try to make sense of it. We begin to explain it.

As we mentioned in chapter 3, this is essentially how our worldviews are formed. Indeed, from a very early age, we begin to try to make sense of the world as we find it. As young children we begin to form our worldviews in basic categories. But we also go through our lives explaining the mundane facts as we find them. Much of this is as a way to explain what we observe and experience. And this process never stops. As we grow cognitively, we begin to be able to think in more complicated terms and categories.

To understand how explanation works, we need to, first of all, understand what an explanation is. The term *explanation* is used in a variety of ways, but, for our purposes, explanations tell us why things happen. An explanation does not merely tell us what happened but why it happened.

Not all explanations are good explanations. Some explanations are better than others. Let's say you come home and see that the window in your apartment is broken out and your TV is missing. You will immediately begin to theorize why this happened and evaluate which of the theories is the best explanation of these facts.

Here are two possible theories:

1. Someone broke into the apartment by breaking out the window and stole the TV.
2. An alien spaceship beamed the TV up out of your apartment and, in so doing, broke the window given the high-pitch frequency of the beam.

We should first notice that both of these theories explain the two facts: first, the window is broken out and, second, the TV is missing. However, we can all immediately see that theory 1 is far better than theory 2. What is it that we see? We can immediately see that theory 1 has theoretical virtues that 2 does not have. Again, a theoretical virtue is an aspect of a theory or explanation that makes it more likely to be true. Since 2 lacks any significant theoretical virtues, we don't take it seriously. In fact, we may even roll our eyes if someone proposed this theory. It is easy to see that theory 1 is far superior, which makes it the best explanation (at least for what we know at this point and given the two proposed theories so far) and, therefore, likely to be true.

Theoretical Virtues

The theoretical virtues that we spot in a theory do much of the work for abductive reasoning. Theoretical virtues are truth conducive. This means when a theory has a theoretical virtue it, in a way, leads us to truth. Having the theoretical virtue makes the theory more likely to be true. When we consider a phenomenon, the theory that has, on balance, the most theoretical virtues to the greatest degree in explaining that phenomenon is the theory that is the best explanation—the one most likely to be true. Just like many of the logical principles we have looked at, we may not have specifically learned or thought about the theoretical virtues before now. Again, reasoning this way often happens on the go. But arguably we are all aware of them and have employed each of these in our reasoning about the world.

Philosophers have spelled out the specific theoretical virtues a number of ways, and they often use different names for the same basic ideas and sometimes have longer or shorter lists of virtues. Given this variety, we will not attempt to be exhaustive. Rather, we will outline five of the main theoretical virtues to give a good sense of what a theoretical virtue is and how it is used to arrive at the most likely explanation.

Consider again the thought experiment above where, upon entering your apartment, you see that your window is broken and your TV is missing. Here is an expanded list of possible theories that would explain what happened. We will reference these as we consider the five theoretical virtues below:

1. Someone broke into the apartment by breaking out the window and stole the TV.
2. An alien spaceship beamed the TV up out of your apartment and, in so doing, broke the window given the high-pitch frequency of the beam.
3. Someone broke into the apartment and stole the TV, and it was your brother-in-law who, with permission, borrowed the TV.
4. Your brother-in-law borrowed the TV.
5. Your brother-in-law borrowed the TV, and, coincidentally, moments after he left a bird flew into the window, smashing the window.

The first theoretical virtue is *internal consistency*. We've already had an occasion to discuss internal consistency in how to evaluate one's worldview. The same considerations apply here. That is, the ideas asserted in an explanation, if it is to be good, must all be logically consistent. Consider the theories above. Theory 3 is not internally consistent. If the brother-in-law had permission to borrow the TV, then it logically can't be the case that he stole the TV. This is because these are contrary ideas. It can't both be true that the brother-in-law stole and borrowed with permission the TV. A theory also cannot be contradictory. As we mentioned in chapter 6, ideas are contradictory when they cannot both be true and they cannot both be false. If a theory has contradictory or contrary ideas, then this strongly counts against the likelihood of the theory being true. These are what we may call *theoretical vices*. A theoretical vice is one that makes the theory less likely to be true and, in this case of clear logical inconsistency, makes the theory false.

Suppose that Smith is on trial for murder (again!), and witnesses place him at the scene of the crime *and* at home. Suppose the prosecutor is logically inept and admits that Smith was at home at the time of the murder but claims he is still guilty of committing a murder that happened on the other side of town. A defense lawyer is going to have a field day with this explanation of the facts precisely because it is not internally consistent. These are clearly contrary claims.

Typically, an internally consistent theory is easy to achieve. Even the alien theory above is internally consistent in that it has no logically contrary or contradictory ideas. Internal consistency has the same issue that airline pilots have. No one notices when the pilot takes a successful flight, but everyone notices when they don't. It is often the case that we don't notice when a theory is internally consistent, but we definitely notice when a theory is not internally consistent. That is, if a theory is making a claim that is either contradictory, contrary, or even self-refuting, then the theory cannot be the best explanation of the world.

A second theoretical virtue, *explanatory power*, is not always easy to achieve, but it is fairly straightforward and quite intuitive. A theory has explanatory power when it explains all the relevant facts. The more facts a theory explains, the greater the explanatory power it has. Notice that theory 4 is lacking in explanatory power. It explains the missing TV, but it does not explain why the window is broken. Suppose you walk into your apartment, and at first you only see the TV is missing. In this scenario, your first thought may be your brother-in-law borrowed it. But the moment you see the broken window, you know this is likely not true. You know, let's say, your brother-in-law would never break the window to get into the apartment to borrow the TV. So a theory is not a good one if it doesn't explain some of the relevant facts it is intended to explain.

One clarification here is that a theory could lack explanatory power in failing to explain something but still be, on balance, a good theory. Even though theory 4 doesn't explain the broken window, it doesn't rule out the broken window. Perhaps there is some further explanation, such as a bird coincidentally flew into the window as your brother-in-law was borrowing the TV (theory 5). This could be added to the explanation to increase its explanatory power. The problem of course with doing this is it seems ad hoc in that we have no independent reason to think a bird flew into the window.[3] We would want to have independent reasons for thinking this part of the explanation should be added (discussed below).

Adding to our theory also makes the theory more complex. The virtue of *simplicity*, our third theoretical virtue, is the idea that if two theories are otherwise equal in explanatory power, the simpler theory is more likely to be true. Discussions of simplicity often make reference to Occam's razor. This idea is associated with fourteenth-century philosopher and theologian William of Occam, who suggests that "entities should not be multiplied without necessity." The idea of Occam's razor is that we should shave away any unnecessary entities from a theoretical explanation. The idea is that if a theory that postulates entities A and B explains all the data just as well as a theory that posits A, B, and C, then the simpler theory is the better one.

It's important to see that the principle of simplicity does not say that just because a theory is simpler it is more likely to be true. If a theory posits only A, and another theory posits A and B, it doesn't follow that the first theory will necessarily be better. It could be that the second theory has greater explanatory power. The idea is, if two theories have the exact same explanatory power and one is simpler, then it is more likely to be true.

For example, sometimes it is thought that atheism has an advantage over theism because it is simpler than theism. Atheism only posits the material world, where theism typically posits God and the material world. But the problem with this line of thinking is that though atheism is simpler, in this

[3] The ad hoc fallacy is discussed further in chapter 12.

sense, it is an inadequate explanation of the world, or so many Christians would argue. If a theory fails in terms of its explanatory power, positing additional entities is often quite warranted.

Suppose there's been a bank robbery, and there's good reason to believe that this is the work of Clyde. But the question is whether Clyde worked alone or if Bonnie was involved. If it's the case there is no reason to think Bonnie was there—that is, all the data can be explained by reference to Clyde alone—then it's likely that Bonnie wasn't involved. If, however, it turns out that a driver was involved and an eyewitness saw Bonnie sitting in the driver's seat waiting outside the bank, then we can't explain everything with Clyde acting alone. Even though it is simpler to think Clyde acted alone, this more-complicated theory, with Bonnie and Clyde both being involved, is the better one given these other considerations.

The fourth theoretical virtue is the principle of *conservatism*, which says that a theory is more likely true when it fits with what we already know about the world. The idea here is that we, as overall rational people, all know quite a bit about how the world works. Again, this is the point that we don't start from a completely neutral point of view, and, in many cases, this is a good thing. We enter any inquiry with a general knowledge of the world. So if a theory requires us to revise most of what we know, then this is a theoretical vice. For example, for us to believe that theory 2 is true, that the missing TV is due to aliens, we would have to revise many well-entrenched beliefs. We would have to believe that aliens exist and that they are going around stealing TVs. This would require substantial change in what we take ourselves to know about the world.

When we are tempted to roll our eyes at a crazy theory, it is often because the view has the vice of being theoretically liberal (i.e., not conservative). That is, it would cause us to revise many of our beliefs. Many skeptical theories are not likely true precisely because they go against most of what we know about the world. Sometimes a philosopher will propose the possibility that we are all brains in a vat that scientists stimulate to give us the experiences of the world. We think our experiences are real objects in the world but, in this scenario, the experiences are all illusory (including experiences of having a body). The skeptic asks how you could know this is *not* the case, since your experiences would be exactly the same if they were produced by real objects through your sense faculties or by scientists stimulating you, like a brain in a vat. Though this skeptical challenge requires a more thorough answer than we have space for here, we should notice that the idea of being a brain in a vat that is stimulated by scientists is rather theoretically liberal. Much of what we think we know about the world would turn out to be false. The far more conservative view would be to believe that our experiences do give us actual knowledge of the world. That is, the brain-in-a-vat view has a theoretical vice, whereas the common sense view has a theoretical virtue.

The final theoretical virtue we will discuss is *independent verification*. An explanation is a good one when other reasons beyond its explanatory power make it likely to be true. When a theory explains data, this is a good thing. However, when we have reasons outside of the fact that it explains the data motivating it, then the theory is even more likely to be true. One reason theory 2, the alien theory, is dubious is that we may have no other independent reason to think it is true. If stealing your TV was the only time aliens have ever visited our planet, then we may never be able to independently verify this. This doesn't mean the theory is false, only that its lacking independent verification counts against it. It seems, as noted earlier, hopelessly ad hoc.

Or consider theory 4, which posits that your brother-in-law borrowed the TV. The problem with saying only this is that it doesn't explain the broken window. So theory 5 adds that the window was coincidentally broken by a bird flying into the window moments after your brother-in-law left with the TV. Again, the problem is that there may be no independent reason for thinking this is true. If feathers were on the ground or someone witnessed the bird flying into the window, then we would have motivation for thinking this theory is true. But, as it is, it is ad hoc.

We are now in a position to see why theory 1, that someone broke into your apartment by breaking out the window and stole the TV, seems so very plausible. First, it is internally consistent. It posits no contradictory or contrary ideas. Second, it explains the relevant facts. It tells us why the TV is missing and why the window is broken. Third, it is simple. It doesn't unnecessarily say that a gang of people broke into the apartment; it just says someone did. There's no real complexity here. Fourth, the theory is conservative. We know that apartments get broken into through windows, and we know that TVs are high-priced items and often are stolen in this way.

This is, as it stands, quite a good theory and easily the best explanation out of the available options. Now, we don't necessarily have independent verification, our fifth theoretical virtue, but that's OK. The best explanation does not need to exemplify all of the virtues. It needs only to have, on balance, the greater number of virtues relative to alternative explanations.

Conclusion

Again, while we can always improve in reasoning abductively, we don't necessarily need training to spot the best explanation. This is an intuitive way in which we choose the best explanation of the world as we find it. If we've misplaced our keys, we'll likely attempt to find the best explanation for the missing keys. If we've been presented with the details of the fine-tuning of the universe, we will naturally attempt to decide the best explanation for these facts. As curious beings designed by God to know, we attempt to explain the world on both ordinary matters that need explanation as well as the formation of our worldview.

Evidence

In a book like this one, there's a tendency to simplify reasoning so that the reader can get a sense of how it all works. We have used syllogism and formalized arguments throughout the book to make plain the logic of arguments. But in the real world, we hardly ever reason this way. We reason on the fly, as it were, on the basis of the evidence we have at the moment. We may have good reasons to believe something, but we may not even be very cognizant of or reflective on those reasons.

Let's say we place our hand near a hot stove. No one is going to stand there and reflect on what reasons one has, or doesn't have, for pulling one's hand away. We are especially not going to come up with a syllogism that formalizes why it would be a good idea to do so. We will make a quick decision and immediately pull our hand away from the stove.

But we of course acted rationally in a case like this even if it is not very reflective. We felt the heat and immediately had good reasons—we had really good evidence—to pull our hand away. We make rational decisions like this all day long. If we needed to, we could later reflect and then articulate (or even formalize) the reasons we have. But we often don't have this luxury in the heat of the moment. We just size up what's going on, and we make a decision on the basis of what evidence is before us. Where do we get the evidence we use to make our decisions? From the moment we open our eyes in the morning, we encounter a barrage of facts. Our world is rich with facts. Many of these facts will be mundane and go largely unnoticed. However, we will use some of what we are aware of as evidence (like feeling the heat from a stove) to form our beliefs (such as, we should pull our hand away).

In this chapter, we are concerned with how to understand evidence and how to believe rationally on the basis of evidence.

The Value of Evidence for Rational Thought

In a famous essay, W. K. Clifford says, "It is wrong always, everywhere, and for anyone, to believe anything upon insufficient evidence."[1] This has come to be known as *Clifford's principle*. Now, Clifford's principle may seem a bit overstated. It's not clear that believing on insufficient evidence is a moral wrong. But it does seem very intuitive to connect having evidence with being rational. If we lack all evidence for a belief, then it seems that belief is not one we hold rationally.

By contrast, if we believe on the basis of sufficient evidence, then it seems quite intuitive to think we are rational in our belief. The reason for this is that evidence links our beliefs to truth. When we form our beliefs on the basis of considering the evidence, then we are intentionally aiming at believing truly. And truth is of course what we, as rational beings, should aim for. As John Locke once said: "He that believes, without having any

[1] W. K. Clifford, "The Ethics of Belief," in *Lectures and Essays*, ed. L. Stephen and F. Pollock (London: Macmillan, 1886), 346.

reason for believing, may be in love with his own fancies; but neither seeks truth as he ought, nor pays the obedience due his Maker, who would have him use those discerning faculties he has given him, to keep him out of the mistake and error."[2] Without a consideration of the evidence, we may happen to believe truly, but it will be only by accident. And it is much more likely that we find ourselves in error.

The value of evidence for rational thinking seems hard to deny (at least, in a rational way). If one wants to rationally deny the value of evidence, it seems one will have to offer evidence for why this is so. If one even just wonders whether evidence is of great value, one will need to seek out and consider the evidence for why we should think evidence is valuable. Any view that denies the value of evidence on the basis of evidence seems, at least on the surface, inconsistent.

What Is Evidence?

So, what is evidence? For our purposes, we will say "evidence" is any fact that indicates the truth of a belief. Having evidence for a claim is being aware of a fact's indicating or pointing to the truth of that claim.

An important part of getting better at believing rationally is understanding what is indicated by the evidence we have. If Smith's fingerprints were discovered on the murder weapon, then most of us know we have evidence to believe Smith committed the crime. But notice we would have to be aware that fingerprints on an object indicate a person has recently handled the object. Most of us know this, and so if we find out Smith's fingerprints were found on the murder weapon, this constitutes strong evidence for us to believe Smith is guilty. So, for something to be evidence, it seems we have to be aware of not only the facts but also what the facts, in a way, point to. When it comes to a criminal investigation,

[2] John Locke, *An Essay Concerning Human Understanding*, ed. A. C. Fraser (New York: Dover, 1959), 413–14.

forensic science is today quite a developed discipline, where the experts can now tell much more about a crime scene than they could in the past. Investigators are, in a way, better able to know what the facts point to in a given situation, and as a result, can have more evidence for what occurred at the scene of a crime.

We, too, can get better at knowing what's indicated by the evidence we have. When we are young, we likely believe just about everything the adults in our lives tell us. But, as we grow, we shouldn't only believe what people tell us. When we realize we believe something only on the basis of one person's opinion, no matter how sincere he or she may be, we may quickly realize we do not have very good evidence. In this case, we should seek out broader evidence.

It's important to mention we can be wrong in our beliefs even when they are based on good evidence.

This is, once again, to emphasize that reasoning about everyday matters will very often be according to nondeductive standards. We almost never enjoy absolute certainty about the things we believe as it relates to the experiences of everyday matters. Typically, the best we can do is have strong evidence for a claim, and this is good enough for rationally believing.

Evidentialism?

We have said if one has sufficient evidence then one is likely rational. But is evidence necessary for rationality? The thesis of *evidentialism* says that one is not rational in believing some claim unless one has good evidence for that claim.[3]

There are philosophers who deny evidentialism. Alvin Plantinga, perhaps the most prominent Christian philosopher of the twentieth century,

[3] This thesis should not be confused with the apologetics methodology that is called "evidentialism." In apologetics, evidentialism is often understood as that evidential arguments from areas such as philosophy, history, and science are necessary for doing apologetics.

has argued, for example, that one's beliefs can be rational (or what he calls "warranted") even if one is entirely unaware of any evidence for the truth of the belief.[4] For Plantinga, the belief must be produced in the right way (by properly functioning cognitive faculties that also satisfy a few technical conditions)[5] for it to be warranted, but he doesn't require one to have any evidence that it has been produced in that way. It just has to be the case that the belief was in fact produced by properly functioning faculties, and so forth. An evidentialist, by contrast, thinks a belief's being produced by properly functioning cognitive faculties doesn't make the person rational unless the person has sufficient evidence for the belief.

This debate gets rather technical in a hurry, and so we won't be able to settle the issue here. However, let's focus on what I call *intellectual assurance*, which is when a person is aware of good reasons that indicate the truth of one of his or her beliefs. So if a belief is merely produced in the right way but one is completely unaware of this, then, by hypothesis, one lacks intellectual assurance. However, if one has sufficiently good evidence for a belief, then one has intellectual assurance for that belief. This suggests a thesis of what we might call *assurance evidentialism*: a person has intellectual assurance for a belief only if one has evidence for that belief. So, even if a philosopher like Plantinga doesn't think evidence is necessary for rationality (or what he calls "warrant"), it seems impossible to have intellectual assurance without it. This is for the simple reason that unless we are aware of facts that indicate the truth of a belief (i.e., we have some evidence), then we cannot be assured the belief is likely truth.

---

[4] See Alvin Plantinga, *Knowledge and Christian Belief* (Grand Rapids: Eerdmans, 2015).

[5] In his most recent work on this, Plantinga summarizes his view: "Put in a nutshell, then, a belief has warrant for a person . . . only if that belief is produced in [him] by cognitive faculties functioning properly (subject to no dysfunction) in a cognitive environment that is appropriate for [his] kind of cognitive faculties, according to a design plan that is successfully aimed at truth." Plantinga, 28.

Suppose I believe that the president of the US is currently in New York City. Let's assume this belief is produced in me by properly functioning cognitive faculties. Perhaps I have, unknown to me, some prophetic ability that has produced my belief that the president is in New York. But notice, from my perspective, the belief just popped into my mind. If I don't have any evidence whatsoever as to the president's whereabouts, then I do not, by definition, have intellectual assurance that my belief is true; the president is in New York. It is not different, from my perspective, if I just guessed where the president currently is, since I am unaware that the belief was formed by a prophetic ability. Again, we can have a properly functioning faculty without being aware of anything that would give us intellectual assurance. By contrast, let's suppose I come to have some evidence that the president is in New York City. Perhaps I watched the news, and it reported that the president is currently in New York City. Now I have intellectual assurance for the truth of this belief.

Intellectual assurance is crucial because without it we have nothing guiding our actions and belief formation. If you want to know who you should vote for in the next election, you will need to look at the evidence to make a rational choice. If you want to know how to do your taxes properly, then you will need to look at the evidence. If you want to know whether your Christian beliefs are true, then you should consider the evidence. If you want to know whether Plantinga is right about evidence, you will also have to work through and consider the evidence. When Plantinga wants to convince you that his theory is the right one, he is going to have to lay out the evidence (e.g., in writing his book).

Surely it is better to possess intellectual assurance for a belief than to lack intellectual assurance. Let's say Smith and Jones both find themselves believing that God exists. But let's say that Smith is familiar with some of the many arguments that point to the truth of God's existence, whereas Jones is not. Even though they may both be equally confident that God exists, it seems that Smith is in a better intellectual situation. Smith has intellectual assurance. He has something that points him to the truth of this belief, and Jones does not. If Jones were to begin doubting his faith, unless he considers the evidence, he very well may drop his belief that God exists. Why? For the simple and rather obvious reason that he lacks any intellectual assurance for its truth. Again, it is intellectual assurance that comes from evidence that guides our actions and helps us evaluate our beliefs.

A Broad View of Evidence

But there is a worry here. The concern could be that there are people who are either not able to or just don't have exposure to the evidence for many of the things they believe. Children, for example, of course aren't able to consider the evidence of the experts, even if they want to. And many adults do not have the time and resources to do so either. Must we say that these are not rational in their beliefs? Are these destined to lack intellectual assurance? Now, this really matters if we are thinking about issues of Christian faith.

Let's take Christians who believe in Christianity and yet lack all training in the evidences of Christianity. Let's imagine a country farmer who lacks all formal college education and even dropped out of high school to work the family farm, and yet the country farmer believes that Christianity is true. Is the country farmer necessarily irrational without this formal training? Of course not. I know too many country farmers with a rich and abiding faith. They may be quite rational in this faith.

The problem here is this assumes an overly narrow view of evidence. The concern about country farmers and children seems to assume only experts have evidence. Does the country farmer lack all evidence for the truth of Christianity? Again, of course not. The farmer could have evidence of all sorts for Christian beliefs. When it comes to God, I take seriously the claims of Scripture that say God is evident in the world. Romans 1:19–20 says, "what can be known about God is evident among them, because God has shown it to them. For his invisible attributes, that is, his eternal power and divine nature, have been clearly seen since the creation of the world, being understood through what he has made. As a result, people are without excuse." King David, in Ps 19:1–2, said:

> The heavens declare the glory of God,
> and the expanse proclaims the work of his hands.
> Day after day they pour out speech;
> night after night they communicate knowledge.

Scripture doesn't say we must have a formal education to see God in creation. His divine attributes can be "clearly seen" in creation. A primary evidence of the existence of God is the pervasive design inherent in the world. The farmer is in the country, after all, and so the farmer has seen the life cycles of animals and crops and how the natural cycle of the seasons and weather all figure into the process of farming. The farmer can, I'd suggest, very easily see design that implies a designer.

Now, the farmer may not be able to give the design argument as a formal argument as we would in an apologetics class, even if the farmer is quite aware of how this indicates the truth of God's existence. The farmer sees a world where the design of God is evident and rationally believes. The point here is that we do not need arguments (especially formalized ones) to be rational in believing. The evidence we have is often experiential. It is experiencing the regularity and design of nature that gives us reason to believe there's a God who stands behind it all.

Our country farmer has also likely been confronted by the reality of God in religious contexts—if the country farmer has seen answers to prayer, and he has had the truth of Christianity testified to him by reliable guides (i.e., preachers and others testifying to the truth of Christianity). As we will detail in the next section, all of this constitutes evidence for the truth of Christianity. Now, this might sound like special pleading. Is it possible for adherents of other religions to have this same sort of evidence for their religious beliefs? And the answer is yes, in principle they could indeed. Let's say people prayed in the name of their religious tradition specifically for something, and it came to pass in an uncanny way. To be consistent, we would have to say that this stands as evidence for them for the truth of their religious tradition in the same way that it does for Christians.

The point here is that adherents of other religions are of course not completely irrational. They believe on the basis of at least some evidence. But just because there is some evidence for the truth of another religion, it doesn't of course mean the tradition is thereby true. This is once again a point about nondeductive logic. Evidence can make a belief likely to some degree even if the belief is false. Uncanny circumstances are sometimes just uncanny coincidences. That is, what one took to be an answer to prayer might have been only pure coincidence. So, while I of course think the evidence is rather strongly on the side of Christianity, there is no problem admitting that there is at least some evidence that points to alternative views. I just don't find the evidence for these compelling.

Evidence, in this view, is rather easy to come by. As long as we are aware of something that points to the truth of our belief, then we do, in fact, have evidence for our belief. People do not typically believe something (especially a cherished belief) on no evidence at all. Now, most of us have a lot of work to do to be more rational in our beliefs. It's easy to have some evidence for our views, but this shouldn't satisfy us precisely because it is easy to come by. So we ought to do the hard work of evaluating our evidence and attempting to have the best evidence we can. That is, we should strive for more and better evidence.

What should be obvious at this point is that evidence is being understood quite broadly here. Having evidence for the truth of Christianity need not require any formal training in science or philosophy or any other discipline. Though children of course are not fully mature when it comes to evaluating the evidence, they can still weigh the evidence for things and rationally believe accordingly. Some children may believe a real, rather rotund guy wearing a red suit shimmies his way down the chimney to deliver presents each Christmas. We typically think of this as an irrational belief, but can we really blame a kid, at a certain young age, for believing that Santa Claus exists? Many kids have the people they trust the most in the whole world adamantly telling them this is true and acting like Santa Claus is real. They also find a variety of presents suddenly showing up on Christmas morning, which their parents insist are from Santa. And what about the milk and cookies that disappear the night before Christmas? This is all indicative of the truth of their belief. Children of a certain young age can have some compelling evidence for believing that Santa Claus is real. But then, for most, they begin to notice countervailing evidence (e.g., an older sibling lets them in on the ruse, or they find the unwrapped presents hidden in the closet before Christmas, or they observe how small a chimney chute is) and eventually come to believe that Santa Claus is not real. Though they have a false belief when they are young, it's certainly not completely irrational given the evidence they have. And it is the evidence they come to have that leads them to the truth as they get older.

We weigh evidence in this same way. It is easy to come by some evidence for a view, but if it is a belief of consequence (such as our Christian beliefs), then we shouldn't settle for easy. Perhaps we grew up in a Christian home, and we had numerous adults telling us that Christianity is true. This constitutes evidence. But we shouldn't stay here. Growing in our faith involves having more and more evidence for the truth of Christianity. We move on from believing it merely on the basis of the evidence of our parents', a friend's, or a pastor's testimony, and our faith becomes our own. As Paul put it, "When I was a child, I spoke like a child, I thought like a child, I reasoned like a child. When I became a man, I put aside childish things" (1 Cor 13:11). He went on to say, "Brothers and sisters, don't be childish in your thinking, but be infants in regard to evil and adult in your thinking" (1 Cor 14:20). Likewise, in all the important areas of our lives, we should seek to have mature thinking. Part of this is assessing the evidence for those beliefs. We can search out better evidence and engage the evidence that would count against our beliefs. And we should be mature and always growing in this way in our Christian beliefs.

Sources of Evidence

In this broad view of evidence, what are the typical sources of evidence?

Two of the most important sources of evidence are experience and testimony. When we talk about experience, we primarily mean sense experience. This is when we have sensations of the world through five senses (e.g., seeing, hearing, and smelling). When we see something with our own eyes or, in some way, experience it for ourselves, we usually thereby have good reasons to believe it. In fact, once we experience something for ourselves, then often no amount of arguments can persuade us to the contrary. When we see someone whom we have trusted and even defended do something untoward, we may cease to believe that person is trustworthy. No amount of convincing otherwise will do. We know what we saw.

Even in the life of Jesus, people were profoundly impacted by being around him and seeing the signs and wonders he performed. This they took to be extraordinary evidence to believe he was who he claimed to be. When Jesus appeared to Thomas personally and conceded to let him touch his wounds, even though Thomas seemed to make this demand from a stubborn heart, Thomas arguably then had even more evidence to believe that Jesus rose from the dead (see John 20:24–29).[6] Or when, in Matt 11:3, John the Baptist sent his disciples to Jesus to ask, "Are you the one who is to come, or should we expect someone else?" Jesus didn't tell them to just have blind faith. He said, "Go and report to John what you hear and see: The blind receive their sight, the lame walk, those with leprosy are cleansed, the deaf hear, the dead are raised, and the poor are told the good news" (vv. 4–5). Jesus seemed to be offering the miraculous experiences in these instances as evidence for being the Messiah.

---

[6] This can be true even though Thomas's demanding this level of evidence seemed to clearly show that Thomas's heart was ill motivated. That is, Thomas wasn't simply wanting to be a careful rational thinker but had a stubborn heart (consider that he says, "I will never believe," v. 25), perhaps because he was hurt at not being among the disciples when Jesus first appeared to them.

But the reality is, we can't always have direct and personal experience of the things we believe. In fact, much of what we know is on the basis of testimony. Testimony includes someone verbally speaking to you about some fact (such as a teacher, parent, or pastor) or reading an accounting of some fact (in a book, website, or a documentary on some topic). In each of these, we are getting testimonial evidence of these facts. People of course do not always tell the truth, and sometimes it is obvious when a source (person, book, website, documentary, etc.) is not trustworthy. But as long we have no reason to doubt a source's integrity, then the testimony of the source gives us at least some evidence to believe. And in cases when we have positive reasons to take a source to be trustworthy, then this testimony may provide us with very strong evidence indeed.

The more consequential the belief, the more evidence we need for trusting their testimony. If we stop and ask directions from a stranger and they answer us confidently, then, unless we have reasons to doubt it, we should believe this testimony. Most people, it seems, are willing to help someone get around in their town. But getting to a destination is usually a matter of relatively small importance. If it turned out the directions were no good, this isn't usually of much consequence.

You shouldn't (and probably wouldn't) ask a stranger on the street for advice about financial investing, career planning, or who you should marry. The stakes, in such cases, are much higher. With these, you will want to talk with someone who knows what they are talking about. In short, we should aim at getting informed advice.

For Christians, much of our beliefs are based on testimonial evidence. We have people who testify to its truth. The Bible says, "How, then, can they call on him they have not believed in? And how can they believe without hearing about him? And how can they hear without a preacher? . . . So faith comes from what is heard, and what is heard comes through the message about Christ" (Rom 10:14, 17). Faith, as Paul said here, comes from hearing the Word of God preached and testified to us. We have multiple layers of testimony here. We have the testimony of the preacher, on the human level. A preacher will assert certain truths to us and, on the basis of the preacher's testimony and assuming we know the preacher to be a reliable guide (i.e., he's not a fast-talking swindler), we are given evidence to believe.

But we can take this one step further. Notice the content of the preacher's message in view here is the Word of God. If we want expert testimony, then we have no better expert testimony than the divinely inspired testimony of Scripture itself. If we know the Bible to be the Word of God, then we have the greatest conceivable testimonial evidence at our fingertips. Again, we are not used to thinking of reading and hearing the exposition of Scripture as evidence. But if testimony is a source of evidence and expert testimony is a source of really good evidence, then it seems there can be no greater expert testimony than a divinely inspired text.

A third source of evidence is a bit more controversial. It is what we may call intuitive or conceptual evidence. There are many things we seem to know not on the basis of experience but because we can grasp the truth with our minds. We can, in a way, just see that certain conceptual claims are true. For example, it seems we can just see that the principle of noncontradiction is true. All we have to do is reflect on it, and once we understand what's being claimed, we can see that it cannot be the case that P and not P at the same time and in the same sense. Or take, for example, simple mathematical facts. When we were kids, we probably memorized our math facts, such as 2+3=5. But as we get older, we, at some point, come to grasp the truth of this on an intuitive basis.[7] Our knowledge of them comes from grasping the concepts with our minds.

[7] These are sometimes called *a priori truths* (and our knowledge of them is called *a priori knowledge*) because we do not depend on (and it, in a way, precedes) observation or sense experience to know these facts. Knowledge that comes on the basis of sense experience is called *a posteriori* or empirical knowledge.

Background Knowledge

Any discussion of evidence needs to also consider the role of our background knowledge. The notion of background knowledge is closely related to the idea of one's worldview. But when we talk about our background knowledge, we are explicitly talking about our beliefs and the intellectual commitments that inform our evaluation of the evidence. Some of these will be worldview commitments, and some may be more mundane and everyday bits of knowledge. But either way, the things we believe operate in the background, affecting what we will count as good evidence.

Though some people fancy themselves as being neutral observers as they evaluate issues before them, I want to suggest that we rarely approach an issue without our background knowledge informing our beliefs. Now it is not all bad for our background knowledge to inform our judgments. That is, though it may seem like neutrality is a good thing when making judgments, it often is not. Take a doctor, for example. A typical doctor has spent years developing his or her knowledge. This is precisely why we pay significant money to get seen by an actual doctor. We want our doctor to be, in a sense, biased toward his or her extensive medical knowledge when the doctor examines us for some possible malady. It would be quite a bad thing if the doctor proceeded in a completely neutral way.

We all bring our background knowledge into the evaluation of virtually any issue. Just like the doctor can't really suspend his or her medical training when considering a medical issue, we can't just suspend our prior beliefs when we consider issues. And this is completely OK so long as we are intellectually honest about it, we are open-minded about possibly being wrong, and we don't unfairly prejudice our prior beliefs.

Consider the following example. Let's say I take forty-five minutes to argue to a group of people that Jesus rose from the dead. I assert that good historical evidence exists for this fact, and I run some of these ideas down. I may mention how early the reports of Jesus's resurrection are, that it's likely we have a variety of eyewitness accounts of Jesus's resurrection, that Jesus's tomb was very likely found empty on Sunday morning by his women followers, and so on. Let's say the audience for my talk is comprised of both Christians and non-Christians. We can be quite sure there will be a difference in how this case is received. If one is a Christian, then one will likely receive this information with openness and acceptance. One might even receive this with great joy, especially if one hasn't heard a robust presentation of the evidence for the resurrection before. It will be, for the Christian, a compelling and convincing case for the resurrection and the truth of Christianity. However, if one is a non-Christian, then one will likely not find the evidence to be very compelling. If the non-Christian is an atheist, then these claims about God raising Jesus from the dead may be something of a nonstarter.

Is this merely a matter of hopeless bias? No! It is a matter of having radically different background beliefs given the different worldviews. A Christian does not believe that Jesus rose from the dead in isolation from any other background beliefs. Indeed the Christian believes God supernaturally raised Jesus from the dead as a part of an overarching plan of the redemption of humankind. But notice this includes an explicit belief in the biblical God. One would need to believe not only that God exists but is interested in working supernaturally in the world before one will ever take seriously the claim that Jesus rose from the dead. If one is an atheist, then it is not so much that the historical evidence is lacking. It's that the whole requisite background beliefs may not be there to consider the evidence as in any way plausible. If you and I didn't believe that God exists as a background belief, then you and I also may not find the historical evidence for Jesus's resurrection very compelling. But with the right background beliefs, then the evidence becomes really compelling.

So what are we to do about this?

There are at least two consequences of the reality of the role our background knowledge plays in our evaluation of evidence. First, we must be reflective about our own background knowledge and the ways in which it informs our evaluation of evidence. We have to realize that, at times, the reason something seems so compelling to us is because of what we already believe. Thus, as we evaluate our beliefs, we must also rationally consider those background beliefs. We need to be careful that we are not unfairly prejudicing our own views given the background beliefs.

Second, understanding the background knowledge someone may be bringing into a discussion is absolutely vital for being able to speak to them in a way that makes an impact. Again, the atheist is likely to reject the historical case for the resurrection, but this is because the atheist doesn't believe in God. So if we are trying to convince our atheist friend of the truth of Christianity, we need to attempt to address these background beliefs. That is, we have to provide reason to believe that God exists and this is what makes sense of Jesus's resurrection. If we don't speak to the background beliefs one has, then one will very likely dismiss the claims we make. In any case, we'll be talking past one another until we settle on the fundamental difference in our views. It's important to back up and figure out where the disagreement starts so that we can address the fundamental thing that's at issue rather than talking past one another.

Conclusion

Evidence matters. Without it, we will lack intellectual assurance for our beliefs. A belief can of course be true without having evidence. We could just guess that Christianity is true, and then we would have a true belief. But if we have no evidence, then we believe truly by accident. We would have no intellectual assurance that Christianity is true. By contrast, if we believe Christianity is true on the basis of good evidence, then we believe truly but also rationally with intellectual assurance of the belief's truth. With this, we can "stand firm and hold to the traditions [we] were taught" (2 Thess 2:15) This doesn't mean we all have to become experts in Christian apologetics. In fact, though it may be very helpful, there's no need for any formal training. Evidence is available in a great variety of places. We can see God in our observation of creation. We can have experiences that point to the truth of Christianity. We may also have a variety of sources of testimonial evidence from preachers, pastors, teachers, or parents. The ultimate testimony is of course the testimony of God himself. He testifies to us through Scripture but also in our devotional pursuits. All of this can constitute the intellectual assurance of Christianity's truth.

Fallacies

We have, so far, been primarily focused on what constitutes good reasoning. We turn now to talk about bad reasoning. The point here is, of course, not to recommend bad reasoning but to help us to become sensitive to common mistakes in reasoning so that we can avoid those mistakes. We want to avoid *fallacies*.

A *fallacy* is a mistake in reasoning. It is a case in which the premises of an argument poorly support the conclusion. The Latin term for this is a *non sequitur*, which literally means "it does not follow." As we'll see, a conclusion can fail to follow from its premises in many different ways. There will be some ways in which the conclusion doesn't follow as a matter of strict deductive logic (i.e., it's invalid). But there will be other fallacies where the premises are just too weak to support the likelihood of the conclusion (i.e., it's weak).

There are a lot of ways to go wrong in making an argument. Some mistakes in reasoning are quite common. These will get names and will be discussed at length momentarily. But we couldn't possibly canvass every way in which a person could commit a mistake in reasoning. In fact, some fallacious arguments are, in a way, too obvious and silly. For example:

1. Dogs are better than cats.
2. Cats are mammals.
3. Therefore, I will win the lottery today.

This is certainly fallacious reasoning, but it is so bad it doesn't even have its own name. No sane person should believe this conclusion on the basis of these premises.

By contrast, the fallacies we will discuss often look like or resemble good reasoning. They are real mistakes that real people make. In fact, these might feel a bit too familiar because you too have made one or more of these along the way. Again, the value of discussing these fallacies is learning to spot the subtle but common ways in which we make mistakes in reasoning so that we learn to think critically about our own views and the views of others.

Formal Fallacies

The first kind of fallacy is what we call a *formal fallacy*. This has nothing to do with fancy dresses or tuxedos but has to do with a defect in the form (or structure) of the argument. We've already looked at these in some detail because a formal fallacy is when the conclusion of an argument does not follow in a deductively valid way. The formal fallacies for which we have names are arguments that resemble deductively valid arguments, but they are instead invalid. That is to say it will be an argument that is similar to a common deductively valid argument form, but in the case of the formal fallacies, the argument is invalid. Thus, formally fallacious arguments fail on deductive standards.

Affirming the Consequent

The first formal fallacy is called *affirming the consequent.* This fallacious form of argument resembles modus ponens, but, with a careful look, it is clearly different. By way of reminder, modus ponens is:

1. If P, then Q
2. P
3. Therefore, Q

But affirming the consequent swaps premise 2 and the conclusion:

1. If P, then Q
2. Q
3. Therefore, P

An instance of affirming the consequent will always be invalid. Here's an example:

1. If it rained just now, then the streets are wet.
2. The streets are wet.
3. Therefore, it rained just now.

When we think about this argument carefully, it's clear that it is invalid. Premise 1 and 2 could be true, while the conclusion could be false. Here's another instance of affirming the consequent that makes this clear:

1. If Jones ate a peanut butter sandwich just now, then Jones needs a drink of water.
2. Jones needs a drink of water.
3. Therefore, Jones ate a peanut butter sandwich just now.

Even if premises 1 and 2 are true, it certainly does not follow that the conclusion is true. There are many other reasons Jones may need a drink of water (e.g., he just finished a run, he has been working in a hot attic, he just ate something else that's salty, etc.) without having just eaten a peanut butter sandwich. Though this argument form looks similar to modus ponens, the difference makes a big logical difference. Any instance of this argument form is always invalid.[1]

Denying the Antecedent

The second formal fallacy is called *denying the antecedent*. It is similar to modus tollens, except that with modus tollens we deny the consequent of the conditional in premise 1. But, as the name suggests, in this formal fallacy the antecedent is denied, which makes it formally fallacious.

Here's the fallacious form of argument:

1. If P, then Q
2. Not P
3. Therefore, not Q

Here's an example of denying the antecedent:

1. If it rained just now, then the streets are wet.
2. It did not rain just now.
3. Therefore, the streets are not wet.

This is invalid since just because it didn't rain just now, it doesn't follow the streets are not wet. After all, those streets could be wet for some other

---

[1] Recall that just because an argument is invalid doesn't mean the argument is a bad one on the nondeductive standards of reasoning. Any argument whose conclusion is made likely but not guaranteed by the premises is, strictly speaking, invalid. Could an instance of, say, affirming the consequent be nondeductively strong? This is possible, but it would be an awkwardly worded argument. For example, if we walked outside and saw that the streets are wet, we would probably conclude that it had just rained. But it wouldn't likely be because we believe "If it rains, then the streets are wet." It would be because we believe a premise that would say something like "In most cases, wet streets are due to a recent rain."

reason. It could again be that a water main broke or that it snowed last night and the snow has just melted. If either of these scenarios were true, then premises 1 and 2 could be true and the conclusion would be false since the streets are wet.

Affirming the Disjunct

The final formal fallacy that we'll consider is called *affirming the disjunct*. This is an invalid argument form that looks like the following:

1. P or Q
2. P
3. Therefore, not Q

This is reminiscent of a disjunctive syllogism. But in the disjunctive syllogism, we *deny* one of the disjuncts and thereby affirm the other. Remember that when it comes to a typical disjunction we are assuming the inclusive-or, which means P and Q can't both be false, but here they *can* both be false. So this is a formal fallacy because even if P is true it doesn't follow that Q is false.

Consider this example:

1. Either Joe gets a second job, or he goes into debt.
2. Joe gets a second job.
3. Therefore, he does not go into debt.

Unfortunately, there are many ways to go into debt. It might be true that the situation Joe is facing means that if he doesn't get a second job, he will go into debt. But just because he gets a second job, it doesn't follow that he will not go into debt. He, or someone in his family, may have to get an expensive surgery, or his second job may not provide enough money to keep him out of debt. If any of these situations occurred, both premises would be true, but the conclusion false. So the argument is formally invalid.

Contrast the formally fallacious argument with the following valid argument:

1. Either Joe gets a second job or he goes into debt.
2. Joe does not get a second job.
3. Therefore, he goes into debt.

Here, if both premises are true, then the conclusion is guaranteed to be true.

We should note that all invalid arguments are formally fallacious. But when we are talking about nondeductively strong and cogent arguments, we don't typically talk in terms of them being formally fallacious, and even nondeductively cogent arguments are, strictly speaking, invalid. This is because formal fallacies only have to do with deductive validity, and if we are considering whether an argument is nondeductively strong or cogent, we are not applying the deductive standards of logic. So while all nondeductively strong arguments, where the truth of the premises do not entail the truth of the conclusion, could be said to be formally fallacious, for simplicity's sake we'll reserve the criticism of being formally fallacious for arguments that resemble the deductively valid argument forms.

Informal Fallacies

The second kind of fallacy is called an *informal fallacy*. The defect in an argument with an informal fallacy is not in the form or structure of the argument but a mistake in the support the premises offer to the conclusion.

Informal fallacies come in two categories. The first is when one or more of the premises are logically irrelevant. As we discussed in chapter 5, premises give us good reason to believe the conclusion of an argument when they are logically relevant to the conclusion. We stated this idea in the following way:

> For any two statements A and B, A is logically relevant to B if in the case that A is true, B is to some degree likely to be true.

Logical relevance is the reason that premises give us reason to believe a conclusion. But if the premises of the argument are logically irrelevant, then this is of course fallacious reasoning. They do not give us reason to believe the conclusion.

The second form of informal fallacies is *fallacies of inadequate support.* Sometimes premises may be logically relevant to the conclusion of an argument, but they only provide weak support. That is, they fail to adequately support the conclusion; the premises do not make the conclusion at all likely because of some fallacious mistake.

Just like the formal fallacies, the informal fallacies we will discuss will be ones that resemble a good argument, or at least they, on the surface, have some appeal. Though there is a potentially infinite number of ways to make mistakes in our reasoning, we give names to common mistakes that may appear, at first glance, to be good. We will consider twenty-five common informal fallacies.

Twenty-Five Common Informal Fallacies

Fallacies of Irrelevance

1. Ad Hominem

The term *ad hominem* means literally "to the man." Let's say that Jones claims, "Caesar crossed the Rubicon in 49 BC." And then suppose Smith claims, "This must be false because you are a member of X political party. Anyone who is a member of X political party is a bad person, and so I don't believe anything you say." Smith's argument is the following:

1. Jones is a member of X political party.
2. Members of X political party are bad people and, for this reason, should not be believed.
3. Therefore, Jones's claim that Caesar crossed the Rubicon in 49 BC is false.

This is clearly a bad argument. Being a member of a certain political party, even if the political party has immoral policy platforms, doesn't make one unable to make true historical statements. Even if the accusation is true, bad people can still make a true claim about Caesar's crossing the Rubicon.

The ad hominem is when a premise of one's argument is directed at the person, usually as some kind of attack, in a way that's irrelevant to the truth or likelihood of the conclusion. In fact, it is sometimes called the fallacy of personal attack. The badness of Jones's political party is really quite irrelevant to whether his claim about Caesar crossing the Rubicon in 49 BC is correct. Even if Jones does have a personal defect given his political membership, this is beside the point.

In John 8:42–47, Jesus lays out a case for why he is from God and why the Jews should believe him in this testimony. The Jews respond, "Aren't we right in saying you are a Samaritan and have a demon?" (v. 48). Now, this is, of course, false, but it is a clear ad hominem, since it is an irrelevant personal attack. Consider this argument:

1. Smith says that the Bible is historically unreliable.
2. Smith is a raging alcoholic.
3. Therefore, Smith's claim that the Bible is historically unreliable is false.

It is so easy to dismiss a challenge to the Christian faith like this by pointing to a character flaw. But we need to engage the ideas of the person rather than how the person making the claim may happen to behave. To dismiss this challenge by calling this person an alcoholic has nothing to do with the historical reliability of the Bible. Just because the person has this moral failing, it of course doesn't mean we have addressed the objection to the reliability of the Bible. The ideas still have to be critiqued on their own terms even if they are presented by flawed people.

Now, this doesn't mean that it is always an ad hominem to say something negative about a person's moral character. That is, a person's character is sometimes logically relevant to the claims that a person makes. In a court case, let's say, the defense attorney might attempt to show that a witness's testimony for the guilt of the accused should not be believed because the witness is a known liar. In this case, it is completely appropriate to point out character flaws. If clear instances exist where a witness has been willing to lie before, then this is logically relevant to whether they are currently lying or at least whether the person is trustworthy. It certainly doesn't mean the accused is innocent. The witness could be telling the truth that the accused is guilty. It is just that the witness's testimony can't be trusted given these character flaws.

2. Tu Quoque

It often doesn't sit well with us when people tell us what to do, and then they themselves don't do what they've said. Many celebrities have told us to stay off of drugs only to be caught possessing drugs or having to check into a rehabilitation center for drug addiction. Though no one likes a hypocrite telling them what to do, being hypocritical is often logically irrelevant to the rationality of one's claims. Because a celebrity is not able to stay off drugs, it doesn't follow that his or her claim that drugs are harmful to you is false. The *tu quoque* (literally, "you too") fallacy is when we dismiss someone's claims because he or she lives hypocritically in light of those claims.

For example:

Smith: Capitalism is evil since it exploits the poor factory workers.
Jones: Don't you own an iPhone?
Smith: Well, yes.
Jones: Capitalism must not be too evil, then.

Here again, just because Smith is hypocritical, it doesn't mean that capitalism is therefore morally appropriate. Jones has committed the tu quoque fallacy. Smith's hypocrisy is irrelevant to whether capitalism is immoral. Jones should present reasons to think Smith's view is false rather than merely calling out the hypocrisy.

This is, of course, not to say that we shouldn't try to be consistent with the claims that we make. When someone is hypocritical, they very well may lose credibility with their audience. That person may even lose their platform to speak against some issues. The celebrity who is caught actively doing drugs will likely and rightfully be pulled off the anti-drug campaign. But their claims are not dubious just because they don't live up to them. To think so would be a tu quoque.

3. Equivocation

English can be a frustrating language to learn. One reason is that many English words have more than one meaning. As we have already pointed out in chapter 6, the word *bank* can mean a financial institution, the side of a river, a row of certain objects; or, as a verb, it can mean to save something up or to bounce a basketball off of a backboard. The term *plant* can mean the green thing that grows in a garden; it could mean the place where items are built, assembled, and produced (such as an automobile plant); or when someone is brought into a group to serve a secret purpose, such as spying on the other members. Given the fact that words can have more than one meaning, mistakes in reasoning occur when one moves from one meaning of a term to another meaning within the argument. This is called the *fallacy of equivocation*. Consider the following argument:

1. If a plant gets regular sunlight and plenty of water, then it will grow.
2. The Ford motor plant gets regular sunlight and has plenty of water.
3. Therefore, the Ford motor plant will grow.

Clearly, here one is equivocating on the term "plant." Premise 1 is referring to the green thing that grows in a garden, and in premise 2 the term refers to a place where automobiles are built. Premise 1 is quite irrelevant to the rest of the argument because it is talking about garden plants.

Here is another example:

1. Brad is a nobody.
2. Nobody is perfect.

3. Therefore, Brad is perfect.

This has the structural appearance of being a good argument. It looks like the following argument form:

1. A is B.
2. B is C.
3. Therefore, A is C.

If this were right, then this would be a valid argument. But this is not right since the meaning of "nobody" shifts from premise 1 to premise 2. This is obviously fallacious (after all, it says "nobody is perfect" and "Brad is perfect," which is a contradiction). The argument equivocates on the term *nobody*. In the first premise, being a "nobody" means one is not well-known. However, when the term "nobody" is used in the second premise, it is used more literally to mean that there's no one who is perfect. This is the fallacy of equivocation.

We should recall that whenever we symbolize we must keep the meaning of the terms the same. If we use a letter to symbolize, every instance of that letter must be the same. So the argument form should look like this to reflect the different meanings of "nobody":

1. A is B.
2. F is C.
3. Therefore, A is C.

With this accurate symbolization of the argument, we can clearly see the irrelevance of the claims.

4. Red Herring

Sometimes the premises of an argument don't support the conclusion, and this is obvious. But other times premises seem designed to distract from the fact they do not support the conclusion. This is the *red herring fallacy*.

The name of this fallacy comes from when one wanted to throw a bloodhound off of a scent, one could drag a smelly fish across the scent trail. The very strong smell of the fish is intended to distract the bloodhound from the trail. Similarly, the fallacy uses statements (often emotionally charged ones) to throw someone off the trail of an unsupported argument despite the fact that the statements are logically irrelevant to the conclusion of the argument.

Politicians are often guilty of the red herring. For example:

> Political candidate: "We should have universal health care. There are poor people dying right now from treatable conditions!"

The premise that poor people are dying right now from treatable conditions is being used to support the conclusion that we should have universal health care. No one wants to appear heartless and uncaring about people who are sick and in need of health care. But it is not a good reason, at least by itself, to institute universal health care. If universal health care will bankrupt our country and the whole health-care system crashes, then this would ultimately lead to even more people dying from treatable conditions. To distract by the emotional appeal of people in need is a red herring.

Or consider this example:

> **Reporter:** "You took bribes from special-interest groups to support their causes. This is morally wrong. What do you have to say for yourself?"
>
> **Politician:** "Well, what is morality? There are a lot of opinions here. It's important to note that we all are allowed to have our own view on this."

While it is true there are many opinions about morality, it doesn't actually address the charge that this politician took bribes. The response seems designed to make it seem like the politician answered the question while simply changing the topic.

5. No True Scotsman

When we are part of a group we cherish, we tend to have an idealized version of the group in mind. If you are an American (or any other nationality with great national pride, such as the Scots), then you may tend to think that all true Americans act in certain ways. The *no true Scotsman* fallacy occurs when one equates the idealized version (i.e., how we think all Americans should act) with a more minimal version (i.e., what it minimally takes to be an American).

Consider this dialogue, for example:

Jones: "All Americans are honorable."
Smith: "Joe is an American, and he is not honorable."
Jones: "Well, Joe is not a true American, then."

This is a fallacy because being an American does not require one to be honorable. Many Americans are of course honorable, and we may want all Americans to represent the country in an honorable way, but one does not cease to be an American when one fails to be honorable. To think so commits the no true Scotsman fallacy.

We should note that one has not committed the no true Scotsman fallacy when a group is identified by certain beliefs (as opposed to, say, one's nationality or citizenship) and one of those beliefs is not held. One is an American by virtue of being a citizen of the United States. Consider, for example, what it is to be a Christian. Being a Christian, in a broad sense, is defined by believing certain fundamental doctrines. Arguably, to be a Christian, certain essential beliefs must be held. Without believing that God exists, that Jesus rose from the dead, or that the Bible is generally truthful would seem to put one at odds with being a Christian. It would be similarly problematic if one claimed to be an atheist but then also claimed to have a personal relationship with an actually existing God. These, so understood, are not instances of the no true Scotsman fallacy.

6. APPEAL TO EMOTIONS

Emotions are powerful things. A persuasive speech is almost always going to be one that appeals to emotions. If a speech is devoid of all passion, then it is unlikely to persuade even if it enjoys airtight logic. However, being persuasive is not the same as giving a good argument. We can be persuaded by a bad argument when the argument is given with tremendous passion and emotional appeal, but this is believing on fallacious reasoning. The *appeal to emotions fallacy*, then, is supporting a claim with emotional appeals to the exclusion of good evidence.

Kid: "I don't want to eat the casserole."
Parent: "There are starving children in Africa who have nothing to eat at all. Eat the casserole!"

Though this is a well-worn tactic many parents have used to get their child to eat dinner, it is, strictly speaking, fallacious reasoning. Just because starving children are in Africa and we have this emotional appeal, it doesn't mean the kid should eat the casserole. Eating the food will not, by itself, help address the lack of food in other parts of the world.

Emotions are of course not bad things. Again, they can be very persuasive, and persuasion of the truth is a good thing (discussed more fully in chap. 13). The problem is when we use emotions as our sole guide to the truth. We can feel the emotional appeal of something that is completely false. It is rational evidence that leads us to truth.

7. POST HOC, ERGO PROPTER HOC (THE POST HOC FALLACY, FOR SHORT)

It is said that Billy Beane, the vice president of the Oakland Athletics, will not watch his own team play at the ballfield. There's a scene in the movie *Money Ball* that portrays Beane's career as general manager of the Athletics. Beane decides to watch his team when they are up 11–0, having won nineteen previous games. After only a few moments of him being in the ballpark, the opposing team rallies and ties it up 11–11. Beane immediately leaves, and the Athletics go on to barely pull it out in the bottom of the ninth. Beane seems to be inferring that his presence at the game caused the Athletics to almost lose the game. The only reason to think this is that the team started losing following (i.e., post hoc literally means "after this") Beane entering the ballpark. But this commits the *post hoc fallacy* because even though the team starting losing after he started watching the game, it doesn't mean that Beane's watching the game *caused* them to lose (*ergo propter hoc* means "therefore because of this").

The *post hoc fallacy* is when one hastily takes the fact that B follows A to be adequate support to believe that A is the cause of B. Beane's presence at the game was irrelevant to how the team was playing. People can sometimes be superstitious and believe that certain actions can causally influence the results of something. Coincidences happen, and they can seem uncanny. But unless we know of or have some reason to think there's a causal connection between the events, it is fallacious to assume, simply, one thing happens after something else.

8. False Equivalence

The *false equivalence fallacy* is committed when two things that may share some similarity are falsely equated as being the same in some other respect or in all respects.

Consider this argument:

1. There's evidence that John F. Kennedy was shot by a lone gunman from the book depository.
2. There's also evidence to suggest there were multiple gunmen, involving a government conspiracy.
3. Therefore, these are both equally rational to believe.

This is fallacious reasoning because, though there is some evidence for both of these, they are decidedly not equal in evidence. Just because the conspiratorial theory of multiple gunmen may have some evidence, it would be fallacious to think this makes these theories equally rational.

Sometimes this equivalence has an emotional component. Hitler was an evil person and committed unbelievable atrocities, but he did also lead a nation. So there will be some similarities between Hitler and virtually any other world leader. But just because a leader may share a similarity with Hitler obviously doesn't make that person morally equivalent to Hitler.

1. The president of the United States has introduced austerity measures.
2. Hitler also introduced austerity measures.
3. The president of the United States is basically Hitler.

The fact that the president of the United States and Hitler both instituted austerity measures is irrelevant to their moral equivalence. Equating the president of the United States with Hitler in this case is obviously fallacious reasoning.

This last example is reminiscent of a fallacy sometimes referred to as *reductio ad hitlerum.* If we were to make a "worst person of history list," Adolf Hitler would almost certainly rank at, or near, the top. This, in turn, makes for a unique way of responding rhetorically (and fallaciously) to arguments. Again, no one wants to be equated with Hitler or his actions. The reductio ad hitlerum fallacy, coined by Leo Strauss, is where one draws a parallel between a person's view or actions and Hitler and then acts like the view is therefore defeated because of this parallel. For example, in the movie *Office Space*, the main character, Peter, is trying to convince Joanna that her restaurant is evil because it makes the servers wear "flair." He says, "You know, the Nazis had pieces of flair that they made the Jews wear." It's of course a ridiculous argument but nicely illustrates an attempt to give a reductio ad hitlerum.

9. Gambler's Fallacy

Let's say you are flipping a coin, and you've gotten tails nine times in a row. You can't believe it. You realize that nine consecutive tails is highly improbable. You check to make sure it is a fair coin, and it is. Now ask yourself this question: What is the likelihood that the tenth flip will be heads? You are, after all, due to get a head, right? The *gambler's fallacy* is when one thinks the probability of some event is affected by previous events that have occurred when the two events are independent. If you think the tenth flip is more likely to be heads than tails, then you are guilty of the gambler's fallacy. This is because the probability of getting heads is the same on the tenth flip as it was on the first flip: it's always 1 out of 2 or 50/50 for each flip (again, on the assumption that we are dealing with a fair coin). This is because the likelihood of each flip is independent of the previous flips, so it doesn't matter how many times in a row you get tails. The likelihood of getting heads (or tails) is always 50/50.

Here an example of the gambler's fallacy:

1. In playing cards, I have gotten ten bad hands in a row.
2. Therefore, I should bet it all on the next hand since I'm due for a winner.

We should note that a series of independent events can be very unlikely when the aim is getting some specific event. So if we set up a game using coin flips where you win if you get three heads in a row and you lose if you get anything else, then the likelihood of getting the winning combination of three coin flips is 1/8 (1/2 x 1/2 x 1/2). Thus the likelihood of losing is quite a bit higher in this case because there are more ways to lose (seven ways, in fact) and only one way to win. However, the likelihood of getting any other single combination of coin flips is all the same (i.e., 1/8). Getting three heads in a row is no more unlikely than getting a heads-tails-heads, tails-tails-heads, or tails-tails-tails combinations.

Or take getting a winning hand in cards. Typically, a winning hand is far less likely because, in most card games, there are many more ways to have a losing hand than a winning hand. For example, you are far more likely to get a losing hand in poker than, say, a royal flush. However, every specific hand in poker is equally likely, which happens to be 1/2,598,960. So, if someone gets a royal flush, is this unlikely? Yes, it is extremely unlikely. But it's actually no more unlikely than any other specific hand. So, when we think the likelihood of our next hand will be anything greater than 1/2,598,960 given the course of our previous hands, then we've committed the gambler's fallacy.

10. Argument from Silence

It is sometimes said that the absence of evidence is not necessarily evidence of absence. Just because we don't have evidence for something, and especially a certain desired kind of evidence, it doesn't mean the event didn't occur. To think so is to commit the *argument from silence fallacy*. If someone is on trial for a crime, and let's say there are no eyewitnesses, it certainly doesn't mean the person did not commit the crime. If there is no evidence at all, the person is going to go free given the presumption of innocence in our legal system. Even still, that doesn't mean that the person did not commit the crime; it just means they cannot be held legally accountable.

Similarly, when something lacks a certain kind of evidence, it doesn't follow that the thing doesn't exist or that the event didn't happen. The Bible records a number of stories not recorded in any other historical works of the time. This is often taken to be evidence that the event was fabricated or that the event is some kind of myth. But these are arguments from silence. It often goes something like this:

1. The Bible records a certain event.
2. There are no nonbiblical records of this event.
3. Therefore, it did not happen.

This is a fallacious argument from silence from nonbiblical or secular records, as it stands, since the conclusion is inadequately supported. Ancient historians (and many contemporary ones) were often quite selective in what they chose to record. This is also true when we tell stories. What seems relevant to one person will perhaps seem irrelevant to another. In fact, most historians were never aiming to give an exhaustive account and often had very limited resources. So they left out details.

In any case, as it is, arguments like these do not provide strong reasons to think the events did not occur. This absence of secular evidence is not necessarily evidence of absence. In many cases, the lack of secular evidence should be expected. Why should, for example, a Persian, Egyptian, or Roman historian care about what is going on in Palestine given that it is relatively small and out of the way? You would expect people who were close to the events to be interested in chronicling the events, and that's exactly what we have in the Bible. One would have to do more than point to the silence from nonbiblical historians to argue that events described in the Bible did not happen.

11. Genetic Fallacy

Our reasons for holding a view may be quite different from the source from which we originally learned it. For example, imagine someone who came to believe in the truth of Christianity because her parents pressured her into it. However, let's say this person goes on to study apologetics and theology, and she devotes her life to believing in the truth of Christianity in a rational way. The fact that her parents pressured her into believing has become really quite irrelevant. It is what initiated the belief, perhaps, but it is certainly not the evidential basis upon which she now believes.

To criticize a person (or a view) for the origin of the view is to be guilty of the *genetic fallacy*. It is fallacious both to criticize someone for where he or she first got the view, and it is fallacious to criticize a view for its actual origin (e.g., critiquing a view because it was first believed by people who lived in a prescientific age). This is a fallacy because the origin of the view or the origin of how one first came to have a view is irrelevant to the rational basis of the view.

Here's an example of this fallacy:

1. You are a Christian because you were born in the Bible Belt.
2. If you had been born in Indonesia, you would likely be a Muslim.
3. Therefore, your Christian belief is suspect.

The argument is fallacious since where the view comes from is irrelevant to whether the person has good reasons to hold to the view. You could point out to the person giving this argument that if he had been born in Indonesia, then he would also likely be a Muslim. Does that make this person's view suspect as well? The point is that we should evaluate someone's position and reasons offered and not simply how the view originated. Now, if it turns out the person holds the view merely because of where the person grew up, then it is of course not an instance of the fallacy. But, for the most part, people have additional reasons (even if not strong) for holding to their views.

12. Strawman

When in a discussion with someone who believes differently from us, we are not always good at accurately representing the other person's view. Sometimes this is an unintentional mistake. However, when we purposefully misrepresent someone's view in either an oversimplified or an exaggerated form that is easily dismissed or argued against, then we are guilty of the *strawman fallacy*. It is as if we have constructed a view that may resemble the view (as a strawman resembles a real person), but it is not the real thing and is easily toppled.

Here's an example of a strawman fallacy:

Jones: "I believe in historic Christianity."
Smith: "I think it is ridiculous that you believe in an invisible bearded guy in the sky."

A strawman is easily seen as irrelevant to the view one is critiquing because it literally isn't the view one is critiquing. No serious Christian believes that God is a bearded guy in the sky. This is merely a strawman. We should note that sometimes people have radical beliefs, and it is not a strawman to represent those beliefs. The point is that we should do that as accurately as we can. It's often helpful to have the person with whom you are dialoguing specifically lay out the view and ask clarifying questions before we begin critiquing the view.

We should also strive to offer what's sometimes called a "steelman" of a view we are looking to criticize. Here we do the opposite of the strawman. To steelman a view is to present the most plausible version of someone's view. It can sometimes happen in conversation that someone will either misspeak or hold to a view that is easily defeated. Rather than simply defeating a weak view, we should steelman the view. That is, we should point out how the view could be made stronger and more plausible. We may still argue against the view, but we'll be focused on the most plausible versions of the view we are critiquing.

Fallacies of Inadequate Support

13. Ad Hoc

Little invisible fairies can explain anything. Consider the following:

> My car keys are nowhere to be found.
> Little fairies took and hid them.
>
> Yes, I realize my car was going twenty miles per hour over the speed limit.
> It was little fairies who caused my foot to be heavy on the gas pedal.
>
> This apple just fell to the ground.
> Gravity? No, it was little fairies who flew up and pulled the apple to the ground.

Little invisible fairies have explanatory power. We should notice that these fairy explanations can make sense of every detail that needs explaining. It can always just be that fairies did it. The problem of course is that no independent reason exists to think that little invisible fairies are conspiring in the world to do these things. That is, the appeal to fairies does explain the data, but there is literally nothing else going for the explanation other than that. If we have good reason to think that fairies exist, and we have compelling evidence that they often steal car keys, then we may be justified in inferring they took the keys. However, absent these independent reasons, the appeal to fairies is ad hoc. The ad hoc fallacy is when a claim (or theory) has no independent reasons beyond the mere fact that the claim explains the data. There are no compelling reasons to believe that fairies exist, and even if they do, there is no reason to believe they are responsible for any of these instances.

Conspiracy theories are often ad hoc. When someone explains the facts of a situation on the basis of aliens or some deep government takeover bid, the theories usually explain the data fairly well. The problem is that we have no independent reasons to believe that they are true and often have good reasons to reject them. If that's the case, then an argument that employs ad hoc conspiracy theories should be considered weak.

A common response to arguments for God's existence is to claim that the Christian is guilty of a God-of-the-gaps argument. This argument is when someone merely inputs God's existence into a gap in our knowledge in an ad hoc way. So, for example, let's say we notice that our universe is finely tuned for human existence and we ask why. The theist will say that God and his creative work is the explanation for this fine-tuning. But the critic will often assert that it is ad hoc for the theist to simply plug God into the gap of our knowledge.

It is possible that Christians are, at times, guilty of positing a God of the gaps in an ad hoc way. However, many arguments for God's existence are not God of the gaps. That is, they are not set up to say that the inference to God is on the basis of what we don't know (i.e., a gap) but on the basis of what we do know (e.g., fine-tuning). We also have independent reasons for believing in the existence of God because there are multiple independent lines of argument for the evidence of God.

14. Slippery Slope

A *slippery slope fallacy* is when an unwarranted logical jump is made in a series of cause-and-effect statements. Typically, the problem is the connection between the causes and the effects is often rather weak, which then adds up to making the chain of inference extremely weak. These often have the form of hypothetical syllogism:

1. P leads to Q.
2. Q leads to R.
3. R leads to S.
4. Therefore, if P, then S.

Here's an example of an argument with a slippery slope fallacy:

1. Electing this political candidate will lead to the world hating us.
2. If the world hates us, it's only a matter of time before nations around us are provoked.
3. If nations around us are provoked, then eventually we will be attacked.
4. Therefore, if we elect this political candidate, then another nation will attack us.

A slippery slope argument resembles a hypothetical syllogism. But since they are weak causal statements, the premises do not adequately support the conclusion. This can be nicely illustrated with a DirectTV commercial (adapted slightly to show the logical form):

1. If you have cable, then when you call the cable company, you are going to be put on hold.
2. When your cable company puts you on hold, you get angry.
3. When you get angry, you go blow off steam (by playing racquetball).
4. When you go blow off steam, an accident happens (such as being hit in the eye with a racquetball).

5. When accidents happen, you get an eye patch from the doctor.
6. When you get an eye patch, people think you are tough.
7. When people think you are tough, they want to see how tough.
8. When people want to see how tough, you wake up in a roadside ditch.
9. Don't wake up in a roadside ditch.
10. Get rid of cable and upgrade to DirectTV (i.e., this is the denial of the antecedent of premise 1).

The genius of the commercial is the humor. We all immediately see that the argument is ridiculously fallacious. There's virtually no chance that having cable will lead to you finding yourself in a roadside ditch. But why? Because it is commits the slippery slope fallacy. It makes tenuous connections out of the string of causal statements. Though there may be a slight chance of some of these things occurring, cumulatively the argument makes a major leap, and thus, the conclusion is (hilarious but) wildly unsupported.

15. Composition

The *fallacy of composition* is when we think that because something is true of the parts of something, it is true of the whole. For example:

1. The greatest basketball players in the league have joined up on the same team.
2. Therefore, they will be the greatest team.

This argument is clearly fallacious because, as we have seen many times in sports, the greatest individual players do not often make the greatest team. That is, an individual being a great basketball player doesn't necessarily extend to the team's greatness. Just ask the 2004 US Olympic basketball team, which easily had the best roster of any team in the world, with the likes of Tim Duncan, Allen Iverson, and a young LeBron James. In the first round, they were defeated by Puerto Rico, losing by 19 points. They went on to lose two more times to teams whose individual players were, for the most part, not even close to the individual talent on team USA. Those teams just played better together.

Now, there are times when something that is true of the parts is, in fact, true of the whole. If all of the building material for a wall is colored red, then the wall itself (as a whole) will be red. But if the bricks are all circular, it doesn't follow that the wall will be circular. The circularity of the bricks is an example of the fallacy of composition.

What's the difference? When can something true of the parts give us reason to think it is true of the whole, and when is it the fallacy?

The answer is that it is the fallacy when the property of the parts is not extendable to the whole. The color of the bricks is extendable to the color of the wall, but the shape of each brick is clearly not. What makes a team a great basketball team is not the same thing that makes a player individually great. Individual greatness is not necessarily extendable to the whole. Some players really shine when they are the only superstar on the team; they may play selfishly and score a lot of points. But if you have a team of selfish players, then the team members will constantly be competing with one another, and this is a recipe for disaster. A good team needs to be one in which each player supports the others' talents, possibly playing more minor roles.

Thus, to rationally infer that something true of the parts is true of the whole, we must know the property is extendable. If we know this, then we can rationally conclude the property is had by the whole on the basis of it being had by the parts. But if we don't, then the inference is guilty of the fallacy of composition.

16. Division

The flip side of the fallacy of composition is the *fallacy of division*. In fact, it is the converse of the fallacy of composition. The error in reasoning for the fallacy of division is when something true of the whole is inferred to be true of a part.

Here's an example:

1. Jones is the starting point guard on the greatest basketball team in the league.
2. Therefore, Joe is the greatest point guard in the league.

From the fact that there is something true of a whole, it doesn't follow that this same thing is true of a component part. Again, great teams are often made of players who figure out how to play well with one another. The starting point guard on the greatest team will likely be a good player but certainly may not be the best in the league.

Just like the fallacy of composition, there are times in which a property had by the whole is also had by the parts. Once again, when one knows that the property of the whole is due to that property being had by the component parts (e.g., the color of a brick wall will be the color of each brick), then this is a legitimate inference. But if property is not extendable from the parts to the whole, then this is the fallacy of division.

17. Confirmation Bias

We are guilty of *confirmation bias* when we (often subconsciously) select certain evidence that merely confirms our opinions or biases while ignoring other relevant evidence.

For example:

1. I prefer study X that shows flossing is not necessary to maintain dental health (ignoring the thousands of other studies that show flossing to be greatly beneficial to dental health).
2. Therefore, flossing is not necessary to maintain dental health.

The problem here is that there may be some study out there that calls into question the benefits of flossing, but there are thousands of other studies that show just the opposite. This looks like a person who wants to avoid flossing with a clear conscience, and they have confirmed this bias. When there's a confirmation bias fallacy, the conclusion may seem to us as if it is supported by the premise, but it only looks reasonable if one ignores all the evidence to the contrary. Just because one study out of thousands gets the result you want, it doesn't mean your claim is, all things considered, rational to believe. It is inadequately supported.

Confirmation bias occurs rather often in ideological debates. We are very soft on the arguments of people who share our view and then very hard on the arguments of people with whom we disagree. For example, many arguments for Christian truths are quite compelling, but if we find *all* (literally all) arguments for Christian truths compelling, then it is likely we are at some point guilty of confirmation bias. It seems unlikely that every argument is a good one. For example, arguments for the reliability of Scripture based on Jesus's fulfilling messianic prophecies often seem, by themselves, weak arguments. In John 19:31–36, the Roman soldiers did not break Christ's legs while he hung on the cross because he was already dead. This is said to fulfill Ps 34:20, which includes, "Not one of [his bones] is broken." This is a powerful theological point, but it is not going to convince someone who doesn't already believe that Scripture is reliable. This, at most, shows that John claimed Jesus fulfilled the prophecy, not that he actually did. We need to be intellectually honest in cases like this to admit when an argument or line of evidence is weak even if it would otherwise support our view.

18. Bandwagon

It is not always easy to go against popular opinion. But as difficult as it may be, it is clear that popular opinion can be wrong. In our country alone, a majority of people have, at times, thought women should not have the right to vote, that racial minorities did not deserve equal civil rights with whites, that it is morally permissible to own humans as slaves, and so forth. The fact that most people believed these things did not (and does not today) give us good reason to believe them. Mark Twain once wisely advised, "Whenever you find yourself on the side of the majority, it is time to . . . pause and reflect."[2]

The *bandwagon fallacy* (also known as *argumentum ad populum*) is when we appeal to the mere fact that many people believe something as a reason to think it is true. It is a fallacy because majority opinion, by itself, doesn't increase the probability of a claim. Majorities can often be given to emotional sway. When something gets to a popular level, the claim is often a pale reflection of what reasonable people believe, and so we need reasons beyond this to adequately support the conclusion.

The bandwagon fallacy is of course different from the consensus opinion of experts, which is supposed to be an *informed* position of a majority of experts who have converged on a single view. Now, this isn't to say scholars and experts are completely immune to bandwagon arguments. They can definitely jump on the bandwagon from time to time. However, when there is a wide convergence of expert opinions, then this may give us some reason to believe the conclusion.

19. Begging the Question

The following argument is, strictly speaking, valid:

1. P
2. Therefore, P

Notice if the premise is true, then it of course follows that the conclusion is true because, well, they are precisely the same claim. The problem is that this is completely unconvincing. It is technically valid (and potentially sound), but the premise provides inadequate support—as in no support—for the conclusion because the premise simply repeats the conclusion.

An argument commits the fallacy of *begging the question* (also known as *petitio principii*) when the truth of the premises already assumes the truth of

[2] Mark Twain, *Notebook* (1904).

the conclusion. Many arguments that beg the question require us to believe the conclusion *in order to* believe one or more of the premises. It is, in this sense, circular. In a good argument, we want the premises to stand on their own and provide independent reasons to believe the conclusion. Take, for example, modus ponens. We don't have to believe "Q" (the conclusion) in order to believe "If P, then Q" and "P" (the premises). It goes the other way. We would believe the conclusion *because* we believe the premises. But if, in an argument, the only reason to believe the premises is if we already believe the conclusion is true, then the argument is clearly question begging.

Here's an argument that's question begging but less obviously than the argument above:

1. The Bible says that God exists.
2. The Bible should be believed because God wrote it and he can't lie.
3. Therefore, God exists.

This begs the question because premise 2 clearly assumes the truth of the conclusion. Notice we couldn't, in principle, believe both premises without already believing the conclusion.

Here's another argument that is question begging:

1. All religion is simply the product of evolutionary desires for survival.
2. Therefore, all religions are false.

This argument is clearly question begging because premise 1 already assumes that all religions are false. The only way for the claim "All religion is the product of evolutionary desires for survival" to be true is if we already think "All religions are false." If we believe that a particular religion actually describes reality (i.e., isn't false), then we don't believe that all religion is the product of evolutionary desires for survival. That is, the only reason to believe premise 1 is that we believe the conclusion is false.[3]

[3] We should note that occasionally people will say that something begs the question where they do not mean that a conclusion is assumed by a premise. For example,

20. Complex Question

A *complex question* is when one's answering a question straightforwardly has unfairly forced one to admit something. A complex question usually looks like it requires a simple yes or no. However, no matter what the person answers (either yes or no), then the answer implies things the person isn't intending to say. The classic example of a complex question is the following:

Have you stopped beating your wife?

This question asks for a yes or a no. However, if you say yes, then it implies you were previously beating your wife. But if you say no, then this affirms you are currently guilty of spousal abuse. This question is complex since if you are innocent of spousal abuse, then there's no way to directly answer the question without admitting something you hadn't intended to admit.

Now, a complex question by itself is not a fallacy because it is a question and not a statement. Only statements can, properly speaking, be a premise in an argument. However, when a premise is based on a complex question, this is where it becomes a fallacy. It could look something like this:

Jones: "Have you stopped wasting your time going to church every Sunday morning?"
Smith: "No."
Jones: "Since you've agreed it's a waste of time, you therefore shouldn't go."
Smith: "Wait, what?"

---

a politically conservative candidate may say to the progressive candidate, "You may promise to provide free health care, free college tuition, cancel all student loan debt, but this begs the question, How are you going to pay for all of this?" Here someone is asserting that something provocative or undefined requires further explication. This is simply a different turn of phrase and not the begging the question fallacy.

The proper response to a complex question is to not answer the question directly and instead reject what's being implied. For example:

> **Jones:** "Have you stopped wasting your time going to church every Sunday morning?"
> **Smith:** "Church is not a waste of time, and yes, I still go!"

21. False Dilemma

Whenever we say something in the form of P or Q, we mean that one or the other of these is true. There's some other option R that is true, while P or Q are both false. The *false dilemma fallacy* is when one presents a disjunction as if it represents all of the options when it does not.

Imagine the following argument:

1. You can either vote Democrat or Republican.
2. The Democrat candidate is crazy and out of touch.
3. Therefore, you'll have to vote for the Republican.

This conclusion lacks adequate support because the disjunction has not exhausted all the options. Even though we have two major parties in this country, there are often third-party options. And it's of course possible to abstain from voting. So this is clearly a false dilemma.

Here is a disjunction that's given in the famous Euthyphro dilemma, which is one against God being related to morality:

> Either an action is morally good because it is commanded by God, or God commands the action because the action is morally good by some standard other than God.

This is a dilemma in the sense that both of the disjuncts seem to have problems. If an action is morally good because God commands it, then it seems morality is quite arbitrary. God can command anything at all (including random things or even what we consider immoral things), and then those things are morally good. But if God commands the action because the action is morally good, then God's commands are logically irrelevant to something's being morally good. The theist looks to be in a tough spot.

But this is a false dilemma. That is, there is a third option. It could be that an action is morally good by virtue of being grounded in God's moral character. On this option, it is not because he commanded it, and it is not because it is morally good by some other standard. But morality is related to God in that it is grounded in the character of God. This is a third option that avoids the problems.

22. Appeal to Authority

Obviously, it's not always bad to believe authorities, but sometimes it involves fallacious reasoning. In chapter 9, we discussed a nondeductively good argument form called the *argument from expert testimony*. Done properly, this argument form gives us a strong argument. However, we pointed out that not all appeals to authority constitute an argument from expert testimony.

The *appeal to authority fallacy* is when one appeals to an authority on an issue that can't be solved by a mere appeal to authority. For example, if we want to justify that Caesar crossed the Rubicon in 49 BC, we may appeal to the expert authority of a historian. Caesar's crossing the Rubicon, it seems, is a fairly straightforward historical fact. But if we want to justify the claim that God exists or that abortion is morally wrong, we couldn't simply appeal to some authority's opinion. This would be fallacious reasoning.

What makes for the difference?

We can't solve whether God exists simply on the basis of an appeal to an authority because this is a controversial issue. There are experts on both sides of the issue. The same is true with other issues—religious, moral, and political. When it comes to the date of Caesar crossing the Rubicon, this is a settled historical fact. However, if new evidence emerged and historians on ancient Rome became divided over the date of Caesar's crossing the Rubicon, then it would no longer be a matter of appealing to the expert's opinion.

23. Hasty Generalization

A *hasty generalization fallacy* occurs when one makes a generalization on a sample size that is too small. As we discussed in chapter 9, a "sample" is the set of representative instances used to say something about the whole. If we want to say something about a large group of things, it is often not feasible to inspect the group as a whole. We typically will look at a sampling of individuals in that group with the understanding that this will give us reasonable insight into the group as a whole. So if a news agency wants to know how many people in their state will vote for a certain political candidate, they can't feasibly interview every person in the state. Rather they will interview a sampling that will forecast what the larger group thinks of this candidate.

As discussed, the larger the sample size, the stronger the generalization. To say something about all Americans based on two or three instances would be incredibly hasty indeed. To say something about all Americans based on 200 or 300 instances would be better but still quite hasty given that more than 300 million people are Americans. A sampling of 2,000 or 3,000 (or more) selected randomly from different parts of the country will begin to give us an idea what Americans think.

Here's an example of a hasty generalization:

1. I have owned four Toyotas, and they have all been reliable cars.
2. Therefore, Toyotas are reliable cars.

Toyotas are popular vehicles, and many millions of Toyotas have been produced over its long history. Having a good experience with only four Toyotas is a woefully inadequate sample to conclude that Toyotas are, in general, reliable cars. This is a hasty generalization.

24. SPECIAL PLEADING

We are not always consistent. Sometimes we firmly believe in general principles, but from time to time, we make exceptions, especially exceptions for ourselves. When we inconsistently make exceptions for a view, we are guilty of *special pleading*. Here's an example:

1. All other religious texts should not be believed because they lack evidence.
2. But my religious text is self-authenticating, and therefore it is true with no need of evidence.

This is fallacious reasoning because one is exempting one's own view from needing any evidence. There is, of course, a sense in which the Bible is self-authenticating, but this is where the Bible itself bears witness (i.e., provides evidence) for believing that it is divinely inspired. It is not an exemption from needing evidence. Moreover, many who hold to a self-authenticating view of Scripture still think that historical evidence is helpful and important for seeing the Bible as divinely inspired.

Here's another example of special pleading:

1. Science has not figured out how to explain the beginning of the universe from nothing, but it will.
2. All religious views rely on faith in holding to its views and should, for that reason, be rejected.
3. Therefore, that there will, one day, be a scientific explanation of the beginning of the universe is preferable.

It's clear that there is special pleading here since this is an explicit use of faith in future scientific theories. If one was consistent in rejecting any view that relied on faith, then this view should be rejected as well. Instead, we should hold our own views up to the same criteria of evaluation.

25. Fallacy of the Beard

Let's say Smith is going to grow a beard and stops shaving. At what point has he become successful? At what point does unshaved stubble turn into a beard? It's not clear. But this shouldn't mean we can't know that, at some point, Smith does in fact have a beard.

There are many gradual processes where the two extremes of the process (let's call these A and B) are entirely distinct and easily identified, but there is not a definite point along the spectrum at which A suddenly turns into a B. It is easy to see the difference between having a full-grown beard and someone who has no beard. The *fallacy of the beard* occurs when we infer that, given this vagueness, we can't know if someone has a beard or not. We may not know precisely when one goes from not having a beard to having a beard, but this doesn't mean we can't know a good beard when we see it.

Here's another example:

1. Going one mile per hour over the speed limit isn't wrong.
2. In general, adding one more mile per hour to your current speed will not make your speed wrong.
3. Therefore, going forty miles per hour over the speed limit isn't wrong.

If premises 1 and 2 are true, then we can keep adding one mile per hour to our speed and eventually get to forty miles per hour. Obviously, this is a bad argument and not one I would suggest using to try to get out of a speeding ticket. Even if it is correct that adding one mile per hour doesn't generally make a difference in whether one is driving appropriately or inappropriately, it doesn't follow that we can't know when someone is being reckless.

Intellectual Virtues and the Art of Persuasion

We have surveyed the basics of logic and critical thinking. But there's no use having the tools of critical thinking without the skill or the ability to use them well. This would be like spending thousands of dollars to get a shed full of carpentry tools without any knowledge of how they work. Now, all of us have picked up a random tool with the good intention to learn to use it, but it can even be dangerous when we try to operate tools we don't know how to use. In a way, it can be dangerous to use logic in an unskilled way as well. When we try to use the tools of critical thinking without the skill of how to use them, we risk having false ideas, which can be a harm to ourselves and to others.

Discussing the skills or virtues of critical thinking is an ancient discussion. Aristotle outlined not only moral virtues, as many philosophers have done, but also intellectual virtues (how to live skillfully in the world in light of moral oughts). The Bible also has a lot to say on the topics of wisdom and reflection. But our focus will again be on Jesus, the embodiment of wisdom and intellectual virtue.

Jesus as Intellectually Virtuous

As we have emphasized throughout the book, people followed Jesus. This was, at times, because of his signs and wonders. But the majority of the time, it was his teaching that drew thousands of people to follow him. What about his teaching drew people in? The Bible tells us it was the authority of his teaching at which people were repeatedly astonished. Mark 1:21–22 says, "They went into Capernaum, and right away he entered the synagogue on the Sabbath and began to teach. They were astonished at his teaching because he was teaching them as one who had authority, and not like the scribes." What gave Jesus's teaching authority? He didn't teach like the scribes, who appealed to the authority of rabbinic tradition. Appealing to a rabbinic tradition was similar to a judge in our US legal system where an appeal to previous cases and judgments is made. Scribes quoted certain favored rabbis. Even the Old Testament prophets framed their speech with "thus saith the LORD" (KJV). But not Jesus. He said, "Truly I tell you." Now, any nutcase could say "truly I tell you," and of course that wouldn't alone give authority to what was said. But people were astonished and took Jesus to have authority. It seems there had to be some qualities about Jesus and his presentation that indicated his authority.

I would like to suggest that at least part of this had to do with Jesus's intellectual virtues. A virtue is an aspect of excellence that is had by someone or something. In chapter 10, we discussed theoretical virtues. These were virtues or excellences of a theory. But people can have certain excellences too, which can be characterized as a skill or ability. People can be morally virtuous, and they can be intellectually virtuous. A moral virtue has to do with actions and behavior. We live morally virtuous lives when our actions are morally excellent and skillfully aimed at living according to moral oughts. By contrast, an intellectual virtue has to do with knowing the truth. Having intellectual virtue is having habits and skills to be logically astute in ways that result in knowledge and truth.

Jesus perfectly exemplified intellectual virtue. His teaching was compelling because he was seen as someone who was offering truth and a knowledge of the world. It's not that people always understood what Jesus said. Indeed, as we have seen, even disciples left frustrated without understanding (e.g., John 6:60, 66). But, at the same time, his teaching was logically and biblically unassailable. The crowds saw what happened to others who tried to object to Jesus's teaching or to catch him in some logical trap. As we've already pointed out, Jesus was always logically and intellectually smarter.

Also, Jesus was always smarter biblically. Jesus regularly said, "it is written," and displayed a masterful use of Scripture throughout his ministry. He even, as we've seen, went head to head with and directly challenged the elite religious scholars and their familiarity and understanding of Scripture. For example, in Matt 19:3, the Pharisees tried to trap Jesus by asking whether divorce on any grounds was permissible. Jesus responded, "Haven't you read?" and quoted Gen 1:27 and 2:24. His point was to say the answer is clear in Scripture and that the religious scholars should know better. They were, it seems, duly put in their place.

In chapter 2, we looked at how Jesus displayed intellectual virtue. In this chapter, we zoom out and consider what he teaches us about the intellectual virtues we should display.

Having Ears to Hear

What's striking about much of Jesus's teaching is that it was designed for those with, as he put it, "ears to hear." Jesus wasn't trying to appeal to everyone. Instead he often intentionally obscured the meaning and point of what he was saying (e.g., when he taught in parables). This is striking because most teachers aim to be well understood. We tend to assume that Jesus wanted people to hear and understand his message. But the situation was a bit more complicated than that.

Why would Jesus teach in a purposefully obscured way? He taught using devices such as parables, in one sense, because he wasn't interested in merely communicating information. That is, Jesus wasn't in the business of tickling the ears of people who wanted only an inspiring moral message without calling them to make a change in their lives. Part of the intellectual brilliance of Jesus's teaching is that he taught to bring about actual conviction for people to thereby be changed. A parable makes us lean in and listen carefully with humble hearts to receive the underlying message. Sometimes Jesus's parables were so shocking and downright offensive (e.g., using a Samaritan, whom the Jews typically hated, as the hero of the parable of the good Samaritan in Luke 10:30–35) that audience members would have had to get over themselves to really get the message. So, Jesus was a great moral teacher in the strongest sense of these words. He wasn't after mere head knowledge but a heart knowledge or a moral knowledge applied to their lives. Therefore, he obscured the message so that only the humble hearted would have ears to hear.

We see this in Jesus's response to the Pharisees in Matthew 9, when they questioned why he ate with "tax collectors and sinners" (v. 11). Jesus responded, "It is not those who are well who need a doctor, but those who are sick. Go and learn what this means: I desire mercy and not sacrifice. For I didn't come to call the righteous, but sinners" (vv. 12–13). Even though the Pharisees may not have realized it, Jesus's answer was thick with sarcasm. The Pharisees cast these people into a lowly category not even worthy for Jesus to dine with; Jesus went with it for great effect. You obviously wouldn't spend time with sick people unless of course you were the doctor. It is not that, for Jesus, the Pharisees weren't themselves sinners in need of salvation, but Jesus acted as if this were the case. Why does Jesus spend his time with sinners? It is because these are the ones who know they are sinners and that they are in need of salvation. They have ears to hear. Whereas the Pharisees thought of themselves as righteous and without need. They simply weren't in a position to really listen.

The Pharisees and the other religious leaders displayed intellectual vice. They didn't have ears to hear, and because of this they were not open to seeing Jesus as Messiah. They literally had the Messiah in their midst, performing signs and wonders, offering good intellectual reasons to believe, and yet they rejected him and, along with others, crucified him. This is a clear picture of intellectual vice.

Unlike the religious leaders, we want to have ears to hear. So let's learn to listen to Jesus and listen for truth. Let's allow Jesus to teach us how to have ears to hear. In the following, we will outline four intellectual virtues that will lead us to knowledge and truth.

1. Open-Mindedness

Open-mindedness is probably not the virtue most people would readily associate with Jesus (or, at least, Christians). Christians are probably better known for being narrow-minded or even closed-minded. But I'd like to suggest a major aim of Jesus's ministry is to cultivate the intellectual virtue of open-mindedness in his followers. The Jews, and especially the religious leaders, were often closed-minded toward Jesus. He was not the Messiah the people expected. They thought the Messiah would primarily be a political leader. Jesus didn't fit the bill, and many people couldn't get past it.

We might say that being closed-minded is being narrowly stuck in what's called a *plausibility structure*. Though many competing ideas are out there, we get used to having our own ideas and beliefs. They become familiar to the extent that different ideas feel awkward and seem obviously false, even if we can't say why. This is a plausibility structure, which acts as something of a filter where certain familiar ideas seem automatically plausible (i.e., possibly or even probably true) and competing ideas seem implausible (seemingly false). Lesslie Newbigin understood a plausibility structure as "patterns of belief and practice accepted within a given society, which determine which beliefs are plausible to its members and which are not."[1]

The problem of course is that some unfamiliar ideas that strike us an implausible may be true. Rejecting everything that is out of step with our plausibility structure will undoubtedly cause us to reject something that's true. When we are unwilling to evaluate our plausibility structures, to the extent that we are resistant to considering even the possibility of an alternative view, we thereby have a closed mind, and a completely closed mind is an intellectual vice.

Jesus, in his subversive gospel message, aimed to break people out of their plausibility structures. This is again why he urged having ears to hear, without which people were apt to remain lost. Part of what it is to have ears to hear, is to have an open mind in the relevant sense. But we need to be careful here because, as Aristotle pointed out long ago, virtue is the mean between two extremes. We can lack a quality and we will then lack the virtue. But we can also have a quality in excess and therefore lack virtue. For Aristotle, the virtue is found in the intermediate between the extremes. Take courage, for example. If one acts cowardly, then one of course lacks courage. But if one acts rashly and takes unnecessary risks in the face of danger, then this is of course not to act virtuously. The excess of any virtue ironically becomes vice.

Open-mindedness can also be taken to a vicious extreme. Perhaps when we are beginning an inquiry or looking at a new topic, we will want to consider all possibilities equally. If we have no settled views on some matter, then it would be quite foolish to strongly prefer a particular view. We should be open to a variety of views as we begin to form our opinions. However, once we begin to settle on certain views, it would be a vicious extreme to continue to be completely open to all views. It seems our minds should begin to shut. That is, once we have surveyed and evaluated the most rational views on some matter, we should not stay completely open-minded any longer.

---

[1] Lesslie Newbigin, *The Gospel in a Pluralist Society* (Grand Rapids: Eerdmans, 1989), 8.

G. K. Chesterton once said, "An open mind is really a mark of foolishness, like an open mouth. Mouths and minds were made to shut; they were made to open only in order to shut."[2] This is perhaps a bit overstated but makes an important point. What we might call perpetual open-mindedness, where we never settle on the truth, is certainly not a virtue. To be open-minded to the extent we think all views are equally rational is not acting with intellectual virtue. As evidence comes, then it seems we should rule out the least rational and settle on the most rational view. It's not that we become thereby perpetually closed-minded to opposing views. New and better evidence should always get a hearing, and we should remain open to that possibility. It's just that since not all views are equally reasonable, especially after some rational inquiry, if a view proves to be false or irrational, then it seems to be a good idea (and extremely rational) to count that view out as likely unless there is new evidence to suggest a second look.

The virtue of open-mindedness, then, is the willingness to consider the possibility of all views in a sense of honestly considering the evidence presented for the view, even views that strike us as initially implausible. The reason we should be open-minded is, it's at least possible to be wrong in any one of our beliefs. By giving an opposing view a hearing, we may find that the opposing view turns out to be true. But even if we don't change our view, by taking seriously an opposing view, we are now able to show the opposing view to be false. That is, we have become even more rational in our beliefs, and this is why it is an intellectual virtue.

The mistake of many of the Jews in Jesus's day was that they had closed their minds so completely and absolutely that no amount of evidence would get them to reconsider. Jesus called for those with ears to hear not because he wants us to accept any idea that comes our way. Rather, he wants us to be willing to give him a hearing to demonstrate that he is who he claims to be.

It was really important for me, in my Christian journey, to have an open mind about alternative views. At one point in my life, I came to seriously

---

[2] G. K. Chesterton, *Illustrated London News*, October 10, 1908.

doubt my faith and the truth of Christianity. Consequently, I systematically considered as many alternative worldviews as I could. I tried to truly have an open mind and approach these without bias. In complete honesty, I found myself surprised at how badly supported non-Christian worldviews (including atheism and agnosticism) are compared to the support and evidence for Christianity. Many other religious views do not even think in terms of evidence and objectivity.

My mind came to be shut on Christianity. It would take quite a lot, at this point, to unseat my Christian intellectual commitments, but it is possible. I am open to hearing counterevidence and not simply dismissing it out of hand. Sure, I *could* change my mind, but it is not likely because I have been evaluating the evidence for a long time now and have found Christianity to be, by far, the most reasonable view. So here I am, I have been completely open-minded along the way, and I'm willing to reconsider; but at this point, I am largely shut on the truth of the Christian way.

2. Intellectual Prudence

The second intellectual virtue recommended in the life and teaching of Jesus is the virtue of *intellectual prudence*, which is being intellectually careful and discerning. Having intellectual prudence is doing our due diligence in forming our beliefs and discerning truth. In some ways, intellectual prudence is what balances open-mindedness. It's only after doing our due diligence that we may begin to close our minds on truth.

A theme that runs throughout the New Testament is to, as John put it, "test the spirits to see if they are from God" (1 John 4:1). Earlier John commended his readers to "let no one deceive you" (1 John 3:7), which is the same thing Jesus said in Matt 24:4: "Watch out that no one deceives you." Jesus is telling us, his followers, to be intellectually prudent in who we listen to. This same sort of attitude was expressed by those in Berea when they received the gospel from Paul and Silas. Acts 17:11 says, "The people [of Berea] were of more noble character than those in Thessalonica, since they received the word with eagerness and examined the Scriptures daily to see if these things were so." Unlike the Thessalonians, the Bereans received the word with eagerness. But it wasn't only eagerness; they exercised prudence in examining whether this message was indeed biblical.

At one point in his ministry, Jesus was about to send out his twelve disciples to do ministry for the first time. Jesus gave them an interesting charge: "Look, I'm sending you out like sheep among wolves. Therefore be as shrewd as serpents and as innocent as doves" (Matt 10:16). Now, we might expect Jesus to have urged his followers to be morally blameless (i.e., innocent as doves). To be guilty of sin, especially among those who were hostile, would have invalidated the disciples' ministry. But what did he mean in urging them to be as shrewd as serpents? Jesus was not commending deception to his disciples but encouraging them to be prudent in the midst of hostility. Just as Jesus had been persecuted in this work, the disciples would also be persecuted.

Jesus was saying that the disciples were to be careful because they would be vulnerable (like sheep) among those who would do them harm (the wolves). Things could go very badly for them. The idea, then, was that the disciples should be discerning and thoughtful in how they ministered to people because they could have made it needlessly worse on themselves, which would ultimately harm their gospel witness. It seems that the disciples should have never been ashamed or afraid to share the gospel, but to be belligerent in attempting to witness to the gospel was imprudent. Doing this would only get them locked up, and the gospel may not go out. Instead, the disciples needed to be strategic and shrewd in how they approached people with the gospel. But in all of it, they should of course have been blameless and innocent. They were going to encounter persecution no matter what, but they needed to be both cautious and discerning as well as innocent and blameless.

Intellectual prudence is largely what we've been advocating throughout the book. We should think critically and reflectively about life and especially about our Christian faith. This is a matter of intellectual prudence. The Bereans were described as being of noble character for their prudence. When we follow this example, we too may be virtuously prudent in having a well-grounded faith.

3. Intellectual Trust

The third intellectual virtue is *intellectual trust.* The Bible of course puts a high value on trust, especially as it relates to the concept of faith. Indeed, it is through faith that we are saved (Eph 2:8). The call of the gospel is to venture ourselves in trust in Christ and the reality of the gospel. We entrust ourselves to the fact that God loves us and sent his Son to die for us and rise from the dead, defeating death.

Though faith in Christ is certainly not a purely intellectual exercise, it of course involves intellectual trust, which is when we depend on a reliable guide in a way that leads us to truth. We need good guides in life to direct us. We would be lost if we didn't have sources upon which we can depend for leading us to truth. Chances are, most inquiries would end in abject failure were we to go about it alone. Imagine you want to build a bridge over a one-hundred-foot span, and the bridge must be sturdy enough for a car to drive over. But suppose you are not allowed to use any advice from people, books, or instructional materials. Though this is a relatively simple engineering feat, it would take most of us a lifetime of trial and error to get it right—and some of us would never succeed. Without having sources of advice and instruction that we can trust, our knowledge would be greatly diminished.

Now, it is always possible that we get bad advice and instruction. We can, at times, be overly trusting and intellectually gullible. Again, this is the idea that any virtue when taken to an extreme becomes something of a vice. If we are building a bridge, we shouldn't, for example, put equal trust in an expert bridge engineer and a guy who has never built anything in his life. The one will have the experience of building many different bridges (having undoubtedly trusted in the advice of others in prior experiences of bridge building), and the other will have, if you are lucky, driven over a few bridges along the way. One of these deserves our trust, and the other does not. So we shouldn't trust just anybody. We need some reason to believe that a source is trustworthy and a reliable guide to truth.

Jesus, himself, is a reliable guide, or so I would argue. The Bible is, at least, clear on this issue as it repeatedly calls us to believe in Jesus. In fact, the most famous verse in the Bible, John 3:16, says, "For God loved the world in this way: He gave his one and only Son, so that everyone who *believes in* him will not perish but have eternal life" (emphasis added). Believing *in* Jesus seems importantly different from merely believing some facts about Jesus are true. Believing in Jesus is where we place our trust in him. And, again, this involves an intellectual trust. Jesus promises it this way: "If you continue in my word, you really are my disciples. You will know the truth, and the truth will set you free" (8:31–32). He is a source of truth since he is, after all, "the way, the truth, and the life" (14:6).

Now, I realize the fact that Jesus claims to be a reliable guide doesn't necessarily make Jesus a reliable guide. I don't have the space here to give a full defense of why we should intellectually trust Jesus. But if he is who he claims to be, then Jesus is the ideal guide and we will find in him, just as countless followers of Christ before us, "the words of eternal life" (John 6:68).

Who did Jesus intellectually trust? Jesus almost exclusively appeals to (and, by implication, trusts) the Word of God throughout his ministry. A clear example of this is when the devil tempted Jesus in the wilderness (Matt 4:1–11). For each temptation, Jesus responded by quoting Scripture, saying, "it is written." Here is the final temptation: "Again, the devil took him to a very high mountain and showed him all the kingdoms of the world and their splendor. And he said to him, 'I will give you all these things if you will fall down and worship me.' Then Jesus told him, 'Go away, Satan! For it is written: Worship the Lord your God, and serve only him.'" As attractive as it may have been to have all the kingdoms of the world handed to him, Jesus appealed to, and thereby trusted, the Word of God. Scripture is of course an expert source of truth given that it is the inspired Word of God. One will find no greater guide or instructions on life and spiritual matters.

Jesus also instituted his church (Matt 16:18). The biblical view of the church is one with overseeing elders at the lead (1 Tim 3:1–7; Titus 1:5–9). One of the primary roles of an elder is to teach and pass on sound doctrine to the rest of the church (2 Tim 2:1). Thus, the structure of the church is one of discipleship. The idea is that Jesus is the head of the church. But Jesus had his disciples, and those disciples were commissioned to make disciples, teaching them the way of Jesus (Matt 28:19–20). And this process of discipleship continues today in the local church. The point is, we are to intellectually trust and be guided by the elders in our church and those more mature around us.

We are not, of course, called to blind trust. Again, the virtue of intellectual trust can be overdone to a vicious extreme. We must exercise prudence in choosing the sources in which we trust. But once we have good reason to trust a source, we can be guided to truth.

4. Intellectual Courage

The fourth intellectual virtue we'll consider here is the virtue of *intellectual courage*. Jesus was upfront about what his followers will face in this life. In John 15:18–20, he said, "If the world hates you, understand that it hated me before it hated you. If you were of the world, the world would love you as its own. . . . If they persecuted me, they will also persecute you." Once again this means more than just our intellectual commitments, but it is certainly not less than our intellectual commitments. Now, if you are a Christian in name only and don't *really* believe that the claims of the Bible are true, then you will likely do just fine. As Jesus put it, the world will love you as its own. Of course, if this is the case, it's not clear why you are identifying as a Christian in the first place.

But for those of us who really believe the claims of Christianity, we will face hostility, and we are called to face down the challenge of persecution. This is a bit of an understatement, but traditional Christian claims are not exactly popular today. In fact, when it comes to the claims on marriage, sexuality, gender, the exclusivity of the gospel, and so on, the world is downright hostile. Staying consistent with the way of Jesus will require the virtue of intellectual courage—when we maintain our intellectual commitments, on the basis of good reasons, in the face of challenge and social pressure. This is an intellectual virtue because simply giving in to social pressure is a really bad way to find truth. What's socially accepted changes constantly. If we try to match with what is socially acceptable, we'll have to change our beliefs so many times it will be hard to keep track.

This is not, of course, to say we shouldn't ever change our beliefs when challenged. If we exemplify the virtue of open-mindedness, then we will give a hearing to challenges and occasionally this will call for us to adjust our views. But if we are changing our beliefs simply because there is social pressure to fit in with others, then this is intellectual vice. The challenge must be a good one, and if we change beliefs, it should be only because it is rational to do so. The opposite of intellectual courage is the one who is "tossed by the waves and blown around by every wind of teaching, by human cunning with cleverness in the techniques of deceit" (Eph 4:14). Paul likened this to being a child who is easily influenced by others. The apostle Peter failed at intellectual courage. When Jesus told the disciples they would all fall away, Peter claimed, "Even if everyone falls away because of you, I will never fall away" (Matt 26:33). Jesus corrected him and said that Peter would in fact deny him three times that very night. Peter responded, "Even if I have to die with you . . . I will never deny you" (v. 35), Though Peter took a valiant swing at one of the servants, he soon afterward straightforwardly denied being a follower of Jesus three times. Peter was of course restored and, from what we know from the book of Acts and of history, never again denied Christ. In fact, when Peter was threatened with jail and possible death if he and the other apostles didn't stop teaching in the name of Jesus, he boldly told the religious leaders, "We must obey God rather than people" (Acts 5:29). Peter found his courage!

In recent years, some high-profile, Christian leaders have come out in support of culturally mainstream views that run against biblical Christianity. These moves away from traditional Christianity are sometimes hailed as courageous. But it is difficult to characterize as courageous giving up the traditional Christian beliefs that are so often ridiculed by a wide majority of the culture. The point is that it's a bit strained to consider embracing the majority view as courageous. It is in a minority view, especially when it must be held in the face of social pressure and even possible persecution, where we see intellectual courage.

Like the other virtues, intellectual courage can be taken to an extreme. Intellectual courage can turn into intellectual stubbornness when we no longer have, on balance, more reason to hold to our beliefs than to reject them. When we have performed our due diligence (i.e., exercised prudence), and it becomes obvious that the evidence for our belief is lacking, then intellectual courage actually dictates that we bravely change our view no matter who this will disappoint. We must, as Socrates urged his interlocuter, follow the evidence wherever it leads.[3] Now, for important and consequential beliefs, we should take our time with this process. It can seem, in a moment, as if we lack sufficient evidence for our view when we are facing a difficult objection and are perhaps experiencing doubt. The reality may be that when we take a step back (and a deep breath), we are quite rational despite having an objection or two we are struggling to answer.

The Art of Persuasion

We are sometimes given the impression that our job, as Christians, is to simply announce the gospel, and if there's not a positive response, we move on, knocking the dust from our footwear. With the intellectual virtues, we aim to become good at knowing. We also aim to be able to persuade. In many ways, these are two sides of the same coin. When we hold our ideas with intellectual virtue, then likely we will be able to persuade others along the way. Still, sometimes we keep these things to ourselves or only speak to those who agree with our Christian convictions. I'd like to suggest that part of fulfilling the Great Commission (Matt 28:18–20) is persuading people of the truth of Christianity.

---

[3] The line from Socrates in Plato's *Republic* is "we must follow the argument wherever, like a wind, it may lead us"; Plato, *Republic*, trans. G. M. A. Grube (Indianapolis: Hackett, 1974), 394d.

Now, let's be clear. It is only the gospel that has the power to save (Rom 1:16). No amount of persuasive argument can ever change the human heart. Most people do not have, most fundamentally, an intellectual problem with being a Christian. It is a heart problem. People suppress the truth and the reality of God; for that reason, Paul tells us, all people are without excuse (Rom 1:18–20). If this is true, then why should we be concerned about persuasion?

Here are three reasons we should develop the skills of persuasion.

First, Jesus used persuasion. When we look at the life and ministry of Jesus, we see a clear precedent for persuading people of the truth of who he is and that people should submit their lives to God in faith. We have already looked at the variety of ways in which Jesus rebutted challenges with insightful arguments. While many religious leaders remained stubborn in their hearts toward Jesus's message, there's little doubt some were persuaded of his claims.

Jesus also made positive arguments to persuade. In Mark 2, a paralytic man was lowered through the roof of a house in which Jesus was teaching. Jesus turned to the paralytic and said, "Son, your sins are forgiven" (v. 5). We are not told in the passage why this man's friends took such drastic measures to get him in front of Jesus, but it likely was not for the forgiveness of his sins. But it was the religious leaders who were the most taken aback. They said in their hearts, "Why does he speak like this? He's blaspheming! Who can forgive sins but God alone?" (v. 7). Everyone (including the paralytic) was thinking that Jesus should just heal this guy and stop talking about forgiving sins.

Now, Jesus could have just obliterated these guys. He could have smoked them with lightning from heaven, and everyone would have known that Jesus had the authority to forgive sins. But he didn't. He attempted to persuade.

Jesus said, "Which is easier: to say to the paralytic, 'Your sins are forgiven,' or to say, 'Get up, take your mat, and walk'?" (v. 9). We should note that the answer to this question is not as clear as we might first think. In one sense, it is clearly more difficult to forgive sins. As these religious leaders rightly asked, who can do this but God himself? But, in a way, it is easier to *say* "your sins are forgiven" because if this is true we wouldn't necessarily be able to see that it is. What would be the visible manifestation of his sins having been forgiven? On the other hand, we may think it is easier to heal someone of paralysis than it is to forgive sins, because a healing is merely physical, whereas forgiving sins is a spiritual state involving our standing with God. But it is harder to *say* this because it will be clear whether the person is healed; he will be able to take up his mat and walk home.

We can imagine these religious leaders being unsure of how to answer the question. But Jesus put his words to action and healed the paralytic. And, with this action, given the argument, he showed them in no uncertain terms his authority to forgive sins.

Here is the argument:

1. If Jesus heals the paralytic, then Jesus is God and able to forgive sins.
2. Jesus heals the paralytic.
3. Therefore, Jesus is God and able to forgive sins.

Once again, Mark gives us the familiar refrain "they were all astounded" (v. 12). In this instance, they were of course astounded, in part, by the miracle. But the context of the miracle mattered. People expected to see a miracle. Jesus claimed to forgive the man's sins and then proved his ability to forgive by the miracle. This claim to forgive caused offense and charges of blasphemy. But Jesus showed persuasively who he really is by giving them what they expected in the first place.

Now Jesus is a hard act to follow. He is of course God and able to use a miracle as evidence for the truth of the claims he makes. It's not easy to emulate that method. But the point remains that Jesus, in his ministry, aims to persuade and this gives us reason to value persuasion in the way of Jesus.

The second reason we have for developing the art of persuasion is that we see persuasion is in the ministry of the apostles. The apostles, at times, also performed miracles, in the power of the Holy Spirit. But this was not usual. They more often made arguments either on the basis of Jesus's works or on the basis of how Jesus perfectly fits the Old Testament predictions of the Messiah. Peter used the fact of the resurrection of Jesus to argue that Jesus was indeed "both Lord and Messiah" (Acts 2:36), and Philip persuaded the Ethiopian that the Isaiah passage he happened to be reading was about Jesus (Acts 8:26–35).

None of the apostles, however, displayed the art of persuasion as obviously and as often as the apostle Paul. In Acts 17, while on his second missionary journey, Paul arrived in Thessalonica. Acts 17:2–3 says, "As usual, Paul went into the synagogue, and on three Sabbath days reasoned with them from the Scriptures, explaining and proving that it was necessary for the Messiah to suffer and rise from the dead: 'This Jesus I am proclaiming to you is the Messiah.'" We should notice a few things about this passage. First, Paul's *usual* custom was to visit the Jewish synagogue and reason with the Jews to persuade them that Jesus was indeed the Messiah. Second, the authority of persuasion that Paul appealed to is the Hebrew Scriptures (i.e., the Old Testament). Why did Paul use the Hebrew Scriptures? It is because this is what the Jews found to be persuasive—the Old Testament was their spiritual authority. If Paul began quoting Greek philosophers, for example, the Thessalonican Jews would have chased him out of the city even sooner than they actually did.

This experience in Thessalonica stands in sharp contrast to Paul's layover in Athens a few stops later (Acts 17:16–34). In Athens, Paul was able to get in front of Epicurean and Stoic philosophers who, to hear what he had to say, took him to the Areopagus, a large outcropping of rocks in Athens where philosophical and legal matters were discussed and debated.

What's interesting here is that Paul, in his speech, did not explicitly appeal to the Old Testament Scriptures. Though he normally appealed to the Scriptures, in this case, he did not. Why? We need to keep in mind who he was talking to. He wasn't talking to Jews but to Greek philosophers. If Paul had tried to make a case out of the Old Testament, like he had in Thessalonica with the Jews, the Athenians wouldn't have given him the time of day. Paul was being persuasive as he appealed to some of their "own poets" and philosophers. Paul was intellectual enough to know what these philosophers believed to the extent that he was seemingly able to quote from their literature off the top of his head. This alone embodies the principles taught in this book. What we see is that Paul packaged the same basic message (that is, the gospel) he had been preaching in the Jewish synagogues in a way that would be persuasive to the Athenians if their hearts were open. As it turns out, some were and some were not. Acts 17 closes with saying some "ridiculed" Paul and his message of resurrection, but some believed.

The final reason is that developing the art of persuasion will make us more effective witnesses for the gospel. C. S. Lewis described himself at his conversion to Christianity as "the most dejected and reluctant convert in all of England" and said that he was "brought in kicking, struggling, resentful, and darting his eyes in every direction for a chance of escape."[4] Lewis didn't want Christianity to be true. It took years of long discussions with his Christian friends and colleagues before he came to a place where he reluctantly submitted in trust to Christ. This was important for Lewis, and it's important for your unbelieving friends who are willing to talk. Though our fundamental problem is a heart problem and it's the Holy Spirit who does the converting work, God can use our attempts to persuade to draw people to him.

It's clear from the example of Acts 17 that we will not always be successful in persuading people of the gospel. If success is measured by conversion, then Paul largely failed in both Thessalonica and Athens. Only a few came to believe. The goal should not be conversion or even persuasion. The goal is to be a faithful witness for Christ. This is of course no excuse for being ill prepared. Part of being a faithful witness is to cultivate the art of persuasion.

We will look briefly at three tips for being persuasive.

---

[4] C. S. Lewis, *Surprised by Joy* (San Diego: Harvest/HBJ, 1984), 228–29.

Tips for Being Persuasive

In today's culture, we often encounter salespeople. Some very talented salespeople effortlessly pitch a product and can make something we don't need quite compelling. However, we often regret our purchase as soon as the sales pitch is over and we are left with something we don't really need. They make the sale but we regret it immediately. Moreover, many salespeople come across as inauthentic and "sales-y." They are often aggressive and pushy.

When it comes to our presentation of the Christian worldview, the first tip for being persuasive is to *be authentic*. We don't want to come across as sales-y and aggressive. It's not persuasive to have a one-size-fits-all pitch or engage in sloganeering. And we don't need it. We are rationally convinced of the truth of Christianity, and we have the evidence on our side. All we have to do to be compelling is lay out the reasons that have compelled us to believe. This occurs best in the midst of an actual conversation.

An important part of being authentic is being honest about your own intellectual journey. When a person raises a difficult objection that you don't know how to answer, admit this. A powerful response to someone, in this situation, is to say, "I don't know." When you merely pretend to know something, you typically lose your credibility. Simply say, "I don't know," and if at all possible, make sure you get back to the person with your best answer after you've researched a compelling answer.

The reason being honest is powerful is because it makes you relatable and shows that person you are genuinely interested in the pursuit of truth rather than only about winning an argument. This shows you are authentic. And when a person brings up an objection that you have struggled through, let him or her know that you have struggled with that idea as well. Walk them through your journey with that objection and have a conversation with them about that. This can be a powerful experience.

A second tip is to *avoid zingers*. A zinger is a rhetorically clever-sounding, bite-sized criticism. They are sometimes insulting (and can even amount to ad hominems) but often in a more passive-aggressive way. An example may be when some Christians tell atheists that April 1 (i.e., April Fools' Day) is National Atheist Day because Ps 14:1 says, "The fool says in his heart, 'There's no God.'" So Christians are, in effect, calling atheists fools. It seems to me this (feeble) attempt at humor is just not worth it and does more harm than good.

Another example of this is seen in *God's Not Dead*, a movie popular among Christians. There is a dramatic scene when the Christian student, tasked with defending God before the whole class, turns to the professor and asks him repeatedly why he hates God. The professor finally admits his hatred for God is because God had taken everything from him in the death of his mother. In a whispered voice, the Christian student asks, "How can you hate someone if they don't exist?"

The thing to notice is that this is not an argument. It doesn't really provide a reason for the professor to reconsider his atheism. He should just say he meant he hates the *idea* of God. Any philosophy professor worth his or her salt would be willing to make this distinction without any problem. This amounts to a zinger that Christians love and that makes unbelievers roll their eyes.

Many zingers find their way to internet memes. These are often accompanied by an image sarcastically expressing something about a person's view. We often see them shared on social media. Memes are not wrong in themselves, but they are hardly an effective way to reach people of different persuasions. Again, they more often alienate and polarize people than foster good discussion.

Rather than zingers, I again suggest conversation. It's worth noting that social media is one of the worst formats for having an actual conversation. Social media works great for zingers. You can write a zinger in 280 characters on Twitter. However, it is quite difficult to have thoughtful conversations on Twitter and other social media platforms.

The third and most important tool in knowing how to do apologetically minded evangelism is *asking good questions*. Suppose someone says to you:

> "Christianity is false because there is too much pain and suffering in the world."

I don't suggest immediately responding to this claim. In other words, don't immediately step onto your soapbox and launch into your well-worked-out solution to the problem of pain and suffering. When you do this, the person's defensive walls will immediately go up, and very little is heard. You may have a knockout-punch solution to this objection. But if it isn't heard, then it's obviously not going to persuade.

Instead of making it a debate, initiate a discussion by asking the following question:

> "Why do you think pain and suffering is a problem for believing in Christianity?"

What often happens is that you begin discussing (actually discussing!) how this difficulty may be resolved. The person may actually have ears to hear the evidence you are going to present. Engaging in a shouting match, with him or her saying, "Evil's a problem" and you saying, "No, it isn't," is not going to be a fruitful approach.

Asking strategic questions does two things. First, it validates them as a person in that you are inviting them into a dialogue rather than forcing them to listen to your monologue. The person becomes a conversation partner in search of the truth rather than simply your audience to whom you are pontificating. You are giving them the floor to back up what was said. By asking good questions, it shows the person you are interested in them and what they have to say.

Second, it pushes the person to support his or her position. It's easy to throw out a claim, but it is much more difficult to substantiate the claim. Our current political scene sometimes feels devoid of any thoughtfulness precisely because candidates and pundits are only engaged in lobbing zingers at each other with little support or evidence for the claims they make. Rather than truth being valued, unfortunately it is whoever is able to make the snappiest quip.

Conclusion: Thinking Christianly

We have looked at a considerable amount of content. For many this may be the first brush with logic and critical thinking. It can feel overwhelming at first, but mastering these concepts will aid you for a lifetime and in all aspects of life (spirituality, relationships, career, etc.). But perhaps even more importantly, we have spelled out a vision for why this matters for the Christian: thinking well and critically is a crucial part of loving and knowing God. What drives this vision is that God created us to be intellectual. We were created with curiosity and a desire for knowledge. As knowers, the most fundamental knowledge pursuit of our lives should be a deep and abiding knowledge of God. It is in this way that we fulfill the biblical command of Jesus to love God with all of our minds (Matt 22:37). But any knowledge of the truth is to be pursued as part of our divine mandate to subdue the earth (Gen 1:28). As the adage goes, all truth is indeed God's truth.

As we've pointed out, our task as believers is to conform our thinking to a biblical worldview. Jesus is our model. After all, Jesus perfectly expressed and lived out a Christian worldview, and so we ought to also at all times and in every way conform our actions and thinking to his. This is why, in the book, we have taken a hard look at how Jesus valued the life of the mind and how he used logic and critical thinking in his ministry.

At times in the church's history, it has embraced this vision and, as a result, created a culture grounded in a Christian worldview that produced our modern society in the globalized West along with revolutions in science, industry, education, and health care, to name only a few. But today, we live in a decidedly post-Christian world. What this means, at least in part, is that Christian thought (i.e., the Christian worldview) is no longer common or taken as seriously. This isn't to say there are not remnants of Christian influence, but thinking explicitly grounded in a Christian worldview is no longer the dominant way of seeing the world in the globalized West. And there are ways it is being driven progressively further to the edges.

But here we are as Christians living within this post-Christian culture. We are Daniels living in Babylon amid a hostile culture and, at times, being commanded to violate our Christian commitments with the threat of reprisal. What does this mean for us? If we spend time consuming cultural goods—such as movies, books, and music—then chances are we have consumed a good dose of post-Christian culture. For the most part, these activities are of course not wrong in themselves. However, they can be decidedly detrimental if we consume them uncritically. Our minds, like a sponge, soak up the facts around us. If we are uncritical, it is not a question of if the post-Christian world will affect us; it is a question of to what degree.

Today, the typical churchgoer unfortunately does not look different from their secular counterparts, except for perhaps what they do on a Sunday morning. But the rest of his or her life is not discernibly different from a secular counterpart. Many churchgoers' primary goal in life seems to be to make good money and buy a nice home, new cars, and the latest devices, take great vacations, and so forth, all with an eye toward making life more pleasurable. This, for some, is simply the American dream. But making this our primary goal in life is not an expression of the Christian worldview.

Jesus tells the Christian to "deny himself, take up his cross daily, and follow me. For whoever wants to save his life will lose it, but whoever loses his life because of me will save it. For what does it benefit someone if he gains the whole word, and yet loses or forfeits himself?" (Luke 9:23–25). Jesus took up a literal cross and carried it toward his execution. We, too, in discipleship, are to take up a cross and follow him. The idea is that when we become followers of Jesus, it's not only that (most of) our Sunday mornings are now busy. We are to give up our lives and follow Jesus in all our ways. Discipleship requires a full embrace of a Christian worldview. As Christians, we are followers of Jesus. In short, we are to look to him, act like him, and even think like him, which, in turn, brings glory to the Father. In short, we are to do life Christianly.

Thinking Non-Christianly

What does it look like to think and do life Christianly? Well, let's first say what it looks like to fail to think Christianly about the world. The reality is, it is not easy to think Christianly in a world that is pervasively at odds with a Christian worldview. Many ideas at home in our culture run contrary to our Christian worldviews. These can, in a way, subtly slip into the thinking of many Christians. We'll consider two ideas that are common in our culture. If we embrace either view, we fail to think Christianly.

Seeing People Naturalistically

The first idea has to do with the human person. When we wonder what a human being is, one common answer is to think of humans as purely physical beings, nothing more than physical and biochemical processes. This is to see the human person naturalistically. We've already had opportunity to talk about the worldview of naturalism at some length. As you may recall, naturalism is the view that all things that exist are natural, material, and physical—nothing is immaterial or supernatural.

By contrast, on the Christian view, the human person is more than a physical thing. Though there are multiple ways to work this out, for many Christian thinkers, the human person is an embodied soul. Though the body is very important (i.e., it is not evil or a kind of soul prison), and we are ultimately designed to be embodied, the Bible makes clear that we can survive the death or separation of our bodies.

In 2 Cor 5:6–8, Paul said, "So we are always confident and know that while we are at home in the body we are away from the Lord. For we walk by faith, not by sight. In fact, we are confident, and we would prefer to be away from the body and at home with the Lord." Paul's preference was to be "away from the body." Notice that if one can be away from the body, then it follows that one is not identical to one's body. Paul was referencing what is known as the "intermediate state" where, if a Christian person dies, his or her soul goes to be with the Lord in an unembodied state. It is this intermediate state that Jesus seemed to refer to as he was hanging on the cross. He told the repentant thief, "*today* you will be with me in paradise" (Luke 23:43, emphasis added). The body of this man was not that day with Jesus in paradise; presumably his body was buried in a common grave for criminals. But he, as a soul, was. In order for these passages to make any sense at all, then we must not be identical with our bodies. Instead, thinking Christianly about a human person means that we consider ourselves and others as embodied souls. It is *you* (as a soul) who goes to be with the Lord when your body dies.

Given this Christian view of the human person, we can, for example, ground human rights and dignity. After all, we are not only souls, but we are souls that bear the image of God, and this gives us dignity and infinite value. On this view, It matters how we treat each other as people who are not merely biological collections of cells and physical processes. If a human being is merely a biological system of cells and processes, then it is exceedingly difficult to see how a human being has inherent dignity and inalienable rights.

The question is, as a Christian, do you think of yourself as an embodied soul or as a physical thing? Do you care for your soul? Do you think Christianly about people you encounter? Do you see them as embodied souls created with infinite worth as image bearers of God? Given the way our culture thinks of human beings, it is easy to allow this idea to "soak in" and forget the infinite dignity inherent in every single human being in how we should love and treat each other.

Seeing Truth Postmodernly

A second idea dominant in our culture that has affected some Christians is a postmodern view of truth. J. P. Moreland defines postmodernism as "primarily a reinterpretation of what knowledge is and what counts as knowledge. . . . On a postmodernist view there is no such thing as objective reality, truth, value, reason, and so forth. All these are social constructions, creations of linguistic practices and, as such, are relative not to individuals but to social groups that share a narrative."[1] Perhaps the most famous slogan of postmodernism is Jean-François Lyotard's characterization of postmodernism as an "incredulity toward metanarratives." Lyotard sees the basic idea of postmodernism as a rejection of overarching stories and claims taken to give objective meaning to the world. On this view, the Bible is not a metanarrative. It is not an objective guide for all people in how to think of reality. The postmodernist doesn't reject the Bible per se but only rejects it as a metanarrative. At most, it provides one story that is no better than a variety of other stories. This allows the postmodernist to respond to Christian claims by saying, "Well, that's true for you, but it's not true for me," since that person may look to a different religious tradition that brings value and meaning to their context.

The biblical view, by contrast, is one of objectivity and exclusivity. Jesus explicitly claimed to be the only way of salvation. In John 14:6, Jesus said, "I am the way, the truth, and the life. No one comes to the Father except

[1] Moreland, *Love Your God with All Your Mind*, 37 (see chap. 1, n. 8).

through me." In Acts 4:12, the apostle Peter said, "There is salvation in no one else, for there is no other name under heaven given to people by which we must be saved." It's difficult to think Jesus and the apostles thought of this as only relevant to Christians in that area and at that time. Jesus called his disciples to, "Go . . . and make disciples of all nations" (Matt 28:19). And again, he said, "you will be my witnesses in Jerusalem, in all Judea and Samaria, and to the ends of the earth" (Acts 1:8). The biblical view is that this is a message for everyone.

The question is, again, as a Christian, do you think of morality, value, purpose, meaning, and truth as objective, or are these things up for grabs? Are there things that are genuinely and objectively morally wrong? And does the Bible give us an objectively true guide to knowing and understanding the world? Unfortunately, many Christians think postmodernly about the truth and moral values.

Thinking Christianly

If we are to have a Christian worldview, we should conform our thoughts and ideas to Christian ways of seeing the world. The idea is that we ought to bring our Christian worldview into every square inch of our lives. It's to think about all our areas of life with a Christian worldview (including the human person and truth and morality, but also our careers, education, relationships, hobbies, property, money, our bodies, etc.).

What is it to live and think Christianly about life? The first thing to say is that we need to be committed to loving God with all of our minds and to approaching our Christian worldview with intellectual faith. We should study and have broad familiarity with the Bible and theology. This is, of course, a lifelong pursuit. The Bible is such that it has no bottom in the sense that we can spend the rest of our lives studying the Bible, and we will never exhaust the amazing riches it offers.

We must also confront our thinking that is contrary to the Christian worldview. Paul told us in Rom 12:2, "Do not be conformed to this age, but be transformed by the renewing of your mind." The idea, is we must excise the ideas of the world around us. We must confront our false ideas and replace them with God's truth revealed in Scripture. Elsewhere the apostle Paul gave us an extreme picture of going to war against ideas that are "raised up against the knowledge of God" (2 Cor 10:5). He said we are to demolish arguments and ideas that run contrary to Christ and that all of our ideas will be captive to Christ.

Approaching life with an intellectual faith and loving God with all of our minds is the starting point. We commit to understanding the Christian worldview so that we can apply it and think Christianly about all parts of our lives.

To see what it looks like to live and think Christianly about our lives, let's consider an example. Let's say you are a businessperson, and you want to think of your career Christianly. You'll have to ask, What is it to do business Christianly? It seems to me that a Christian should consider three areas in bringing his or her work in business under the lordship of Jesus Christ.

The first and perhaps the most obvious is in the area of Christian ethics. If we are to do business Christianly, we ought to do business according to Christian ethical principles. One should not lie, cheat, steal, or take advantage. We shouldn't oppress, exploit, or discriminate unjustly. Instead we should walk in "love, joy, peace, patience, kindness, goodness, faithfulness, gentleness, and self-control" (Gal 5:22–23) and exhibit other moral fruit of the Spirit. It should mean something if someone is a Christian business owner. Unfortunately, Christians do not have the best reputation for always being trustworthy and for being people of integrity when it comes to business. Too many people have tarnished the name of Christ in their business dealings. But if we do this, then of course we are not doing business Christianly. Christians need not be perfect, but they are to have integrity. The world watches us, and we can have an incredible impact by simply treating people fairly and doing what we said we would do.

The second way to do business Christianly is to, in our business, exemplify Christian values. This goes beyond a basic ethical approach, which of course many non-Christians would be committed to as well, and brings in uniquely Christian values. For example, the primary interest of most business owners is the almighty dollar. Of course nothing is wrong with making money. This will always be part of the purpose of having a business. But it's not doing business Christianly if this is the sole driving value. It would be profoundly unchristian to squeeze every last drop of profit out of an industry while mistreating customers and even other employees. Doing business Christianly requires us to think of people (all people) as embodied souls created in the image of God. You of course need your employee, for example, to do the work he or she was hired to do, but we are called to treat people with dignity and respect. On the Christian view, every person has infinite value only by virtue of being human and is deeply loved by God. Thus, we should always aim to be redemptive in the lives of people. We are called to forgive and, if possible, restore someone when there is genuine repentance. Of course, this is not always possible if the sin is too egregious. But if we can, we should act redemptively. This is precisely what we have found in Christ and so should do for others.

The third way one may do business Christianly is to do it living with Christian purpose. How would it change your life today to live in light of our eternal destiny as citizens of the kingdom of Christ? What a game changer for our pursuits both in our accomplishments and our setbacks. Finding success in business is terrific, but we should keep it in perspective in light of eternity. We can maintain our hope and eternal outlook even if our business fails. Thinking of this Christianly, our joy and well-being need not be tied up in finding (or failing to find) success in our business. Success is great, but it is only a small part of the much bigger (i.e., eternal) ultimate purpose for why we are where we are. In the same way, our setbacks in life can be taken in stride. With an eternal Christian perspective, we can trust that a setback hasn't escaped God's sovereign will and that he will provide for our needs.

A secular person can of course live his or her life as if it has ultimate purpose. They can, for example, live incredibly sacrificial lives that aim to benefit the "good of humanity." But it's difficult to see what, on a worldview level, grounds that purpose. What is the purpose in living our lives well if we go to the grave and that's it? The difference, when it comes to a Christian outlook, is that life does not end at the grave. In fact, we become, in a way, more fully alive. The purpose of the Christian life, in all of our pursuits, is eternal and should always aim not at our personal, creaturely comforts but at the eternal glory of God.

Jesus said it this way: "Don't store up for yourselves treasures on earth, where moth and rust destroy and where thieves break in and steal. But store up for yourselves treasures in heaven, where neither moth nor rust destroys, and where thieves don't break in and steal. For where your treasure is, there your heart will be also" (Matt 6:19–21). This is a subversive message. Our natural tendency is to store up treasures here on earth, whether it be as a business owner or any other pursuit. And if this is all there is, then that's exactly what we should do. However, thinking of life Christianly, this is not our primary aim or purpose in life. In fact, there are times when we should purposefully forsake our creaturely comforts in service to the Lord.

Finding God

As Christians, we have the best possible reason for pursuing the life of the mind. We are, after all, pursuing the God of the universe. Thinking critically about life and pursuing the life of the mind is, at bottom, devotional for the Christian. Again, this must start with thinking critically about our Christian worldviews. But it is certainly not limited to this either. Beyond studying the Bible and Christian theology, we can also be motivated to study what historically has been referred to as the "book of nature." The Bible tells us:

> The heavens declare the glory of God,
> and the [sky] proclaims the work of his hands.
> Day after day they pour out speech;
> night after night they communicate knowledge. (Ps 19:1–2)

The sky above testifies to us of the glory of God. Paul wrote, "For his invisible attributes, that is, his eternal power and divine nature, have been clearly seen since the creation of the world, being understood through what he has made" (Rom 1:20).

The point is that this is God's world, and we are its stewards (Gen 1:28). Any study in any area of the created world can be done Christianly and devotionally. That is, we love God with all of our minds when we pursue knowledge of the world in any of its aspects.

The idea is that we have an incredibly compelling reason to study the world around us: in doing so, we can know the Creator of the universe and behold his glory! We can see the attributes of God, but we can also stand in awe and worship at the majesty and exquisite design of God.

APPENDIX: PRACTICE PROBLEMS

* The answer key for these problems can be accessed at https://www.bhacademic.com/logic

Chapter 5

Identify whether the following is a statement or not a statement:

1. The sky is blue.
2. Hey, you over there!
3. Chocolate ice cream is better than vanilla.
4. Birds are flightless creatures.
5. Greetings!
6. A bachelor is an unmarried man.
7. Ouch!
8. What color are you painting your room?
9. There are pencils on my desk.
10. When Caden arrives.

Three Principles of Logic

Identify the principle of logic being expressed:

1. You can't read and not read at the same time.
2. Either you do it or you don't.
3. God is God, no matter what anyone says.
4. Sara isn't sitting and standing at the same time.
5. Jack is C. S. Lewis, and C. S. Lewis is Jack.
6. Socrates is either alive or dead.
7. Either Bigfoot exists or he doesn't.
8. My cup of water is my cup of water.
9. Rene can't be both thirsty and not thirsty at once.
10. Either she sings or she's silent—you can't have both!

Arguments

Identify the premises and conclusions in the following arguments:

1. Reese is a bird. So, she has wings.
2. All men are mortal. Socrates is a man. Therefore, Socrates is mortal.
3. James probably won't be available if he has kickball practice tonight. But kickball was not canceled, despite the rain. So, James probably won't be available tonight.
4. Some dogs are cats. All dogs are polka dotted. So, some cats are polka dotted.
5. If Austin reads a book, he is going to fall asleep. Austin is reading a book. So, Austin will fall asleep.
6. Most pigeons are brown. This is a pigeon. Therefore, it is probably brown.
7. Everything that begins to exist has a cause. The universe exists. Therefore, the universe has a cause.

8. Either the sun is in the sky, or the stars are out. The sun is not in the sky. Therefore, the stars are out.
9. I need to stop by the bank today. But it closes at five, and it's already two o'clock. So, I must head over in the next two hours.
10. If I cook, then I will have food. If I have food, then I won't be hungry. Thus, if I cook, I won't be hungry.

Show Me the Argument

Supply the missing premise in the following enthymemes:

1. The kitchen is dirty. So, Emma hasn't done her chore.
2. The puppy is whining at his dog bowl. Therefore, the puppy must be hungry.
3. If I do my homework, I will pass this class. So, I should do my homework.
4. It's cold outside. So, I should wear a sweater rather than a T-shirt.
5. Legolas is an elf. So, he is quick and nimble.

Identify the premise[s] and conclusion of each of the following arguments (note: some sentences may be neither a premise nor a conclusion):

1. I really don't like Abraham Lincoln. He was a terrible guy! See, socialists are the only people who impose income taxes, and he was the first president to impose income taxes. Did you know that? So, Abraham Lincoln must have been a socialist.
2. There are a number of interesting historical arguments for Christ's divinity. One famous argument proposes three options: Jesus was either a liar, a lunatic, or the Lord. We can see that he wasn't a liar; he would have had to have been a beast of the worst kind to claim that he was God, and Jesus was obviously a very good guy. But was he a lunatic? There are nice lunatics, after all. Well, Jesus didn't act like a lunatic; he actually acted like an extremely rational person.

So, if he was not a liar, and he was not a lunatic, then Jesus must have been the Lord.

3. Megan can only win this game of chess if she's lucky. After all, her opponent is a really sharp player. But luck doesn't actually exist. So, Megan can't win this game.
4. Telling a lie is never morally permissible. And I believe it, because of a story I heard about Corrie ten Boom's niece. Apparently, Cocky told the truth, even though Nazis were after her brothers! So, if even she told the truth in the hardest circumstances, it must never be okay to lie. And, you know, she wasn't just anyone; the ten Boom family were some of the best moral exemplars we can learn from.
5. Under the worldview of naturalism, naturalism itself cannot be a rational belief. See, naturalism purports to be a rational belief about the world. But, under the worldview of naturalism, only cause-and-effect relationships exist. This is a problem because rational belief only exists if there are logical connections between reasons and conclusions, and cause-and-effect relationships are not logical connections.

Logical Relevance

State whether the following premises are logically relevant to the conclusion. If they are logically relevant, also note if the premises falsify, make likely, or entail the conclusion.

1. Premise: I hear sprinklers outside. Conclusion: The vegetable garden is being watered.
2. Premise: Plato was Aristotle's teacher. Conclusion: Aristotle was Plato's student.
3. Premise: My water bottle is empty. Conclusion: I should take a sip from it.

4. Premise: A pilot is traveling faster than the speed of sound. Conclusion: He is traveling at the speed of light.
5. Premise: Matt is a man. Conclusion: Therefore, he is a rational animal.
6. Premise: James is calling Emily on the phone. Conclusion: He must want to talk to her.
7. Premise: 1+1=2. Conclusion: The sky is blue.
8. Premise: TJ's hair is wet. Conclusion: He is completely dry.
9. Premise: Mark is Anna's brother. Conclusion: Anna is Mark's sister.
10. Premise: This book has a black cover. Conclusion: Therefore, the author is a woman.

Deductive Validity

Identify the following arguments as valid or invalid:

1. Either Mark is wearing blue, or he is wearing green.
   Mark is not wearing green.
   As a result, he is wearing blue.
2. All bikes have wheels.
   All rollerblades have wheels.
   So, all bikes are rollerblades.
3. If the dress is blue, then it is white.
   The dress is not blue.
   Thus, it is not white.
4. Everything that began to exist has a cause.
   The universe began to exist.
   Therefore, the universe has a cause.
5. If an animal is a dog, then it has a tail.
   This animal has a tail.
   Therefore, it is a dog.

6. Either I am sitting down, or I am standing up.
   I am standing up.
   Therefore, I am sitting down.
7. Some chairs are brown.
   All chairs are places to sit.
   Which means that some places to sit are brown.

Deductive Soundness

Identify the following valid arguments as sound or unsound:

1. If something is a book, then it doesn't have pages.
   This thing is a book.
   So, it doesn't have pages.
2. All dogs are mammals.
   Collies are dogs.
   So, all collies are mammals.
3. All well-formed arguments are valid arguments.
   Some of the practice problems in this book are well formed.
   So, some of the practice problems in this book are valid.
4. Either unicorns exist or centaurs are real.
   Centaurs are not real.
   Therefore, unicorns exist.
5. All blue things are red things.
   No green things are red things.
   So, no green things are blue things.
6. If the sky is dark, the sun is not up.
   The sun is up.
   So, the sky is not dark.
7. Some cats are not dogs.
   All cats are horses.
   Some horses are not dogs.

Nondeductive Standards

Note whether the following arguments deductively entail or nondeductively make likely the truth of their respective conclusions:

1. Jessica almost always drinks coffee with her breakfast.
   Jessica is eating breakfast.
   So, Jessica is drinking coffee.
2. All philosophers love wisdom.
   Plato was a philosopher.
   Thus, Plato loved wisdom.
3. Most students who complete their homework pass this class.
   Grant completed his homework.
   So, Grant will pass this class.
4. Most Americans eat turkey on Thanksgiving Day.
   Rebekah is an American.
   So, she will eat turkey on Thanksgiving.
5. Either I am wet, or I am dry.
   I am not wet.
   Therefore, I am dry.
6. C. S. Lewis is the author of *Mere Christianity*.
   The author of *Mere Christianity* is the author of *The Lion, the Witch and the Wardrobe*.
   C. S. Lewis is the author of *The Lion, the Witch and the Wardrobe*.
7. If Jeff mows the lawn, his mom normally gives him ten dollars.
   Jeff just mowed the lawn.
   So, his mom will give him ten dollars.

Nondeductive Strength

Identify whether the following nondeductive arguments are strong or weak:

1. Anne is a good, hardworking student.
   So, she will get an A in logic class.
2. Emily is Anne's sister.
   So, Emily will get an A in logic class.
3. John struggles with understanding valid arguments.
   Problem set 22 asks questions about valid arguments.
   Thus, John is going to struggle with answering those questions.
4. There are more women than men in logic class.
   Thus, the women will have a better overall average grade than the men will.
5. There are fewer men than women in the class.
   Therefore, the men will have a better overall average grade than the women will.
6. The person who had the best grade on the first exam will probably have the best grade on the final exam.
   James wishes he had the best grade on the first exam.
   Thus, James will have the best grade on the final exam.
7. The person who had the best grade on the first exam will probably have the best grade on the final exam.
   Jessica had the best grade on the first exam.
   So, Jessica will have the best grade on the final exam.

Nondeductive Cogency

Identify whether the following strong arguments are cogent.

1. Planted seeds normally sprout.
   So, if I plant seeds, they will sprout.

2. Most birds can't fly.
   A dodo is a bird.
   Therefore, it can't fly.
3. When someone flips a light switch in a dark room, the light will turn on.
   So, if I flip a light switch in a dark room, the light will turn on.
4. Comedic plays are supposed to make people laugh.
   Romeo and Juliet is Shakespeare's greatest comedic play.
   Therefore, if I go see it, I will find it very funny.
5. Prince Charles is the firstborn child of Queen Elizabeth II.
   The firstborn child of a reigning monarch typically becomes the next monarch.
   Thus, Prince Charles will be the next monarch of England.
6. Most students who don't do their homework earn straight As.
   So, if you don't do your homework, get ready for an A.
7. Most days, it rains in the rainforest.
   So, if you spend a day in the rainforest, you will experience rain.

Chapter 6

Test for Validity

Use the three-step process to test for validity. Are the following arguments valid or invalid?

1. If Charles goes swimming, Charlotte will jump in with him.
   Charles is going swimming.
   So, Charlotte will jump in with him.
2. Either Charlotte will jump in the lake, or Charity will pick the water lilies.
   Charity is picking water lilies.
   Which means that Charlotte just jumped in.

3. Only the girls are picking water lilies.
   Charlie is picking water lilies.
   In other words, Charlie is a girl.
4. Charlotte either goes by Charlotte or Charlie.
   Chelsey calls her Charlotte.
   So, Chelsey calls her Charlie.
5. Either the boys are fishing, or the girls are playing catch.
   The girls are picking water lilies; they're not playing catch.
   Hence, the boys are fishing.
6. If Chad throws in a fishing lure, he will catch a fish.
   Chad caught a fish.
   Accordingly, he must have thrown in a lure.
7. If Christopher throws in his bait, he will catch a bass.
   Christopher did not throw in his bait.
   As a result, he did not catch a bass.
8. If the outing ends early, then nobody had fun.
   Everyone had fun.
   So, the outing did not end early.
9. Either the group can head home at 4:00 p.m. for dinner, or they can stay and watch the sunset.
   They did not head home at 4:00 p.m.
   Hence, they stayed to watch the sunset.
10. If everyone carpooled home from the meadow, then Charity and Charlotte rode together.
    Charity and Charlotte rode together.
    Which means that everyone carpooled home from the meadow.

Symbolization

Symbolize the following arguments:

Argument	
1. If your dog is the size of a house, then he has a house-sized doghouse. If he has a house-sized doghouse, then he will be inside. In other words, if your dog is the size of a house, he will be inside.	
2. Either the armies will charge, or a minotaur will take over the country. A minotaur will take over the country. Thus, the armies will charge.	
3. If pigs fly, then the sun is up. Pigs fly. So, the sun is up.	
4. Either pears are purple, or roses are red. Pears are not purple. Thus, roses are red.	
5. If fairies exist, then fauns will dance with dwarves and men. Fauns will dance with dwarves and men. So, fairies exist.	
6. If apples are red, then oranges are yellow. Apples are red. Therefore, oranges are yellow.	
7. If we have vanilla, I will make a London fog. We do not have vanilla. Thus, I will not make a London fog.	

8. Either cats are cold, or birds are blue. Cats are not cold. Thus, birds are blue.	
9. If the dwarves are noisy, then our enemies can hear us. The dwarves are noisy. So, our enemies can hear us.	
10. Either the sky is blue, or monkeys can fly. Monkeys can't fly. In other words, the sky is blue.	

The Common Argument Test for Validity

Test the following arguments for validity, naming the form where applicable:

1. I will either cook with olive oil or butter.
   I will not cook with olive oil.
   So, I will cook with butter.
2. If it is light outside, the sun is up.
   It is light outside.
   So, the sun is up.
3. Vegans never eat meat.
   Rachel is a vegan.
   So, Rachel never eats meat.
4. If Emily Dickinson wrote this poem, then it is high-quality work.
   This poem is terrible.
   Accordingly, Emily Dickinson did not write it.
5. If the sky is blue, it's not going to rain.
   The weather report said that there's zero chance of rain today.
   So, the sky is blue.

6. If I am going to make dinner, either chicken or ground beef is defrosting on the counter.
   Chicken is not defrosting on the counter.
   Ground beef is not defrosting on the counter.
   So, I am not going to make dinner.
7. If Henry VIII had not divorced Catherine of Aragon, he would not have married Anne Boleyn.
   If Henry VIII had not married Anne Boleyn, she would not have been beheaded.
   Hence, if Henry VIII had not divorced Catherine of Aragon, Anne Boleyn would not have been beheaded.
8. If I throw in my fishing line, I will either snag the bottom or catch a turtle.
   I will not snag the bottom.
   I will not catch a turtle.
   So, I must not be throwing in a line.
9. Either Augustine wrote the *Confessions*, or Milton wrote *Paradise Lost*.
   Milton wrote *Paradise Lost*.
   So, Augustine wrote the *Confessions*.
10. The founding fathers were smart people.
    George Washington was a founding father.
    Thus, George Washington was a smart person.

Complex Statements and Connectives

Identify the types of complex statements in the problems that follow:

1. Ruth wants to either go hiking or get coffee.
2. If you like detective novels, you will totally enjoy reading Dorothy Sayers.
3. Alex drinks Earl Grey tea if and only if vanilla syrup is added to it.

4. Most kids either love or hate broccoli.
5. No blue things are green things.
6. Bees and butterflies both have wings.
7. If Shakespeare was alive, he wrote *Hamlet*.
8. Good dogs don't bark.
9. Grace is married to Brad if and only if Brad is married to Grace.
10. Plato and Aristotle were both ancient philosophers.

Chapter 7

Truth Tables

Using truth tables, test for the truth values of the following statements, noting when they are tautologies or contradictions:

1. If P, then Q

P	Q	If P, then Q
T	T	
F	T	
T	F	
F	F	

2. S or P

S	P	S or P
T	T	
F	T	
T	F	
F	F	

3. If P, then (not P or Q)

P	Q	If P, then (not P or Q)		
T	T			
F	T			
T	F			
F	F			

4. Not (if A, then B)

A	B	Not (if A, then B)	
T	T		
F	T		
T	F		
F	F		

5. L and (M and not L)

L	M	L and (M and not L)		
T	T			
F	T			
T	F			
F	F			

6. G or (not G or C)

G	C	G or (not G or C)		
T	T			
F	T			
T	F			
F	F			

7. (A and B) or (not A and not B)

A	**B**	**(A and B) or (not A and not B)**				
T	T					
F	T					
T	F					
F	F					

8. Either (if S, then R) or (S and not R)

S	**R**	**Either (if S, then R) or (S and not R)**			
T	T				
F	T				
T	F				
F	F				

9. If (W or not W), then (X and not X)

W	**X**	**If (W or not W), then (X and not X)**				
T	T					
F	T					
T	F					
F	F					

10. If (S or P), then Q

S	**P**	**Q**	**If (S or P), then Q**	
T	T	T		
F	T	T		
T	F	T		
F	F	T		
T	T	F		
F	T	F		
T	F	F		
F	F	F		

Using Truth Tables to Test for Validity

Using the truth table, test the following arguments for validity:

1. If Q, then P
   Not Q
   Therefore, not P

Q	P	If Q, then P	Not Q	Therefore, not P
T	T			
F	T			
T	F			
F	F			

2. J or K
   J
   Therefore, not K

J	K	Either J or K	J	Therefore, not K
T	T			
F	T			
T	F			
F	F			

3. G if and only if E
   G or E
   Therefore, E

G	E	G if and only if E	Either G or E	Therefore, E
T	T			
F	T			
T	F			
F	F			

4. L if and only if V
   Not V
   Therefore, not L

L	V	L if and only if V	Not V	Therefore, not L
T	T			
F	T			
T	F			
F	F			

5. H and not G
   If N, then G
   Therefore, not N

H	G	N	H and not G		If N, then G	Therefore, not N
T	T	T				
F	T	T				
T	F	T				
F	F	T				
T	T	F				
F	T	F				
T	F	F				
F	F	F				

6. A or B
   If B, then G
   Therefore, if not A, then G

A	B	G	A or B	If B, then G	If not A, then G	
T	T	T				
F	T	T				
T	F	T				
F	F	T				
T	T	F				
F	T	F				
T	F	F				
F	F	F				

7. If W, then X
   Either W or Z
   Therefore, Z

W	X	Z	If W, then X	Either W or Z	Therefore, Z
T	T	T			
F	T	T			
T	F	T			
F	F	T			
T	T	F			
F	T	F			
T	F	F			
F	F	F			

8. A or N
   A and N
   Therefore, N or F

A	N	F	A or N	A and N	Therefore, N or F
T	T	T			
F	T	T			
T	F	T			
F	F	T			
T	T	F			
F	T	F			
T	F	F			
F	F	F			

9. Not C
   X and S
   Therefore, S

C	X	S	Not C	Both X and S	Therefore, S
T	T	T			
F	T	T			
T	F	T			
F	F	T			
T	T	F			
F	T	F			
T	F	F			
F	F	F			

10. If R, then S
    If S, then T
    Therefore, T

R	S	T	If R, then S	If S, then T	Therefore, T
T	T	T			
F	T	T			
T	F	T			
F	F	T			
T	T	F			
F	T	F			
T	F	F			
F	F	F			

Chapter 8

Sweeping Categorical Claims

Identify whether the following sweeping categorical claims are inclusive or exclusive.

1. No stars are green.
2. All men need work.
3. No angels are mortals.
4. Bumblebees have stingers.
5. Good men have virtues.
6. None of Jane Austen's books were written by Dante.
7. Monkeys have tails.
8. The Grand Canyon is beautiful.
9. Water is not a solid.
10. Lights are not dark.

Particular Categorical Statements

Identify whether the following particular categorical claims are inclusive or exclusive.

1. Some bears are stuffed animals.
2. Some bikes do not work.
3. Some chairs are brown.
4. Some chairs are not brown.
5. Some birds fly.
6. Some leaves are green.
7. Some people aren't nice.
8. Some of the disciples didn't end up becoming apostles.
9. Some clothes are soft.
10. Some water isn't blue.

Symbolizing Categorical Statements

Symbolize problems 1–5 of section 1 and 6–10 of section 2 in standard form.

Contradictories

Write the contradictories of the following statements:

1. Some maps are blue.
2. All monkeys are brown.
3. Some ice is not cold.
4. No flowers are six feet tall.
5. Some artists are not painters.
6. Some pandas are foxes.
7. No shoes are worn on your head.

Contraries

Write the contraries of the following statements:

1. All food is tasty.
2. No cars are white.
3. All clothes are scratchy.
4. All winters are cold.
5. No hair is curly.

Write the subcontraries of the following statements:

1. Some habits are virtues.
2. Some men are logical.
3. Some gold does not glitter.
4. Some wanderers are not lost.
5. Some logic problems are sound.

Write the subalterns of the following statements:

1. No coats have hoods.
2. All bikes have wheels.
3. All faeries have wings.
4. No books are magnanimous.
5. All bagels are sugary.

Diagramming Categorical Logic

Diagram the following universal and particular statements:

1. All original members of the Detection Club were mystery authors.
2. Some of the original members of the Detection Club are authors of *The Floating Admiral.*

3. No protagonist of the Detection Club is a detective who solves cases by mumbo-jumbo.
4. All members of the Detection Club are worth reading.
5. Some books written by members of the Detection Club are not books that involve twins.
6. No protagonist of the Detection Club is a detective who solves cases by jiggery-pokery.
7. Some Hercule Poirot novels are books that were written during Agatha Christie's tenure as president of the Detection Club.
8. Some Lord Peter Wimsey novels were not written during Dorothy Sayers's tenure as president of the Detection Club.
9. The entirety of his book on Thomas Aquinas was published during G. K. Chesterton's tenure as president of the Detection Club.
10. No story coming from a member of the Detection Club is allowed to utilize more than one secret passage.

Representing Two Categorical Statements

Practice diagramming the following sets of categorical statements to test whether the conclusion follows from the given premises:

1. All bikes are orange.
   All tricycles are bikes.
   Conclusion: All tricycles are orange.

2. No peach trees are blooming.
   All plum trees are blooming.
   Conclusion: No plum trees are peach trees.

3. Some green things are red things.
   No green things are yellow things.
   Conclusion: Some yellow things are not red things.

4. Some metals are not pliable.
   All metals are shiny.
   Conclusion: Some shiny things are not pliable.

5. All black Labradors are dogs.
   Some Labradors are dogs.
   Conclusion: Some Labradors are black Labradors.

6. No zombies are purple.
   Some purple things are flowers.
   Conclusion: Some flowers are not zombies.

7. No cities are countries.
   All countries are political entities.
   Conclusion: No cities are political entities.

8. All elves are magical creatures.
   No centaurs are elves.
   Conclusion: No centaurs are magical creatures.

9. Some books are novels.
   All books are composed of words.
   Conclusion: Some things composed of words are novels.

10. No trees are blue.
    Some blue things are birds.
    Conclusion: Some birds are not trees.

Chapter 9

Determining Strength

Identify whether the following arguments are weak or strong:

1. Yesterday Sara used a blue towel when she got out of the pool. So, she'll use a blue one today.

2. Sara only owns blue towels.
   Sara never borrows towels from other people.
   If we go to the pool today, Sara will use a blue towel to dry off.
3. Sophie likes most classical music.
   In other words, if you show her some new music, she'll like it.
4. Sophie plays the guitar.
   So, if you hand her a banjo, she'll know how to play that too.
5. Sydney gets spicy food every time she goes out to eat.
   Thus, if she goes out to eat later today, she'll probably be ordering spicy food.
6. Sydney likes to cook with bell peppers.
   My conclusion? Her food must be really spicy.
7. Susannah has really good taste in tea.
   Annie likes good tea.
   So, if Susannah offers Annie some tea, she will like it.
8. Susannah eats dark chocolate nearly every day.
   Susannah drinks tea nearly every day.
   Hence, I think Susannah must drink tea with her chocolate all the time.
9. Annie's room is always clean.
   That shows she is a neat freak.
10. Annie never seems to get to bed early.
    She's been up past midnight every day this month!
    So, I think it's safe to say that she'll stay up past midnight tonight as well.

Cogency

Identify whether the following problems are cogent or uncogent:

1. The sun has gone down every day for the past two centuries.
   So, the sun will go down every day for the rest of the year.

2. Every time it has been tested, water at sea level boils at 212 degrees Fahrenheit.
   If someone heats up water at sea level, it will boil when it hits 212 degrees.
3. Most birds can fly.
   A beaver is a bird.
   So, it can fly too.
4. Most bees have stingers.
   A drone is a bee.
   Therefore, it has a stinger.
5. Most presidents of the United States have not served more than two terms.
   Franklin G. Roosevelt was a president of the United States.
   So, he did not serve more than two terms.
6. Most nights the moon is not visible in the sky.
   So, the moon will probably not be visible tonight.
7. Most light bulbs turn on when properly connected to electricity.
   So, if you properly connect a broken light bulb to electricity, it will turn on.
8. Most mammals give birth to their young.
   A platypus is a not a mammal.
   Therefore, a platypus does not give birth to its young.
9. Most dogs are born with tails.
   Corgis are dogs.
   Therefore, Corgis are born with tails.
10. The majority of eggs eaten in the US are chicken eggs.
    So, if you eat an egg in the US, it will probably be a chicken egg.

Chapter 10

How to Reason Abductively

Given the evidence listed, pick the best explanation.

1. Ann walks into her apartment looking tired and sweaty with gym clothes on. Did she:
   a. change into gym clothes before driving to and from class?
   b. just get back from working out?
   c. decide to sunbathe in the park and accidentally fell asleep?
   d. not sleep very well last night, and a neighbor's kid sprayed her with a water gun while she walked downstairs to check the mail?
2. Baseball practice started five minutes ago, and John, who is habitually tardy, hasn't arrived yet. Was he:
   a. kidnapped by the local tramp but also decided to go along with the man because he thought it would be fun?
   b. stuck behind a terrible wreck on the freeway?
   c. asked by his mom to come home because she is sick with chickenpox and needed soup?
   d. distracted on his way to practice?
3. Your dog comes in covered in mud. Did:
   a. a delinquent neighborhood kid decide to pummel him with water balloons full of mud?
   b. he accidentally start a mudslide on the local hill?
   c. he find a puddle to play in after a rainstorm?
   d. he take a trip to the local spa?
4. Megan's watercolor pencils are on her desk when she gets home from work. Did:
   a. her roommate borrow the pencils and return them to her desk rather than putting them in their proper place?

   b. her dog get the pencils out of the cabinet she stores them in and put them on her desk?
   c. the neighbors' kids slam into their shared wall while tussling with so much force that the pencils fell out of the cabinet onto her desk?
   d. her action figurines come to life and have a sketching session, leaving the pencils on the desk because they nearly got caught in the act?
5. Rebekah sniffs a shirt as she pulls it out of her closet and decides it smells bad. Did:
   a. an angry neighbor sneak in and spray her clothes with perfume?
   b. small animals get into her closet and make a nest in the shirt?
   c. she pull it out of her dirty laundry basket because she wanted to put it in the washing machine?
   d. it sit in her closet so long that it started to smell musty but only sat in the closet for a day?
6. When Jessica went to the oven to check on the chicken she was cooking for dinner, she found it was burned. Did:
   a. a small animal get into her house and accidentally turn the temperature up?
   b. her husband attack the oven with a ray gun as part of his latest adventures as an aspiring inventor?
   c. a thief sneak in and replace her well-cooked meal with a burnt one without stealing anything?
   d. she misread the recipe she was following and set the oven to 425 instead of 325?
7. Ruth comes into her living room to find her favorite vase smashed on the floor. Did:
   a. her cat accidentally brush against it while walking on the counter?
   b. a vindictive ex-boyfriend break in intending to destroy exactly that vase?

   c. a gust of wind blow so hard through the broken window that the vase toppled over?
   d. the house of cards she was building fall over next to it?
8. The balloons you set up as décor for last night's birthday party are all deflated in the morning. Did:
   a. one of your guests sneak back in with a BB gun to have a game of target practice?
   b. you fail to tie the balloons properly?
   c. the neighborhood cat decide to try his claws out on the colorful little bouncy things he found hanging up?
   d. an alien sneak in with his favorite knife to commit an act of mass murder and confuse balloons for people?
9. Julie's fiddle-leaf fig died over the course of the last week. Did:
   a. her pet parrot chew away at its roots every night while she was asleep?
   b. a guest poison the plant while visiting five days ago?
   c. she overwater it?
   d. her roommate decide to chop it in half in a fit of rage, but its trunk is still intact?
10. All the chocolate has disappeared from your secret stash. Did:
   a. you eat it all in a sleep-walking sugar craze?
   b. ants find it?
   c. your trusty friends take your declaration of intent to diet next week a little too seriously and stow it all away?
   d. it turn out that your secret stash wasn't so secret after all; your significant other ate the last two chocolate bars last week?

Theoretical Virtues

Looking back at the problems in the previous section, use the theoretical virtues to explain why the answer you chose is the best one. Also, pick one incorrect option from each problem, and list which theoretical virtues it fails to exhibit.

Chapter 12

Formal Fallacies

Identify the form of the following valid and fallacious arguments:

1. If Jones connects with the ball, he will hit a home run.
   Jones did not hit a home run.
   So, Jones did not connect with the ball.
2. Smith will either tackle Brown, or Brown will not be given a free kick.
   Smith will tackle Brown.
   Thus, Brown will be given a free kick.
3. If Sara is better than Mark at ping-pong, she will win the game.
   Sara is not better than Mark at ping-pong.
   Therefore, she will not win the game.
4. If Ben goes on a hike, Anne will go on a hike.
   Anne will go on a hike.
   So, Ben will go on a hike.
5. If Nate makes the right move, Jen will lose the foosball game.
   Nate made the right move.
   Thus, Jen will lose the game.
6. Either Keith will make the basket, or Jordan will steal the ball.
   Keith will not make the basket.
   Therefore, Jordan will steal the ball.
7. If Edward does not parry his blade, John will score a point.
   John will not score a point.
   Therefore, Edward will parry his blade.

8. If Emma is not careful, Seth will hit the birdie slyly over the badminton net.
   Emma will be careful.
   So, Seth will not hit the birdie slyly over the badminton net.
9. If Jessica sets the ball right, Hannah will make it over the net.
   Hannah will make it over the net.
   Thus, Jessica will set the ball right.
10. Either Sophia will draw a hopscotch square, or Anna will not have fun today.
   Sophia will draw a hopscotch square.
   So, Anna will have fun today.

Fallacies of Irrelevance

Identify the following fallacies:

1. Brad says that pandas are not real.
   But Brad doesn't like chocolate ice cream, and all people who dislike chocolate ice cream are silly.
   So, pandas must be real.
2. Make sure to stop by and adopt a puppy—just look at how cute they are wagging their tails!
3. George is super annoying, so if he was the one who told you that Anna is a painter, don't believe it.
4. Look, there is no evidence that humans were created ex nihilo. Thus, humans were not created out of nothing.
5. Atheists think there is no such thing as morality and, thus, they must think it doesn't matter how you live your life. But that's just accepting immorality. Therefore, atheism is a false view.
6. Mom: "Anna, make sure that you vacuum your bedroom at some point today."

Anna: "Sorry, I can't! I'm going to be busy all day and won't get back till dinner time."

7. Make sure to eat all of your veggies. The boogie monster will get you if you don't!
8. Aaron's mom told him that it is important to keep his room clean.
   But his mom's room is the dirtiest in the house.
   So, it must not really matter if he keeps his room clean.
9. This thing is an orange.
   All orange things taste good.
   So, this orange must taste good.
10. Miss Brown says that I should read more books because they will be good for me.
    But Miss Brown is a teacher, and teachers always say things like that.
    So, I don't need to read more books.
11. There is no way Jones tried to bribe his professor for a better grade; good students never do that sort of thing.
12. Gardener: "Make sure that you give that rose bush plenty of sunshine and enough water."
    Homeowner: "Well, it's been pruned just right, so we should be good."
13. God created the world, and carpenters are creators too. So, carpenters must be gods!
14. So far, two pink gumballs and five red gumballs have come out of the machine. So, a pink one will come out next.
15. Bridgett must like tea; no Englishman could ever despise the stuff.
16. Susan doesn't like the taste of this dish.
    But her taste in music is terrible.
    So, she must be misjudging.
17. Mr. Carter told me that I shouldn't use the chop saw in his shop.
    But he uses it all the time!
    So, it must not actually be bad for me to use it.

18. Apples are fruit, and pineapples are fruit. Apples taste amazing, so pineapples must too.
19. Megan has had so much bad luck this year that I bet things around her are about to turn for the better!
20. After I stepped on a sidewalk crack, it started to rain. So, stepping on the crack must have caused my bad luck.
21. Mayor Jones says that the city needs to raise taxes to avoid going into debt.

    But Mayor Jones is a communist, and they always want to raise taxes for no good reason.

    So, the city doesn't need to raise taxes to avoid going into debt.
22. There is no evidence that Joel stole the book from Brad. So, Joel didn't steal it.
23. Sam, that dog over there, has a lot of hair, four limbs, and a tail. That guy Matt also has a lot of hair and four limbs. So, Matt must have a tail.
24. All right, kids! Line up next to the door. You know it always makes Miss Sara smile when you do.
25. Julie says that cutting off too many leaves while pruning is bad for houseplants.

    But I've seen the pile of leaves she just took off of her ivy vine—it was huge!

    So, taking off a lot of leaves must not really be a problem.
26. Professor: "You should set aside some sacred time for your studies."

    Student: "But I really don't like the topic we're covering in class."
27. Christians say that gods don't exist.

    So, it must be the case that their god doesn't exist.
28. The goalkeeper has saved three penalty kicks in a row. So, he will definitely save this next one too.
29. After I ate some veggies, my stomach started to hurt. I bet the asparagus did it.

30. There is no evidence that aliens brought human beings to earth, so aliens did not bring humans beings to earth.

Fallacies of Inadequate Support

Identify the following fallacies:

1. Parent: "Either you eat all of your food or none of it."
   Jessica takes a bite.
   Parent: "All right—that means you have to eat it all."
2. Be careful hanging out with Ann. If you let her in the club, all seven of her sisters are going to want to join too.
3. The world is flat; it looks and feels that way every day.
4. Matt: "Have you stopped holding to the ridiculous theory that God created the world?"
   Joan: "No, I haven't."
   Matt: "Well you should, since you just agreed it is ridiculous."
5. No, you can't teach Mark how to use a knife. If he even touches one, he will cut himself so bad that he will need to be taken to the hospital.
6. I couldn't find my logic homework.
   My dog must have eaten it.
7. This tea kettle is made of metal, so its handle is made of metal too.
8. Dogs are better than cats. At least, that's what Mr. Peters says, and he is a world-renowned zoologist. So, it must be true.
9. Yes, Officer, I do think you should give people tickets for running a stop sign, but I don't deserve one because I am new to the area and didn't see it.
10. This cake has salt and salted butter in it, so it must be salty.
11. You should order the latest phone. Everyone's doing it.
12. "But, Mom, you said it was OK for me to sip from your cup! So, I did a couple of times. You shouldn't be mad that I finished it."

13. You can either hate me and correct me or love me and let me do what I want—there is no other option.
    You don't let me do what I want.
    So, you hate me!
14. This soup tastes really bad.
    A thief must've snuck into the house while it was simmering and added something to it.
15. If you don't do your homework today, you'll end up failing the class and flunking out of college!
16. Rudolf's nose is red, so Rudolf is a red reindeer.
17. I have known seven parrots personally, all of whom loved to be scratched on the head. So, parrots love to be scratched on the head.
18. Everyone who matters has signed up for a campus club. You should too.
19. We Christians believe that the Bible is divinely inspired. Why? Because it says so in 2 Timothy.
20. Sara: "Have you stopped listening to that modern hip-hop trash?"
    Anne: "Nope!"
    Sara: "Well, seeing as how you just agreed that it is trash, you need to stop listening to hip-hop."
21. Yes, of course I think that kids should get in trouble for slapping their classmates. But Bobby is a good kid, so I don't think you should punish my son.
22. Both of the succulents Mark owned died rather quickly. So, succulents must be easy to kill.
23. If you set aside five dollars to spend out of your savings, you will not deplete them. So, take out as much as you want; it's just five dollars on repeat, so your account will never run dry.
24. Aaron can choose to be a girl if he wants to be. Gender is a choice, after all.
25. Tulips are the world's prettiest flowers. A lot of well-respected florists, including Ms. Meadows, say so.

26. Students who fail to turn their homework in on time should fail this assignment. My homework should be accepted for this assignment even though it is late. A zero on this assignment will make me fail the class, and that is not an option.
27. This stuffed animal is fuzzy and soft, so its plastic eye must be fuzzy and soft too.
28. A person is either alive and well or dead and gone.
    The apostle Paul is not alive.
    So, he is completely gone—he no longer exists.
29. Apples taste better than pears. Why? Because John Jones is a professional chef, and he says so.
30. Megan says that she doesn't like wearing a seatbelt. Why? Because Aaron survived a car crash thanks to not wearing his seatbelt. So, Megan thinks that not wearing a seatbelt in the car is a good idea.

SUBJECT INDEX